On Behalf of the Child

Child Welfare, Child Protection and the Child Care Act 1991

EDITED BY
HARRY FERGUSON
& PAT KENNY

A. & A. FARMAR

British Library Cataloguing in Publication Data
A CIP catalogue record for this book
is available from the British Library

Cover design by Bluett
Copy-editing by Pat Carroll
Index by Helen Litton
Designed and set by A. & A. Farmar
Printed by Betaprint

ISBN 1 899047 01 8

A. & A. Farmar
Beech House
78 Ranelagh Village
Dublin 6

Contents

Foreword   *William R. Duncan*   *vii*

Introduction   *Harry Ferguson and Pat Kenny*   I

Part I: GENERAL PERSPECTIVES

1. The Child Care Act 1991: An Overview   *Paul Barron*   9

2. Child Welfare, Child Protection and the Child Care Act 1991:
   Key Issues for Policy and Practice   *Harry Ferguson*   17

3. The Child Care Act 1991 and the Social Context
   of Child Protection   *Pat Kenny*   42

4. Family Support and Child Welfare: Realising the
   Promise of the Child Care Act 1991   *Robbie Gilligan*   60

5. Section 5 of the Child Care Act 1991
   and Youth Homelessness   *Eoin O'Sullivan*   84

6. The Implications of the Child Care Act 1991 for
   Working with Children in Care   *Helen Gogarty*   105

7. Parents, Families and Access to Children in Care: The
   Implications of the Child Care Act 1991   *Sile Gallagher*   121

Part II: PRACTICE PERSPECTIVES

8. A Programme Manager's Perspective   *Michael McGinley*   145

9. A Perspective from the Courts   *Liam O. McMenamin*   158

10. A Child Psychiatry Perspective   *Don C. McDwyer*   162

11. A Paediatric Perspective   *Catherine Ryan*   176

12. A Public Health Nursing Perspective   *Anna Kelly*   186

13. A General Practice Perspective   *Eamon Shea*   203

14. A Social Work Perspective   *Val O'Kelly*   212

15. A Child Psychology Perspective   *Kieran Woods*   225

Conclusion: Towards an Integrated System of Child Care Services
   Harry Ferguson and Pat Kenny   238

Index   243

Acknowledgements

We would like to acknowledge the generous support of the North Western Health Board and Mr Donal O'Shea, Chief Executive Officer, which made this project possible. The idea for this book first arose out of a conference on the implications of the Child Care Act 1991 hosted by the North Western Health Board in January 1993. We are particularly grateful to Mr Michael McGinley, Programme Manager, for his unstinting financial and moral support for the book from the outset.

We are grateful to each of the contributors for responding to strict deadlines and finding time to produce drafts within already busy schedules. We sincerely hope that the book repays their efforts.

The burden of producing this book was greatly eased by the support we received from administrative staff in the Letterkenny office of the North Western Health Board and the Department of Social Studies, Trinity College, Dublin.

We owe a great deal to Anna Farmar who was exceptionally helpful and supportive in guiding us through the process of production of this book and conscientious to a fault in taking the manuscript through the final stages.

Finally, we would like to record our heartfelt thanks to Mary Sheridan, and Joanne and Eoin Kenny for their tolerance and support throughout.

Harry Ferguson
Pat Kenny
15 December 1994

FOREWORD

William R. Duncan

The editors of this book rightly describe the Child Care Act 1991 as one of the most important pieces of social legislation ever to reach the statute books in the Republic of Ireland. The Act contains for the first time a clear recognition of the state's obligations (acting through the agency of the health boards) with respect to the protection of children at risk. In this sense it may be viewed as fulfilling one of the most solemn obligations imposed on states by the *Convention on the Rights of the Child* (Adopted by the General Assembly of the United Nations on 20 November 1989.) Article 19 of that Convention, which has now been ratified by approximately 170 states including Ireland, reads:

> 1. States Parties shall take all appropriate legislative, administrative, social and educational measures to protect the child from all forms of physical or mental violence, injury or abuse, neglect or negligent treatment, maltreatment or exploitation including sexual abuse, while in the care of parent(s), legal guardian(s) or any other person who has care of the child.
>
> 2. Such protective measures should, as appropriate, include effective procedures for the establishment of social programmes to provide necessary support for the child and for those who have the care of the child, as well as for other forms of prevention and for identification, reporting, referral, investigation, treatment, and follow-up of instances of child maltreatment described heretofore, and, as appropriate, for judicial involvement.

On the level of principle, the Act of 1991 sets out to achieve a balance between the sometimes conflicting considerations of, on the one hand, giving primacy to the child's interests and, on the other hand, respecting parental rights and the privacy of the family unit. The stress placed on family services and support, and the graded approach to family intervention implicit in the Act (the least necessary to protect the child), are balanced by an increase in the range of interventions at the disposal of health boards and by a marginal shift towards easing intervention in emergency cases. At the same time there is new and welcome insistence, inspired partly by Constitutional developments, on the independent rights of the child, and in particular the child's right to have his or her voice heard in decisions affecting his or her future.

The success of the Act will depend on many variables, including the adequacy of resources devoted to its implementation, and the manner in which its provisions are interpreted by the health boards and the courts. But most important of all will be the quality of decision-making by the professionals who are charged with its implementation. A fine legislative scheme cannot guarantee good child care practice. The best it can do is provide a supporting framework within which are exercised those professional judgements which day-in day-out determine the quality of public care for our children. It is therefore of great importance that the objectives, as well as the small print, of the Child Care Act 1991 be widely discussed and understood by all the professionals groups involved in child care. For this reason alone this book, by entering the debate and promoting such understanding, renders a considerable public service.

One of the perennial problems for child care and protection has been the tendency for the several professional groupings involved—in social work, the health care services, education and the law—to operate in isolation from one another, against a background of distinctive professional cultures and sometimes divergent professional objectives. The need for the different professions to appreciate each other's roles and work methods, and to engage in effective communication and co-operation on behalf of the child, is a key requirement of modern child care practice. One of the strengths of this book lies in its emphasis on this interdisciplinary imperative. This is amply illustrated in the perspectives offered in the first part of the book; it is evidenced also by the wide range of skills and experience represented by the authors of the chapters in Part II.

The Child Care Act 1991 had a gestation period of perhaps twenty-five years. The extended labour involved in its implementation, as the various regulations to be made under the Act are prepared and the additional resources to help make the Act effective are put in place, seems likely to take another five. It is vitally important that this period of preparation be used to generate the widest possible understanding and discussion of the Act. This book makes a substantial contribution to this process, and sets a fine example by drawing together in constructive dialogue the different professions involved in fulfilling that most important of State obligations, the care and protection of our children.

INTRODUCTION

Harry Ferguson and Pat Kenny

By any standards, the 1990s have been extraordinary in terms of public and political concern about child welfare and child protection in Ireland. Since the foundation of the Irish state, those concerned with problems such as child abuse have struggled to make them public and political issues. This has changed dramatically since public disclosure of the 'X' case in 1992, the Kilkenny incest case, and the tragic case of Kelly Fitzgerald, as well as disclosures concerning the abuse of children in care and the investigation into Madonna House children's home in Co. Dublin. A process of pushing child protection and welfare into the political limelight culminated in late 1994 in the extraordinary events surrounding the case of the known child abuser Father Brendan Smyth, so mishandled by the Church authorities over a period going back some forty years, and the alleged mismanagement of the case in the Attorney General's office which eventually brought down the coalition government. These events have served to illustrate in the most dramatic terms the need for major reforms of child care law, policy and practice.

The Child Care Act 1991 represents one of the most important pieces of social legislation ever to reach the statute book in the Republic of Ireland. There are a number of reasons for this claim. Firstly, the Act has been such a long time coming. It is the first piece of comprehensive child care legislation enacted since the formation of the Irish state. In tandem with the legal provisions arising out of the Irish Constitution, the 1908 Children's Act—a piece of legislation enacted by the British state—has provided the legislative framework for child care practice in this country for almost the entire twentieth century (Shatter, 1986; Duncan, 1987).

A second reason why this piece of legislation is so important is that since the Act reached the statute book, the events referred to above have shown the urgent need for legislative change, events which themselves have begun to hasten the process of implementation of the Act. Of particular importance in this process is what became known as the 'Kilkenny incest case' and the report of the investigation into it (McGuinness, 1993). The recommendations of the *Report of the Kilkenny Incest Investigation* led to a firm commitment from the Government to implement the Child Care Act 1991 in full by 1996 (Department of Health, 1994).

The process of analysing the many implications of the Kilkenny Report for child care policy and practice has begun, and this book makes a further contribution to that important task (Buckley, 1993; Ferguson, 1993; Ferguson, 1994; Kenny, 1993; McGrath, 1993). But although it has been the issue of child abuse which has placed child care on the political agenda and come to dominate public debates, the Child Care Act, and this book, are by no means restricted to consideration of how child abuse should be identified, investigated and managed. Naturally, the issue of child protection constitutes a key theme of this book. But our aim has been to be inclusive and to provide an outline and analysis of the full range of child welfare and protection services relevant to contemporary policy and practice and the Act. We are concerned, therefore, to offer perspectives on services in relation to youth homelessness, family support and children in care as well as on child abuse. Indeed, it could be argued that we need to give more attention to those child welfare services in order to counter the increasing tendency for child care services to be equated only with child protection.

This book has been produced at what is, by any standards, a key, formative moment in the history of Irish child care services. Published work on child care is still very limited in this country, although this is beginning to change (*see*, for example, Gilligan, 1991). Despite its significance, the process of analysing the implications of the Child Care Act has only begun (*see* McGuinness, 1992; O'Connor, 1992; Gilligan, 1993; O'Sullivan, 1993).

INTRODUCTION

This is the first book of its kind to examine not only the Child Care Act, but also child welfare, child protection and Irish child care policy and practice *per se*, from a multiplicity of perspectives. It is intended to have a broad appeal to policy makers and practitioners from across the range of relevant disciplines, as well as to academics, students and commentators in the media. The contributors are drawn from a wide range of backgrounds, in policy-making and administration, academia, management and frontline child care practice.

The chapters offer a range of perspectives relevant to child welfare, child protection and the Child Care Act, organised into two sections. Part I covers general perspectives. Chapters 1–7 provide overviews of the Act's content, identify key trends and policy and practice issues and analyse in detail the general implications of the Act for particular services of child protection, child welfare and family support, youth homelessness and children in care, their parents and families. Part II considers the implications of the new legislation in more detail from the perspectives of the professional groups and disciplines responsible for translating it into practice.

Each author addresses three main themes: first, his or her perspective, the agency function and general orientation and the tasks involved in its child care work. The author considers the factors shaping this perspective and the occupational culture and outlook of the professional group in question, such as training, key ethical issues, professional status and theoretical framework. Secondly, each author offers a perspective on the implications of the Act for each discipline, covering the broad policy and practice parameters of the Act. The contributors' primary concern in this respect is to cover the operational implications of the Act from their professional perspective and to offer an interpretation of what it will mean in policy and practice. Thirdly, each author addresses the key theme of multi-disciplinary co-operation and co-ordination and explores the relevant inter-professional and inter-agency issues that will arise when working under the Act.

It should be clear from this that the aim of this book is not simply to set out what is in the Act, however important a task that is, but to analyse criti-

It's aim is to analyze critically

cally its implications for child welfare and child protection policy and practice. In so doing, what is offered is less a prescription for action than an attempt to map out the broad policy and practice parameters of the Act from a range of perspectives. What is offered throughout constitutes much more than mere speculation. Analysis of the likely impact of the Act is based on projections from current trends, research evidence and hands-on experience of working with children and families.

With the exception of Paul Barron, Harry Ferguson, Robbie Gilligan and Eoin O'Sullivan, the contributions are from professionals who work in the North Western Health Board area. The book should not, however, be read as a policy document of the NWHB on the Act, nor as relevant only to that region. The contributions are relevant to child care policy and practice throughout Ireland. No effort has been made to force the contributions into some kind of false uniformity of policy and practice perspectives on the meaning of 'child welfare' and 'child protection' or consensus as to how the Act should be interpreted and put into operation. On the contrary, the book is intended to provide a reference point for information sharing, debates and progressive models of implementation of this historic piece of legislation.

It is of fundamental importance today that the plurality of perspectives on child welfare and child protection are understood and taken account of in policy and practice. It is hoped, therefore, that this text will be read in its entirety. However, each chapter can be read as a discrete contribution so that those interested in particular perspectives can turn directly to the relevant chapter for an outline of what is in the Act and an analysis of the likely implications it has for child care policy and practice in relation to their specific concerns.

Inevitably, perhaps, given that *On Behalf of the Child* explores a full range of 'professional' perspectives on the Child Care Act, there is a strong bias towards representing the views of the 'expert'. It was beyond the scope of this book to include the consumer perspective. We are mindful of the enormous powers that professionals have over the lives of children and parents, and have tried to give attention to their perspectives and the scope within the Act to promote the ability of professional groups to work in partnership with and empower parents and children.

This book represents a contribution to what needs to be an ongoing process of reflection, research, training and planning which will enable professionals (and indeed the public) to reach a deeper understanding of their own and others' perspectives on child welfare, child protection and the Act. We hope that the book can make some contribution to promoting such understandings of child care policy and practice in the Irish context and strengthen all our abilities to work effectively on behalf of the child.

References

Buckley, H. (1993), 'The Kilkenny Incest Investigation: Some Practice Implications', *Irish Social Worker*, Vol. 11, No. 4.

Department of Health (1994), *Shaping a Healthier Future: A Strategy for Effective Healthcare in the 1990s*, Dublin: Stationery Office.

Duncan, W. (1987), 'Child, Parent and State: The Balance of Power', in W. Duncan (ed.), *Law and Social Policy*, Dublin: Dublin University Law Journal.

Ferguson, H. (1993), 'The Latent and Manifest Implications of the Report of the Kilkenny Investigation for Social Work', *Irish Social Worker*, Vol. 11, No. 4.

Ferguson, H. (1994), 'Child Abuse Inquiries and the Report of the Kilkenny Incest Investigation: A Critical Analysis', *Administration*, Vol. 41, No. 4.

Gilligan, R. (1991), *Irish Child Care Services: Policy, Practice and Provision*, Dublin: Institute of Public Administration.

Gilligan, R. (1993), 'The Child Care Act 1991: An Examination of its Scope and Resource Implications', *Administration*, Vol. 4, No. 4, pp. 345–70.

Kenny, P. (1993), 'Child Protection: A Professional Dilemma', *Irish Social Worker*, Vol. 11, No. 3.

McGrath, K. (1993), 'The Effects on Those at the Heart of the Kilkenny Inquiry', *Irish Social Worker*, Vol. 11, No. 4.

McGuinness, C. (1992), 'Social Work and the Law', *Irish Social Worker*, Vol. 10, No. 4.

McGuinness, C. (1993), *Report of the Kilkenny Incest Investigation*, Dublin: Stationery Office.

O'Connor, P. (1992), 'Child Care Policy: A Provocative Analysis and Research Agenda', *Administration*, Vol. 40, No. 3, pp. 200–19.

O'Sullivan, E. (1993), 'Irish Child Care Law—The Origins, Aims and Development of the 1991 Child Care Act', *Childright* (June), No. 97.

Shatter, A. (1986), *Family Law in the Republic of Ireland*, Dublin: Wolfhound Press.

PART I: *General Perspectives*

Chapter 1

THE CHILD CARE ACT 1991: AN OVERVIEW

Paul Barron

Introduction

The Child Care Policy Unit was set up in the Department of Health in mid-1993. The new unit's role relates to the formulation and implementation of policy on child care and family welfare with particular reference to child abuse, youth homelessness and family violence and to overseeing the delivery of appropriate services through the health boards and voluntary agencies. In the short to medium term the unit's main work will relate to:

- the preparation of the regulations, guidelines and protocols required for the implementation of all remaining sections of the Child Care Act

- the development of child care services in accordance with the provisions of the Child Care Act

- the implementation of the recommendations of the *Report of the Kilkenny Incest Investigation*

- the development of appropriate responses to the growth in youth homelessness

- an examination of the need for improvements in adoption legislation, including the introduction of an Adoption Contact Register

My aim in this chapter is to provide an overview of the Child Care Act 1991. It should be emphasised that this summary has been prepared for general guidance only and does not purport to be a legal interpretation.

Part I: Preliminary

The Act contains 79 sections in all, 16 of which have, at the time of writing, been implemented (*see* page 16).

Section 1 empowers the Minister to bring the provisions of the Act into effect on a phased basis.

Section 2 defines a 'child' as a person up to eighteen years old. The main effect of this is to raise the age up to which health boards are responsible for children, and to which children may be admitted into care, from sixteen to eighteen years. The new definition applies to the provisions of this Act as they are brought into operation; however, it does not apply to proceedings under the Children Act 1908; for example, the age limit for fit person orders remains at sixteen years.

Part II: Promotion of Welfare of Children

Section 3 places a statutory duty on health boards to identify and promote the welfare of children who are not receiving adequate care and protection and to provide a range of child care and family support services. In performing these functions, health boards must regard the welfare of the child as the first and paramount consideration, have regard to the rights and duties of parents, give due consideration to the child's wishes and have regard to the principle that it is generally better for children to be brought up in their own families.

Section 4 deals with voluntary care. It enables health boards to receive into care, without reference to the courts, orphans and abandoned children and, with parental consent, children whose parents are unable to care for them for any reason.

Section 5 requires health boards to make available accommodation for homeless children.

Section 6 requires each health board to provide an adoption service or to arrange to have the service provided by a registered adoption society. It may assist, financially or otherwise, a society with which it has made such an arrangement.

Section 7 provides for the establishment of a child care advisory committee in each health board area to advise the board on the performance of its functions under the Act. The members who are appointed by the health boards must include persons with a special interest or expertise in child care and representatives of voluntary bodies providing child care services.

Section 8 requires health boards to have a report prepared annually on the adequacy of child care services in their areas.

Sections 9 and *10* enable health boards to make arrangements with voluntary bodies to provide child care and family support services on their behalf and to grant-aid such bodies.

Part III: Protection of Children in Emergencies

Section 12 provides that a garda may, without warrant, remove a child to safety where there is an immediate and serious risk to the health or welfare of the child and where it would not be sufficient to wait for the health board to apply for an emergency care order. It also grants gardaí powers of entry, without warrant, and enables them to be accompanied by other persons (for example, social workers) in effecting the removal. A child who is removed by a garda must be delivered up to the health board as soon as possible so that the board can apply for an emergency care order. Where no sitting of the District Court is due to be held within three days, it will be necessary to arrange a special sitting to consider the application. It will not be lawful for the board to retain custody of the child beyond the three-day period unless the Court makes an emergency care order.

Section 13 empowers the District Court to make an emergency care order authorising the placement of a child in the care of a health board for up to eight days where there is reasonable cause to believe that there is an immediate and serious risk to the child's safety which necessitates placement in care. The Court may also make an order if a child is likely to be at risk if removed from the place where he or she is for the time being, for example, where a child is in hospital and it is suspected that he or she might be abused on returning home.

Part IV: Care Proceedings

Section 17 enables the District Court to make an interim care order placing a child in the care of a health board until a decision is reached on an application for a care order. This is designed to 'bridge the gap' between the expiration of an emergency care order (after eight days) and the determination of an application for a (full) care order. An interim care order may be made for eight days or, if the parents consent, for longer than eight days and may be renewed from time to time.

Section 18 provides for the making of a care order where the District Court is satisfied that the child has been or is being assaulted, ill-treated, neglected or sexually abused, or the child's health, development or welfare has been or is being avoidably impaired or neglected, or the child's health, development or welfare is likely to be avoidably impaired or neglected.

A care order may be made until the child attains the age of eighteen or for a shorter period, which may be renewed if the Court is satisfied that grounds for the making of a care order continue to exist. Where a child is the subject of a care order, the health board shall do what is reasonable to safeguard and promote his or her welfare and shall have authority to decide whether the child should be placed in foster care or residential care, give consent to necessary medical treatment, give consent to the issue of a passport to enable the child to travel abroad for holidays, etc.

Section 19 enables the District Court to make a supervision order authorising a health board to have a child visited at home to ensure that he or she is being cared for properly. The grounds for a supervision order are similar to those for a care order, but the standard of proof required is less stringent; for example, for a supervision order the Court must be satisfied that 'there are reasonable grounds for believing' that the conditions may exist, whereas for a care order the Court must be 'satisfied' that the conditions do exist. Decisions on the frequency of parental visits will be a matter for the health board, although the parents will have a right of appeal to the courts if they believe that the level of supervision is too intrusive. The board may ask the Court to direct the parents to bring the child to a day care centre, child guidance clinic, hospital, etc. A supervision order applies for up to twelve months and is renewable.

Section 20 provides that where, in any proceedings under the Guardianship of Infants Act 1964, the Judicial Separation and Family Law Reform Act 1989 or any other proceedings for the delivery or return of a child, the Court considers that it may be appropriate for a care order or a supervision order to be made, the Court may adjourn the case and direct the health board to undertake an investigation into the child's circumstances and to consider whether it should apply for such an order. Where, following an investigation, the health board decides not to apply for an order, it will be required to inform the Court of its reasons for so deciding.

Part v: Jurisdiction and Procedure

Section 24 requires the Court, having regard to the rights and duties of parents, to regard the welfare of the child as the first and paramount consideration in any proceedings in relation to the care and protection of children.

Section 25 empowers a court to make a child a party to all or part of care proceedings and, where appropriate, to appoint a solicitor to represent the child. Where a solicitor is appointed by the Court, the costs and expenses incurred will be paid by the health board involved unless the Court orders otherwise.

Section 26 enables the Court to appoint a guardian *ad litem* for a child involved in care proceedings. Any such appointment will lapse if the child is made a party to the case. The costs will be borne by the health board concerned.

Section 27 enables the Court to obtain a report from any person on any question affecting the welfare of the child. The report may be received in evidence at the proceedings and the person making the report may be called as a witness.

Section 29 provides that care proceedings will be heard in private and will be as informal as possible. It also prohibits the wearing of wigs and gowns and requires care proceedings to be heard at a different place or at different times or on different days from those at which ordinary sittings of the Court are held.

Section 31 prohibits the publication or broadcast of any matter that would serve to identify a child who is the subject of care proceedings.

Part VI: Children in the Care of Health Boards

Under *Section 36* a health board may place a child in foster care or in a residential centre, or for adoption where he or she is eligible for adoption, or it may make other suitable arrangements, which may include placing the child with a relative.

Section 37 requires a health board to facilitate reasonable access between a child in care and the parents or any other person who has a bona fide interest. A person who is dissatisfied with the access arrangements made by a health board may apply to the District Court which may make an order as it thinks proper regarding access. A health board may apply to the Court for an order authorising it to refuse to allow a named person to have access to a child in its care.

Sections 39, 40 and *41* require the Minister to make regulations governing the placement of children in foster care, in residential care and with relatives respectively.

Section 43 requires the making of regulations governing the circumstances in which a health board may remove a child from foster care or any other placement.

Section 44 provides for regulations requiring health boards to undertake regular reviews of children in care.

Section 45 enables a health board to provide 'aftercare' support and assistance for children who were formerly in care.

Part VII: Supervision of Pre-school Services

Section 50 enables the Minister for Health, in consultation with the Ministers for Education and for the Environment, to make regulations for securing the safety and promoting the development of children attending preschool services. The regulations will cover pre-schools, play groups, day nurseries, crèches and other services which cater for pre-school children.

However, care provided by relatives is exempt and the provisions will not apply to a person taking care of not more than three pre-school children from different families in his or her own home.

Section 51 requires persons carrying on pre-school services to notify the local health board.

Section 52 imposes a statutory duty on persons carrying on pre-school services to take all reasonable measures to safeguard the children concerned.

Under *Section 53*, health boards will be required to arrange for the inspection of pre-school services in consultation, where appropriate, with the Department of Education.

Section 56 empowers health boards to provide pre-school services and to make available information on pre-school services.

Section 57 provides that a person guilty of an offence under this part may be fined up to £1,000 or imprisoned for up to twelve months and, in addition, may be disqualified from operating a pre-school service.

Part VIII: Children's Residential Centres

Section 60 provides that it will not be lawful for any person or body to operate a residential centre for children unless it is registered with the local health board.

Section 61 provides for the registration by health boards of these centres subject to regulations to be made by the Minister. These may include standards in relation to care, accommodation and facilities, staff numbers and qualifications etc. in the centres.

Section 62 provides for appeals to the District Court against decisions of health boards in relation to registration.

Section 64 provides that a person guilty of an offence under this part shall be liable to a fine of up to £1,000 or twelve months' imprisonment, or both, and may be disqualified from operating a residential centre.

Section 66 brings the staff of certain children's residential centres within the scope of the Local Government Superannuation Scheme.

Part IX: Administration

Section 69 enables the Minister to supervise health boards in the performance of their functions under the Act.

Section 72 reserves certain functions to chief executive officers of health boards, particularly those functions which relate to the care of individual children. These functions may be delegated by chief executive officers to other officers of the boards.

Part X: Miscellaneous and Supplementary

Section 74 makes it an offence to sell solvent-based products to children where it is known or suspected that they will be misused. Provision is made for fines of up to £1,000 or twelve months' imprisonment. A garda may seize any substance in the possession of a child in a public place which the garda has reasonable cause to believe is being misused by that child in a manner likely to cause him or her to be intoxicated.

Sections in operation (as of December 1994)

Section 1	Short title
Section 2	Interpretation
Section 3	Functions of health boards
Section 5	Accommodation for homeless children
Section 6 (part)	Provision of adoption service
Section 7	Child care advisory committees
Section 8	Review of services
Section 9	Provision of services by voluntary bodies
Section 10	Assistance for voluntary bodies
Section 11	Research
Section 66	Superannuation of certain staff
Section 69	Powers of Minister
Section 71	Prosecution of offences
Section 72	Function of chief executive officers
Section 73	Expenses
Section 74	Sale of solvents

Chapter 2

CHILD WELFARE, CHILD PROTECTION AND THE CHILD CARE ACT 1991: KEY ISSUES FOR POLICY AND PRACTICE

Harry Ferguson

, 1 9 2 1

The Child Care Act 1991 represents a landmark in the history of child care in Ireland. Here we have the first major piece of child welfare legislation to be enacted since the foundation of the Irish state. It is crucial, therefore, that not only the content but also the potential impact of the Act are evaluated and their implications for child welfare and protection mapped out in full. Here is an opportunity to create something new in Irish social policy and practice, to rid ourselves of all the old technical legal problems, the resource issues, and the philosophical stumbling blocks to achieving good child care practice.

This chapter presents a historical overview of the development of the Act, and discusses key issues for policy and practice that arise from its implementation. In particular, some key trends in child welfare and child protection practice are identified and related in a general way to the philosophical issues and models of child care policy and practice relevant to the Act.

The Child Care Act 1991: Historical Background

The 1908 Children Act, together with the Irish Constitution, have heretofore provided the main legal framework for child care. From the late nineteenth century until the 1960s, Irish child care services were provided largely by voluntary agencies. The Irish Society for the Prevention of Cruelty to Children (ISPCC), first established under the umbrella of the UK National Society for the Prevention of Cruelty to Children (NSPCC), which administered child protection in Ireland until 1956, was the main casework agency at work on behalf of the child. Residential child care services, meanwhile, were (and still are) provided mostly by religious orders (Ferguson, 1993).

With the 1970 Health Act, which established health boards, state agencies took over primary responsibility for the provision of child care services. Under the 1908 legislation the legal basis of the duties of health boards has always been ambiguous. For example, strictly speaking, health boards have no statutory duty to investigate child abuse cases. While the *Child Abuse Guidelines* (Department of Health, 1987) do clarify procedural issues and give a pivotal management responsibility for child abuse to the director of community care and health board community care teams, such guidance is not legally binding. For many years Irish professionals have been aware of the inadequacies of the legal framework arising from outdated legislation. As long ago as 1971, the ISPCC wrote: 'The Children Act, 1908, together with its amendments, *must* be brought up to date' (ISPCC, 1971, p. 5, emphasis in original). Two years later the Society was even more specific:

> There are many instances where we feel that if we had better legislation for the protection of children, we could provide a better service. We would like to see the possibility of getting a 'Supervision Order' so that we could be given a chance to work with more difficult families within their home environment. This is not possible under existing legislation, and as a result we sometimes have to remove children because of non-co-operation of parents. (ISPCC, 1973, p. 70)

Twenty years later, the supervision order is indeed an important new measure that the 1991 Act introduces. The momentum for reform of child care services had begun following the publication of the Kennedy Report in 1970 (Kennedy, 1970). It continued with the establishment in 1973 of the Task Force for Child Care Services. While it was due initially to report on recommendations for change within six months, its *Final Report* was eventually published in 1981 (Task Force on Child Care Services, 1981;

Gilligan, 1991). Following an abortive attempt to get a Child Care and Protection Bill through the Dáil in the mid-1980s, it was another full decade before the Child Care Act reached the statute book in July 1991.

From the outset, the Government signalled its intention to implement the 1991 legislation on a phased basis. Matters did indeed move along relatively slowly and by the end of 1992, just 16 of the 79 sections had been implemented (Barron, this volume; Gilligan, 1993). The context of implementation and level of public interest in child care changed dramatically in March 1993 when the Kilkenny incest case hit the headlines. It involved a twenty-seven-year-old woman who, from the age of ten, had endured extreme physical and sexual abuse at the hands of her father. Within a week of the case being made public, an inquiry, headed by Senior Counsel Catherine McGuinness, was instituted by the Minister for Health, Brendan Howlin. Its terms of reference were to

> carry out an investigation, insofar as the health services are concerned, of the circumstances surrounding the abuse . . . and in particular to establish why action to halt the abuse was not taken earlier, and to make recommendations for the future investigation and management by the health services of cases of suspected child abuse. (McGuinness, 1993, p. 11)

The *Report of the Kilkenny Incest Investigation* was published on 18 May 1993 (for a full analysis, *see* Ferguson, 1994a). The Child Care Act was central to its concluding recommendations:

> We cannot recommend too strongly the urgent need to provide the necessary resources and to implement the remaining sections of the Act and in particular Parts III, IV, V and VI which deal with the taking of children into care, court proceedings and the powers and duties of health boards in relation to children in their care. (McGuinness, 1993, p. 95)

The publication of the report resulted in an immediate response from the Government in the form of a commitment to release £35 million over the following three years to implement the Child Care Act 1991 in full by the end of 1995. However, the target date for full implementation has since been pushed forward to the end of 1996 (Department of Health, 1994).

Thus, in Ireland the political culture surrounding child welfare and state intervention into the family is such that nothing can ever be certain. It does appear, however, that the social, political and legislative impasse surrounding child care services is over, as the inquiry into the Kilkenny case was instrumental in making child care a political issue: it will not as easily disappear from the public agenda as before (Ferguson, 1994b). The process of pushing child welfare and protection into the political limelight culminated in late 1994 in the extraordinary events surrounding the handling by the Catholic Church and the Attorney General's office of the case of the child abuser Father Brendan Smyth, which precipitated the fall of the Coalition Government. As one chapter of history closes, at ground level the work of interpreting the Act, developing services and consolidating and changing practice standards has begun in earnest.

Irish Child Care Law and Policy: Philosophical Issues

Whatever is eventually achieved in the area of child welfare and protection, the dilemmas addressed by the Child Care Act are anything but new. In regulating parent–child relations, all liberal Western nation-states are faced with the central challenge of balancing the rights of parents to rear their children autonomously, while at the same time endeavouring to protect the welfare of the child. The Constitution of 1937 has been crucial in the management of this balance in Irish child care law, policy and practice. It enshrined the protection of the family from undue interference by the state and tilted the balance institutionally towards the enhancement of parental rights and the minimum intervention end of the continuum (Duncan, 1993). Here was the genesis of a sensitive and largely minimalist approach by the Irish state to intervention into the family which soon found its way into child protection and welfare discourse (Powell, 1992). In 1954, under the heading 'Home or No Home', the Dublin branch of the ISPCC quoted Article 41, Sections 1 and 2, of the Constitution:

> 1.1 The State recognises the Family as the natural primary and fundamental
> unit group of society, and as a moral institution possessing inalienable and

imprescriptible rights, antecedent and superior to all positive law.

1.2 The State, therefore, guarantees to protect the Family in its constitution and authority, as the necessary basis of social order and as indispensable to the welfare of the Nation and the State.

2.1 In particular, the State recognises that by her life within the home, a woman gives to the State a support without which the common good cannot be achieved. (*Bunreacht na hÉireann: Constitution of Ireland*, 1937)

The Society argued that this principle constituted 'perhaps the greatest of rights of the child which we are continually fighting to maintain [which] is the right to a secure and happy home with its family'. At the same time, the Society sought to defend itself against what it saw as the 'mistaken impression in the minds of many people that we regard the committal of children to Industrial Schools as a sovereign remedy for unhappiness or unsuitable conditions in the home. A poor home, they say, is better than no home' (Dublin and District ISPCC, 1954, p. 7). Such commentary reflected the tensions involved for professionals in reconciling their use of powers under the 1908 Children Act with the principle of minimum intervention into the family prescribed by the Constitution. Child welfare and protection were constructed in such a way as to be run through with powerful tensions and contradictions (Task Force on Child Care Services, 1981, p.182; Ferguson, 1993).

The Child Care Act 1991 both extends the traditional philosophical underpinnings of state–family relations arising from child care law and the Constitution and introduces a number of important clarifications. By and large, the 1908 Children Act was restricted simply to outlining negative criteria upon which professionals responded to children who had had criminal offences committed against them or who were being cruelly treated. In a general sense, the 1991 Act transcends that negativity and is an altogether more constructive piece of legislation in that it places positive duties on health boards to act on behalf of the child both in anticipation of and in response to adversity (McGuinness, 1992). The spirit and underlying philosophy of the 1991 Act are therefore crucial.

The Act (Section 24) requires the Court—having regard to the rights and duties of parents—to 'regard the welfare of the child as the first and paramount consideration' in any proceedings in relation to the child's care and protection. Due consideration must be given in decision-making to the child's wishes. Health boards are, however, also to 'have regard to the principle that it is generally in the best interest of a child to be brought up in his or her own family'. The primary emphasis is on the provision of support and assistance by the state so that children can remain at home. Only in exceptional circumstances are children to be taken into care. The overall aim is for the state to support in a humane way the role of parents rather than supplanting it.

General Implications of the Act

Against this background, the Child Care Act introduces a number of important substantive clarifications. Until now, the precise role and duties of the Irish state and its professionals in child care have been unclear in many crucial respects. A vital overall function of the 1991 Act is to clarify the nature and scope of the powers and duties of health boards in child care practice. In specific terms the Act:

- extends the legal definition of a 'child' to eighteen years

- places a positive duty on health boards to promote the welfare of children in their area—including the identification of children who are not receiving adequate care and protection

- places a statutory duty on health boards to provide family support services

- extends and refines the powers of health boards and gardaí in the protection of children in emergencies

- clarifies the role of the courts and procedural issues arising from care proceedings and introduces a range of new orders

- sets out clearly the powers and duties of health boards over children who are in their care

- enables a health board to provide 'aftercare' support for children who were in their care

- places a duty on health boards to provide voluntary care for appropriate children

- creates scope for formal development of pre-school services

- requires health boards to make available accommodation for homeless children

- gives to District Justices the power to make access orders

- places a duty on health boards to provide an adoption service

- creates conditions for systematic review of the 'adequacy' of services, and structures of accountability through child care advisory committees

The single most important area of clarification of the Act is that it places a duty on health boards 'to promote the welfare of children in its area'. Even more specifically, Section 3(2)(a) requires health boards to 'take such steps as it considers requisite to identify children who are not receiving adequate care and protection and co-ordinate information from all relevant sources relating to children in its area'. Section 8(2) specifies the categories of children likely to be included here as:

- children whose parents are dead or missing

- children whose parents have deserted or abandoned them

- children who are in the care of the board

- children who are homeless

- children who are at risk of being neglected or ill-treated, and

- children whose parents are unable to care for them due to ill health or for any other reason

Identifying Children at Risk and Promoting the Welfare of Children

A key overall issue for policy and practice arising out of the Act is the opportunity it presents to develop an integrated child care system that provides a balance of services for all the categories of vulnerable children referred to. The prospects for finding this balance and the likely impact of implementation of the Act have to be evaluated in the context of current trends in policy and practice. One of these categories, 'children who are at risk of being neglected or ill-treated', has come to dominate health board practice in recent years. During the 1980s the numbers of child abuse cases reported to health boards increased ten-fold: from 406 cases in 1982 to 3,856 cases in 1991.

A key question in the light of the new duties of health boards under the Act to identify children at risk is: who identified these cases? Table 2.1 summarises the available information on sources of referral in child abuse cases in Ireland in the 1980s.

Table 2.1 Sources of referral in child abuse cases in Ireland, 1982–7

	Per cent
Neighbours and relatives	19
Self referrals	7
Official sources	62
Anonymous and miscellaneous	12

Source: Department of Health, *Child Abuse Statistics*, selected years.

These figures amply illustrate the importance of professionals to the identification of children at risk since the early 1980s. The discipline of medicine alone (hospitals, general practitioners, area medical officers and public health nurses) accounted for over half of the reports within the 'official' category, which amounts to 36 per cent of all reported cases. The work of public health nurses is a good example of initiatives taken by health board staff to identify children at risk. In the early 1980s, nationally, public health nurses reported 18.5 per cent of cases investigated. By 1987, the proportion was down to 11.4 per cent, but of a much higher total of cases reported. The actual numbers of cases identified by public health nurses more than doubled during the 1980s, to a 1987 figure of 187.

It is important to recognise the profound historical transformation that has occurred in reporting patterns in child abuse cases. In my own research into the history of child protection, I found that up to the 1950s only some 20 per cent of cases reported to the ISPCC came from professional sources. Policy initiatives such as the Child Abuse Guidelines—the first edition of which was published in 1977—have been crucial in changing professional awareness of child abuse and establishing reporting procedures.

Thus, a striking feature of recent trends is the crucial role that health board staff have *already* played in identifying these child abuse cases. However, despite this major historical transformation, more will be required under the Act. A key question is: are professionals doing enough to identify children at risk? The Act requires health boards actively to seek out children who are not receiving adequate care and protection. It is not enough simply to wait passively for children to come to the attention of the services. They must be sought out. This can be understood on two levels: the need to develop a more pro-active approach on behalf of suspected abused children; and the need to identify and respond to children who are at risk from a range of adversities other than physical and sexual abuse or neglect.

In relation to the identification of child abuse, we might usefully compare our situation with the USA, for example, where mandatory reporting of child abuse has been in operation since the 1960s. There, paediatricians alone report in the region of 12 per cent of all reported cases of child abuse, a figure that does not include paediatric examinations of children to clarify allegations of abuse made from another source (Dubowitz and Newberger, 1989). In comparison, Irish professionals are under-reporting, a view that is supported by the *Report of the Kilkenny Incest Investigation*, which recommends the introduction of mandatory reporting of child abuse—as did the Law Reform Commission *Report on Child Sexual Abuse* (Law Reform

Commission, 1990). Mandatory reporting was in fact included in the original Child Care Bill but was defeated in the Dáil debates and excluded from the eventual Child Care Act.

The Kilkenny Report recommends that professionals 'probe' much more deeply the causes of injuries to children, and develop protocols and other means of co-ordinating information about children at risk of child abuse (McGuinness, 1993). We now know that abused children present to the health services in a number of ways. But the Kilkenny case illustrates the need for professionals (as well as lay people) to be pro-active on behalf of a particular category of abused child about whom we have come to understand more in recent years; those, like 'Mary', the survivor in the Kilkenny case, who are not psychologically ready or able to disclose by confiding in an adult because of the legacy of many years of accommodating to abuse (*see* Ferguson, 1994a). Particular efforts need to be made to identify these children, who often require professional advocates who are willing to take risks on their behalf (Richardson and Bacon, 1991). Despite official support for the introduction of mandatory reporting, there is little reason to be optimistic about the prospects of its introduction in Ireland. In its absence, the new duties placed on health boards to identify children at risk of child abuse take on an even greater significance in the light of the Kilkenny case.

The complexity of this task can be further grasped by considering another level at which identification has relevance under the Act: the need to develop a system that can identify and respond to children who are at risk from a range of adversities other than abuse. It is common to hear professionals recount with irritation that social workers today appear uninterested in their concerns about vulnerable children unless something quite serious is about to happen or has already happened. These tensions reflect the fact that a static number of community child social workers has had to deal with huge increases in the volume of child abuse cases. The generic service offered by these frontline professionals has been rationalised, and savings in time and resources have been made in the traditional child welfare and preventive work of social workers, which has been drastically cut back. As a result, formal 'entry' to the child care system and the threshold for provision of social work and support services appear to be lower for children at high risk of abuse than for other children in need. Such organisational pressures mean that to ensure a response to their concerns about a case (indeed, to get it treated *as* a 'case') the onus is increasingly on referring agents to convince social workers of the 'dangerousness' of the case (*see also* Parton and Parton, 1989). In the process child *care* has been reframed as primarily child *protection*.

One consequence of this is a trend towards equating child abuse in the public—and it seems the administrative—mind with extreme child sexual abuse and physical violence. It is, of course, vital that every effort is made to sustain recognition of sexual abuse. But equal consideration should be given to the nature and scope of other forms of childhood adversity. Although it gets much less publicity, child neglect has in fact always been the most common form of child abuse worked with by professionals in Ireland. In the decades up to the 1960s as many as 90 per cent of cases investigated by the ISPCC were categorised as 'neglect' (ISPCC, 1957). With increased awareness of physical and sexual abuse in the 1970s and 1980s, child protection has come to involve a relatively smaller proportion of cases that are defined as neglect. Thus, by 1989, 34 per cent of the cases investigated by health boards were classified as sexual abuse, 8 per cent as emotional abuse and 11 per cent as physical abuse, while 47 per cent of cases were still categorised as neglect (Department of Health, 1982–9). Child sexual abuse has always gone on and what these trends reflect is the impact of changing public and professional awareness and reporting of the problem (*see* Ferguson, 1991).

As a result of the increased sensitivity to sexual abuse from the late 1980s, considerable resources have gone into establishing specialist units in many areas of the country to assess child sexual abuse. Neglect is recognised by the specialist services insofar as it presents as a problem in the lives of some sexually abused children. For instance, in a study of 512 confirmed cases of child sexual abuse in the Eastern Health Board region during 1988, child neglect was also present in 22 per cent of the families,

Definition of neglect.

according to social workers (McKeown and Gilligan, 1991).

The most widely accepted official definition of what is today termed 'persistent or severe neglect' is 'exposure to any kind of danger including cold and starvation which results in serious impairment of the child's health or development including non-organic failure to thrive' (Birchall, 1989; McGuinness, 1993). Skilled investigative techniques are important here to aid in assessments of neglect. That medical evidence can be crucial is implicit in the notion of 'non-organic failure to thrive', which means that wilful neglect is considered when no organic reason can be found for a child being underweight. As well as starvation or poor diet, failure to thrive can arise from emotional problems, where parents may disengage emotionally from the child in question and withdraw care. This kind of scapegoating of a particular child usually has deep psychological roots and arises from a legacy of chronic unmet needs and developmental blocks within the parents themselves. An example of this pattern of child abuse was evident in the tragic and highly publicised Mayo case of fifteen-year-old Kelly Fitzgerald, whose parents were convicted of 'wilful neglect' in October 1994.

The majority of neglect cases involve milder concerns, however, such as parents leaving children unattended, recently (re)defined as 'Home Alone' cases, and various other problems in coping with child care. While we should avoid invidiously comparing and prioritising the harmful effects on children of different forms of adversity, it is justifiable to examine what does, or does not, get done on behalf of children who experience different kinds of adversity. An awareness of this kind of situation has given rise, internationally, to concern about the 'neglect of neglect'. Child care experts have begun to suggest that much more attention needs to be given to the more extensive and, some argue, equally damaging problem of neglect (Wolock and Horowitz, 1984). Thus, while child neglect is still being recognised and worked with by professionals, the challenge is to rediscover it as a specific policy issue and to put more resources and expertise into responding to it.

This should be done through the provision of a whole range of child care services, and not just child protection. Neglect correlates very strongly with poverty and social deprivation. This does not mean that all poor people neglect their children. It means, rather, that those especially vulnerable people often lack the personal and communal resources (such as supportive social networks) to survive the adversity of chronic social disadvantage that characterises the lives of so many children and parents in this state. In this sense, the neglect of neglect plays into political neglect of child care provision in general. Many suspected 'neglect'/routine child care cases involve borderline care of children in families who are poorly integrated into social networks, who may be 'outsiders'. The provision of greater material resources and family support services for vulnerable households under the Child Care Act can make some contribution to alleviating potentially serious neglect situations. The management of this interface between child protection and family support systems and the definition of problems and identification of children who should be referred for particular services constitutes one of the key issues for policy and practice under the Act.

The significance of these trends in changing awareness and definitions of child care problems and the dominance of child protection within child care—indeed, the fact that child care has all but *become* child protection—can be further established by considering what actually happens to those children who are the subjects of child abuse referrals and who do enter the child protection system. Research shows that a relatively small proportion end up receiving a service of any kind, as cases get screened out at every stage through the system.

Jane Gibbons' (1993) study of the use of child protection registers under the 1989 Children Act (England and Wales) examined 1,888 referrals that raised child protection concerns in eight UK local authority social services departments. She found that as many as 26 per cent of reported cases were filtered out of the system after checks with other agencies without any further investigation; further inquiries had not justified putting the concerns to the family. Another 50 per cent were filtered out by the investigation. In 49 per cent of referrals the allegations were regarded as unsubstantiated. This left 24 per cent of referrals to be considered at a child protection case conference. Only 7 per cent of cases referred for neglect reached the child protection register. Most were screened out of the system at an early stage, *usually without the offer of other services*. Gibbons concludes that:

> Too many families struggling with child rearing in difficult circumstances who come to the attention of social services departments are prematurely defined as potential child protection cases rather than as families containing children in need. Too many investigations take place that produce neither protective action nor the offer of any service.

My own similarly focused research into Irish practice is not advanced enough to identify proportions of cases being filtered out at each stage. But the evidence suggests that the general pattern in Ireland is similar. Enormous energy is put into information gathering and investigations which, in a high percentage of cases, end up offering little or nothing to the families. This is not because professionals are in any sense uncaring. On the contrary, for the most part, they appear to be only too well aware of what they cannot offer because a system of family support services is not in place to which needy cases can be referred. Thus, meeting the challenge of developing a child care system which balances child protection and the development of other services will require, at a minimum:

- health boards taking seriously the definition of children not receiving adequate care and protection to include children dis-advantaged by circumstances other than abuse

- a commitment to spending equivalent amounts on family support, youth homelessness, and after care services as on investigation of child abuse

- providing clear working definitions of child abuse

- raising the threshold of concern that defines the point of entry to the child protection system, so that fewer cases are dealt with and money is diverted into family support

Unless the delivery of services is planned in this way, on current trends identification of children who are not receiving adequate care and protection is in danger of becoming, in practice, focused on high-risk child abuse cases and a child protection concern *only*. Social workers can now do little or no preventive/family support work. It also appears that another (unintended and unplanned) consequence of these trends is that the threshold of seriousness of 'at risk' cases supervised alone by professionals such as public health nurses has also risen, as they have to contain cases that social workers cannot accept as referrals.

There is ample scope under the Act to provide family support services for parents who are having difficulty coping, and for households in which children are homeless, for example. It is a question of building institutions and policies and developing a mind-set which can take the child care system in that direction while at the same time improving the technology of practice around child protection. Under the Act, health boards have a statutory duty to offer services to all family members of children who are not receiving adequate care and protection, and to do so through negotiation and not simply imposition (Thoburn, 1993). The new regulations in the Act regarding pre-school services are welcome and services such as family resource centres and accommodation for homeless young people have a vital role to play (*see also* Gilligan, this volume; O'Sullivan, this volume). The focus must be on children who experience a range of adversities due to social neglect arising from poor housing, poverty and marginalisation. The travelling community is an obvious target group in this respect. The provision of such services does, of course, have major resource implications. While resources are crucial, the issues of philosophies of child care practice and the surrender of power by professionals are also of vital importance. The aim should be to regard the users of services as citizens rather than as stigmatised 'problem' groups.

Children in the Care of Health Boards

Most children in Irish society do, of course, remain with their parents. One objective of the Act is to increase the likelihood of this happening. On the

Important to compare with Canada

other hand, the number of places required for children in care is set to increase to accommodate the new provisions for sixteen–eighteen-year-old children (Gilligan, 1993). Nationally, there are in the region of 2,700 children—or 2.2 per 1,000—in the care of health boards at any one time (Department of Health, 1991). A significant trend is that comparatively more of these children are in care because of a court order than ever before: 50 per cent today compared to 24 per cent in 1983 (Department of Health, 1991).

This trend has constituted a further increased demand on the static pool of social workers, as an increasing amount of professional time is devoted to court work and its aftermath, such as supervising access visits (*see* Gallagher, this volume). Such work will increase for social workers and child care workers under the Act, as Section 37 requires the health board to 'facilitate reasonable access' between a child in care and his or her parents or any other person who has a bone fide interest in the child.

The Act provides for boards to accept children into voluntary care, with parental consent. In other respects, the Act clarifies the responsibilities of health boards to provide a *quality* child-centred service, by holding case reviews (Section 44), having regard to the child's heritage and maintaining contact with the family of origin. The scope provided within the Act for health boards to place children in care with relatives is potentially a very significant provision.

The Protection of Children in Emergencies

If there is one overriding criterion for the assessment of 'good' child care practice in Ireland, as in other liberal Western democracies, it is the extent to which professionals balance the rights of parents to freedom from state interference and children's rights to protection. One of the most important overall implications of the 1991 Act is to reconstruct this balance (or, in fact, to construct it explicitly in Irish child care legislation for the first time). On the one hand, the Act widens the scope of professionals to intervene in parent–child relations. The powers given to the gardaí (through Section 12) to remove children without warrant in cases of 'immediate and serious risk' are as substantial as the equivalent powers they had under the 1908 Act. They are, however, curbed somewhat by the requirement that the health board apply to the District Court for an emergency care order (ECO) within three days of the child having been removed to safety.

The ECO gives judges the (new) power to give to the health board the right to have the child examined/assessed by doctors and psychiatrists. On the other hand, the ECO and the interim care order (ICO) will bring in a new set of checks and balances to the much maligned and out-of-date place of safety order (POSO) (*see* Law Reform Commission, 1990). The ECO (Section 13) is granted on the grounds that 'there is reasonable cause to believe that there is an immediate and serious risk to the child's safety' that necessitates his or her placement in care. It lasts for a maximum of eight days (as opposed to 28 days for a POSO). After eight days the board must apply for an ICO (Section 17) if it wishes to pursue care proceedings. Parents are given a new right to challenge the application for an ICO. In effect, the nature of professionals' power to protect children in emergencies is greatly clarified, as are parental rights. It remains to be seen how, in practice, 'immediate and serious risk' will be interpreted by the courts and how the District Court is 'satisfied' that the grounds for a care order (Section 18) are to be proved.

Jurisdiction and Procedure

In addition to refining child protection powers and the powers and duties of health boards to children on care orders, the Act introduces an important new order—the supervision order (SO). The SO (Section 19) appears to have considerable potential to assist health board staff in their protective work with children who have been identified by them as being at 'high risk'. A major reason that health board professionals have experienced difficulties in monitoring children in high-risk child abuse cases—such that some children have died—is that professional involvement has been on a purely voluntary basis (*see*, for example, Government Information Service, 1982; London Borough of Greenwich, 1987; Violence Against Children Study Group, 1990).

Such 'failures' are in no small part due to the weakness of the current legal framework, which provides little or no statutory means for professionals to remain involved in such difficult cases on anything other than a tenuous voluntary basis. Thus under a supervision order a significant shift could occur in the level of safety and protection that can be given to many children currently known to be at high risk of (further) abuse in situations where the conditions for fit person orders cannot be met. One senior legal commentator has noted that there is

> a slight danger that a court when faced with an application to take a child into care may use a Supervision Order as a kind of compromise which is not too hurtful to the parent, even in cases where the welfare of the child really demands that he or she be taken into care. (McGuinness, 1992, p. 18)

Whether or not this will happen will depend, in part, on the availability of a coherent conceptual framework about the nature of child abuse and core principles of child protection. In short, an extensive knowledge base is required to do the kinds of effective child-centred work demanded under each section of the Act. Thus, these are not simply technical questions about if, and how often, parents are to have access to children in care, or professionals are to be allowed to supervise children in their own homes. It is also necessary to explore what precisely is meant by notions such as 'supervision'. There is considerable evidence now to suggest that, for example, simply 'seeing' children in the limited sense of setting eyes on them is not enough. Professionals will need to work directly with children at risk to ensure their safety and engage therapeutically with them to promote their recovery from adversity (Ferguson, 1994c).

The Act provides for new stipulations to be made by the Court that supervision can mean that the child 'attend for medical or psychiatric examination, treatment or assessment at a hospital, clinic or other place' (Section 19 (4)). In the enforcement of these supervisory conditions, professionals not only have to be clear about their respective roles, but must also feel comfortable in the use of authority and be prepared to work against considerable parental resistance. Research suggests that this is usually best achieved by an open approach that involves parents in decision-making, uses formal written agreements with parents and other significant adults, and as far as possible avoids alienating them from the decisions that are being made about their lives (Corby, 1987; Thoburn, 1993). The active participation of parents in decision-making will be a key feature of practice under the Act. The maximising of such a 'partnership' model of intervention requires that professional involvement take place on as planned and co-ordinated a basis as possible.

Ultimately, good supervision and a supportive organisational response are crucial to promoting child care practice that is not only effective, but also 'safe' for all concerned. The safety and security of workers must be promoted, otherwise professionals may, consciously or unconsciously, avoid violent people and confrontational situations. Worker safety is fundamental to promoting child safety and well-being (Milner, 1993; Ferguson, 1994c).

Child Care and Legalism

One consequence of the Act is that the law will play a much greater part in decision-making and monitoring professional practice. Already, the trend is for professional judgements to be placed more under the microscope and this will accelerate under the Act (for a similar argument re UK trends, *see* Parton, 1991). Not only will the courtroom evidence of social workers, psychologists, psychiatrists, public health nurses, gardaí and paediatricians be scrutinised in a new way, but also in some respects their clinical freedom is likely to be compromised. The much tighter time-scale for decision-making in the protection of children in emergencies and powers given to judges through supervision orders are examples of the much stronger role the judiciary will have to play in decision-making and monitoring of previously quite sacred areas of professional discretion and practice. This is one area where considerable efforts have to be made to develop ongoing inter-professional communication and mutual understanding between child care professionals and judges.

Court cases are set to become livelier, more contested affairs as the respective positions and powers of the health board, children and parents are represented in a new way by the legal profession. It is a cause of some relief, therefore, to see scope being made for the child's voice to be heard, either through being made a party to the proceedings and having a solicitor (Section 25), or through the appointment of a guardian *ad litem*. It is all too easy when considering these issues to ignore the child's voice. But as a child who was the subject of a confirmed sexual abuse case said to a researcher about the importance of ascertaining the child's perspective: 'Consult them. Don't just go ahead with the investigation. We've got brains and can make decisions. Take account of us. We are people' (Taylor *et al.*, 1993, p. 157).

Conclusion

In reviewing trends in child care policy and practice, I have emphasised the need to seize the opportunity provided by the implementation of the Act to plan for and develop an integrated system of child care services. Ultimately, the climate within which the Act is interpreted and implemented is crucial to this. In recent years child care issues have begun to reach the public domain in Ireland in a new way. There are more articles, official reports, and the beginnings of research and legislative interest. The very existence of this Act is itself a reflection of this. As is characteristic of advanced modern societies, the media play a key role in moulding perceptions of child care problems and practices. For instance, as I have argued elsewhere, the entire construction of the Kilkenny case relied fundamentally on the way in which the media took up the story (Ferguson, 1994a; 1994b). And that process of construction was crucial to making child welfare and protection a political issue.

Back in 1973, when nothing had happened in response to hopes of legal reform, the ISPCC observed with frustration that 'Concern for deprived children is not a party issue' (ISPCC, 1973). In the 1990s child welfare and protection are party political issues in a way that they were not before. The investigation into the Kilkenny case was central to this. It marked a new political interest in child care, triggered an injection of funds, and set a public agenda against which political action will be measured in terms of whether the recommendations of the report have been implemented.

Yet it is important to recognise the implications of child care becoming a political issue. Child care has been placed on the public agenda, but the mood is increasingly one in which child care professionals are more accountable and open to criticism. Professional judgements will increasingly have to be made in a fundamentally changed political context. Public attention and pressure around a number of issues will increase. People will question whether professionals are doing enough to protect children. Claims are more likely to be made that professionals are abusing their powers by misdiagnosing and falsely accusing parents of child abuse, a perception that has already led to the formation of the Accused Parents Aid Group (APAG), composed of parents who say they have been wrongly accused of child abuse. There will be discussion about the trustworthiness of professionals and the implications of disclosures about the abuse of children in care in Madonna House and by Father Brendan Smyth, for instance, through which it has come to public knowledge that the safety of children cannot be guaranteed even by taking them into care (*see*, for example, the *Sunday Tribune*, 3 July 1994).

A sign of the times is the recently published book by Denis Howitt (1992), *Child Abuse Errors: When Good Intentions Go Wrong*, which draws on interviews with falsely accused parents and attempts to popularise the notion that child protection work is error-ridden. The resulting pressures on professionals to 'cover themselves' and indulge in 'defensive practice' threaten to push them even more firmly into a child protection system and away from the need to respond to all children in adversity and develop support services for vulnerable households, homeless young people, and so on.

The importance in this climate of promoting positive images of child care practice and professionals cannot be emphasised strongly enough. That is why it is so necessary to be sensitive to a historical perspective and recognise even small-scale gains and achievements. It means actively seizing the opportunity that is provided by the implementation of this Act to define how good intentions can go right. This process should include critical reflection on what respective professional intentions actually are, and how they can be achieved—be it with respect to child protection, family support, children in care or homeless children. Often professional intentions do not 'go right' because the resources are not there to make them happen. There are—as ever in the Irish context—major resource issues to be confronted. Equally, however, success in key areas, such as identifying and co-ordinating information concerning children at risk and generally working effectively under the Act, will depend on attitude, the values and philosophies professionals bring to their practice, and attention to the process of multi-disciplinary working (Reder *et al.*, 1993).

Continued efforts will have to be made to keep the less glamorous categories of children, such as homeless youths, on the public agenda (O'Sullivan, this volume). In a sense, this remains true of the entire range of child care services. Above all, how the Child Care Act works out in policy and practice will depend heavily on sustaining the political will necessary if the Act is to be fully implemented, if effective work is to be done with the broad range of child care problems that are known to exist and if we are to ensure that, as far as is humanly possible, good intentions do 'go right'.

References

Birchall, E. (1989), 'The Frequency of Child Abuse—What do we Really Know?' in O. Stevenson (ed.), *Child Abuse: Public Policy and Professional Practice*, Hemel Hempstead: Harvester Wheatsheaf.

Bunreacht na hÉireann: Constitution of Ireland (1937), Dublin: Stationery Office.

Corby, B. (1987), *Working with Child Abuse*, Milton Keynes: Open University Press.

Department of Health (1982–9), *Child Abuse Statistics*, Dublin.

Department of Health (1987), *Child Abuse Guidelines*, Dublin.

Department of Health (1991), *Statistics on Children in Care*, Dublin.

Department of Health (1994), *Shaping a Healthier Future: A Strategy for Effective Healthcare in the 1990s*, Dublin: Stationery Office.

Dublin and District ISPCC (1954), *Branch Annual Report*, Dublin: ISPCC Archives.

Dubowitz, H. and Newberger, E. (1989), 'Pediatrics and Child Abuse', in D. Cicchetti and V. Carlson (eds.), *Child Maltreatment: Theory and Research on the Causes and Consequences of Child Abuse and Neglect*, Cambridge: Cambridge University Press.

Duncan, W. (1993), 'The Constitutional Protection of Parental Rights', in J. Eekelaar and P. Sarcevic (eds.), *Parenthood in Modern Society*, Dondrecht, London and Boston: Kluwer Academic Publication/ Martinus Nijhoff.

Ferguson, H. (1991), 'The Power to Protect Abused Children: Reflections on Child Protection and the Cleveland Affair', *Irish Social Worker*, Vol. 10, No. 1.

Ferguson, H. (1993), 'Surviving Irish Childhood: Child Protection and the Death of Children in Child Abuse Cases in Ireland since 1884', in H. Ferguson, R. Gilligan and R. Torode (eds.), *Surviving Childhood Adversity: Issues for Policy and Practice*, Dublin: Social Studies Press.

Ferguson, H. (1994a), 'Child Abuse Inquiries and the Report of the Kilkenny Incest Investigation: A Critical Analysis', *Administration*, Vol. 41, No. 4, pp. 385–410.

Ferguson, H. (1994b), 'Lessons of Kilkenny Incest Case Must Not be Forgotten', *The Irish Times*, 1 March, Dublin.

Ferguson, H. (1994c), 'Managing to Practise Child Protection: Key Elements of a Child-centred Approach', *Irish Social Worker*, Vol. 12, No. 1.

Gibbons, J. (1993), *The Operation of Child Protection Registers*, Norwich: Social Work Development Unit, University of East Anglia.

Gilligan, R. (1991), *Irish Child Care Services: Policy, Practice and Provision*, Dublin: Institute of Public Administration.

Gilligan, R. (1993), 'The Child Care Act 1991: An Examination of its Scope and Resource Implications', *Administration*, Vol. 4, No. 4, pp. 345–70.

Government Information Service (1982), Press Release issued on behalf of Department of Health, on the Minister's Examination of the Circumstances Surrounding the Deaths of Children in Two Eastern

Health Board Cases, 26 July, Dublin.

Howitt, D. (1992), *Child Abuse Errors: When Good Intentions Go Wrong*, London: Harvester Wheatsheaf.

ISPCC (1957), *Annual Report*, Dublin: ISPCC.

ISPCC (1971), *Annual Report*, Dublin: ISPCC.

ISPCC (1973), *Annual Report*, Dublin: ISPCC.

Kennedy Report (1970), *Report on the Reformatory and Industrial Schools System*, Dublin: Stationery Office.

Law Reform Commission (1990), *Report on Child Sexual Abuse*, Dublin: Law Reform Commission.

London Borough of Greenwich (1987), *A Child in Mind: Protection of Children in a Responsible Society. Report of the Commission of Inquiry into the Circumstances Surrounding the Death of Kimberly Carlile*, London.

McGuinness, C. (1992), 'Social Work and the Law', *Irish Social Worker*, Vol. 10, No. 4.

McGuinness, C. (1993), *Report of the Kilkenny Incest Investigation*, Dublin: Stationery Office.

McKeown, K. and Gilligan, R. (1991), 'Child Sexual Abuse in the Eastern Health Board Region of Ireland in 1988: An Analysis of 512 Confirmed Cases', *Economic and Social Review*, Vol. 22, No. 2, pp. 101–34.

Milner, J. (1993), 'Avoiding Violent Men: The Gendered Nature of Child Protection Policy and Practice', in H. Ferguson, R. Gilligan and R. Torode (eds.), *Surviving Childhood Adversity: Issues for Policy and Practice*, Dublin: Social Studies Press.

Parton, C. and Parton, N. (1989), 'Child Protection: The Law and Dangerousness', in O. Stevenson (ed.), *Child Abuse: Public Policy and Professional Practice*, Hemel Hempstead: Harvester Wheatsheaf.

Parton, N. (1991), *Governing the Family: Child Care, Child Protection and the State*, London: Macmillan.

Powell, F. (1992), *The Politics of Irish Social Policy, 1600–1990*, Lampeter: Edwin Mellen Press.

Reder, P., Duncan, S. and Gray, M. (1993), *Beyond Blame: Child Abuse Tragedies Revisited*, London: Routledge.

Richardson, S. and Bacon, H. (1991), *Child Sexual Abuse: Whose Problem? Reflections from Cleveland*, Birmingham: Venture Press.

Task Force on Child Care Services (1981), *Final Report*, Dublin: Stationery Office.

Taylor, C., Roberts, J. and Dempster, H. (1993), 'Child Sexual Abuse: The Child's Perspective', in H. Ferguson, R. Gilligan and R. Torode (eds.), *Surviving Childhood Adversity: Issues for Policy and Practice*, Dublin: Social Studies Press.

Thoburn, J. (1993), 'Some Issues of Decision-making in Child Protection', in H. Ferguson, R. Gilligan and R. Torode (eds.), *Surviving Childhood Adversity: Issues for Policy and Practice*, Dublin: Social Studies Press.

Violence Against Children Study Group (1990), *Taking Child Abuse Seriously: Contemporary Issues in Child Protection Theory and Practice*, London: Routledge.

Wolock, I. and Horowitz, B. (1984), 'Child Maltreatment as a Social Problem: The Neglect of Neglect', *American Journal of Orthopsychiatry*, Vol. 54, No. 4, pp. 530–43.

Chapter 3

THE CHILD CARE ACT 1991 AND THE SOCIAL CONTEXT OF CHILD PROTECTION

Pat Kenny

Introduction

This chapter discusses the Child Care Act 1991 from the perspective of child protection. The main provisions discussed are those concerned with the protection of children from abuse that has happened or that might happen. However, the Child Care Act has a wider scope than this, and all the uncertainties about the family in society and the state's role in protecting and controlling the family are manifest in this one aspect of the law. When discussing the Child Care Act, many of the assumptions we make about the family and the state must be considered. Thus this chapter, while maintaining a narrow focus on child protection and the new Act, incorporates a much wider debate.

The discussion is based to a great extent on experience gained in child protection practice in one social work department, in Donegal, under the North Western Health Board, and is informed by relevant literature. A brief description of that department is followed by a discussion of some of the literature on child protection practice.

The organisation of health boards is described in Chapter 8 of this book (McGinley, this volume). Each of the eight health boards has social work departments, one for each community care area. This is, of course, in addition to other community care services, such as psychology, public health nursing, environmental health, area medical officers and supplementary welfare. Each community care area is headed by a director of community care. As well as other duties, the director is responsible for the overall monitoring and co-ordination of child abuse cases (*see* Department of Health, *Child Abuse Guidelines*, 1987, p. 8).

Donegal is one of two community care areas in the North Western Health Board region, the other being Sligo/Leitrim. Each social work department is headed by a senior social worker. In Donegal, the department is organised into specialist teams, including teams working with child protection cases, foster care, specialist counselling of children in care, community workers and hospital-based social workers working with medical and psychiatric patients as well as two social workers working with elderly people in the community. The total number of social workers in Donegal is twenty. I am currently employed in a specialist post in work with child sexual abuse, attached to the child protection team.

In relation to child abuse referrals, our case load has increased dramatically over recent years (*see* Table 3.1).

Table 3.1 Child abuse referrals, 1984–9, North Western Health Board

	Referrals
1984	9
1985	23
1986	49
1987	150
1988	122
1989	82

Source: Department of Health, *Child Abuse Statistics*, 1984–9.

The increase in referrals reflected an increased level of concern in Irish society about children who were being abused, rather than an actual increase in the rate of child abuse. The increase in referrals of child sexual abuse was, according to McKeown and Gilligan (1991), due mainly to the efforts of women's groups, who were involved in highlighting the issue. Other areas in the country experienced similar increases in the rate of referrals, and in 1987 the Government decided to open two specialist units for the assessment of suspected cases of child sexual abuse in Dublin. At around the same time funding was provided for other health boards, including the North Western Health Board, to employ professionals in specialist posts in child sexual abuse work. The North Western Health Board has two such posts, one for each community care area.

When discussing the practice of one health board, it is often helpful to look at the ways other health boards approach the same practice. In the limited scope of this chapter only the briefest assessment can be made. However, by looking at trends in other parts of the country of children coming into care we begin to see interesting differences in practice. This is directly relevant to discussion of the implications of the Child Care Act 1991, in so far as it reminds us that child protection is affected by the individual perceptions of professionals as well as wider social and political imperatives, and is, therefore, subject to various local tensions. British research into the social and political context of child protection is discussed later, to highlight possible reasons why child protection can vary so much from area to area.

The Social and Political Context of Child Protection

Responses to child abuse differ from area to area in this country, as in other countries. Different responses become manifest in the way children in need of care and protection are received into care, as well as in the numbers of children actually received into care. The Department of Health's *Survey of Children in the Care of Health Boards in 1991* revealed that the proportion of children in care because of child abuse varies from 27 per cent in the Longford/Westmeath area and 26 per cent in the Cavan/Monaghan area to as low as 3 and 4 per cent respectively in the Sligo/Leitrim and Louth community care areas (*see* Table 3.2 , p. 46, and Figure 3.1, p. 47).

Different community care areas have very different numbers of children in care as a result of child abuse. This may reflect different ways of identifying and responding to child abuse rather than different rates of child abuse.

Taking a local example, we see that many more children are received into care in Donegal as a result of child abuse than in Sligo/Leitrim at 24 per cent and 3 per cent respectively. However, these two community care areas take broadly similar numbers of children into care, with slightly higher numbers in Sligo/Leitrim. There is no evidence to suggest that more people abuse their children in particular areas.

There is no clear relationship between the numbers of children in care and the reasons children are in care. In 1991 the Sligo/Leitrim area had slightly more children in care than neighbouring Donegal, but in Donegal 24 per cent of children in care were in care because of abuse, while only 3 per cent of Sligo/Leitrim children were in care for that reason. The figures reflect different ways of defining or responding to problems rather than a difference in underlying behaviour. Across the country, the number of children put into care (as a proportion of the total population of children in each county) also varies widely. In Tipperary it is 15 per 1,000, in Cavan only 8 per 1,000; in Roscommon and Wexford the figure is only 5 per 1,000. The average is just over 7 per 1,000. Some professionals and members of the public worry that what they see as too great a willingness to diagnose child abuse will lead to more and more children coming into care. The figures suggest that this has not been the case (*see* pp. 46 and 47).

In the context of the Child Care Act 1991, the rate of usage of the Act for child protection purposes may well vary from area to area. This is already reflected in the usage of court orders to secure children's places in care under the 1908 Children Act. There are wide variations in the use of court orders. Taking our local example again, Donegal uses more court orders than Sligo/ Leitrim, and has a higher number of children classified as in care as a result of child abuse. There also seems to be some relationship between the use of court orders and the identification of child abuse as the reason for reception into care. But the relationship is by no means linear and, as we shall see later, many factors influence the way cases are dealt with. To take another example, Louth and Wexford have very similar levels of children in care as a result of abuse. Yet the use of court orders to take children into care is quite different (Department of Health, 1991).

Table 3.2 Statistics of children in care in 1991

Area	No. of children in care	% in care of total pop. (all ages)	% in care because of abuse	% in care by court orders
Roscommon	27	0.05	11.1	25.9
Wexford	51	0.05	7.8	19.6
Galway	97	0.05	16.5	39.2
Mayo	67	0.06	16.4	41.8
Carlow/Kilkenny	71	0.06	15.5	57.7
Donegal	84	0.065	23.8	78.6
Meath	68	0.065	16.2	61.8
Clare	60	0.065	10.0	45.0
Waterford	62	0.07	6.5	16.1
Kerry	91	0.07	16.5	37.4
Cavan/Monaghan	83	0.08	26.5	19.3
Laois/Offaly	91	0.08	15.4	35.2
Sligo/Leitrim	68	0.08	2.9	23.5
Louth	81	0.09	3.7	40.7
Limerick	152	0.09	18.4	50.6
Cork	383	0.09	11.5	45.4
Longford/Westmeath	99	0.10	27.3	49.5
Tipperary (SR)	87	0.11	16.1	41.4
Tipperary (NR)	87	0.14	19.5	36.8

Source: Department of Health, *Survey of Children in the Care of Health Boards in 1991* (1991).

This is relevant because, in considering the implications of the Child Care Act 1991, we must acknowledge that factors other than the availability of the law influence practice. These factors are likely to be connected with the particular views of professionals working in child protection and their perception of what society regards as the best way to respond. They may also be a reflection of the views of managers and policy makers in particular

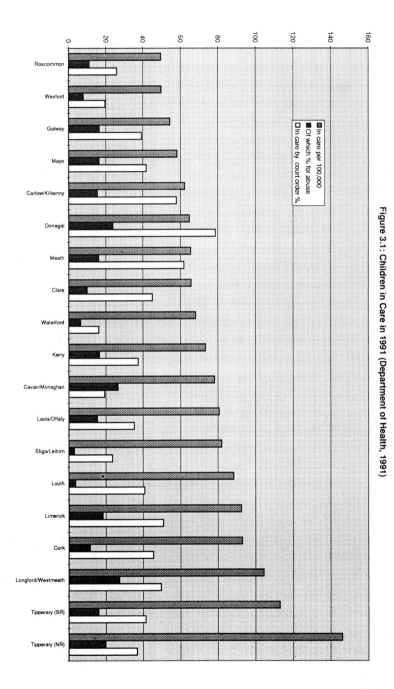

Figure 3.1: Children in Care in 1991 (Department of Health, 1991)

areas. We will see that all these factors have a role to play in the way child protection is carried out, and hence in the way this new piece of legislation will be used. The social tensions involved in child protection are reflections of an ambivalent social response to child abuse, which is concerned both to protect children and at the same time to protect the privacy and primacy of the family. These social tensions have direct implications for practice and become manifest in differing professional attitudes and approaches. How this actually works in practice has been the subject of research carried out in Britain discussed below.

How Child Abuse is Defined and Responded To

Probably one of the most difficult areas of child protection practice is defining what is child abuse and what is not. To the lay person this may seem an utterly ridiculous or even reprehensible statement for a professional involved in child protection to make. At times of crisis or when more serious cases of child abuse are published, it is often possible to define child abuse with ease. But for the few cases that reach the public domain there are thousands that do not. And the way they are defined involves much more than considering the state of the child or children.

Robert Dingwall and his colleagues have studied how child abuse cases are diagnosed in Britain (Dingwall *et al.*, 1983). According to them, decisions about child abuse are reached in a 'social and political context'. They argue that issues pertaining to child abuse, such as definitions of abuse, different types of intervention, and who is responsible for dealing with it are placed in a social construct of moral understanding, rather than being technically defined. Quoting Gelles (1975), this point is illustrated:

> In other words there is no objective behaviour we can recognise as child abuse
> . . . when I speak of the social construction of child abuse I mean the process
> by which: (a) a definition of abuse is constructed; (b) certain judges or gate-
> keepers are selected for applying the definition; (c) the definition is applied by
> applying the labels 'abuse' and 'abuser' to particular individuals and families.
> This social process of defining abuse and labelling abusers should be an impor-

tant facet in the study of child abuse.

Thus the scene is set for a debate about child abuse which seeks to understand the role of the various gatekeepers in child protection, their definition of the problem and their efforts to intervene.

To justify this claim, Dingwall and his colleagues studied cases of child abuse in three areas of Britain. As a result of their research the authors suggest that if child abuse were defined under a 'strict liability' model, all cases of injury to children would be assumed to be the result of parental negligence. In this context the only evidence that would be considered would be the 'clinical presentation' of the child. The result would be many more children taken into care, according to the authors. Of course, this would not be acceptable in this country any more than in Britain.

Other ways of considering definitions and decisions are required. Dingwall and his colleagues argue that two types of evidence are used in the assessment of child abuse cases: 1) clinical evidence, having to do with the clinical presentation of the child, and 2) social evidence, having to do with the factors existing in the family that might explain the clinical state of the child. Thus injuries to the child might be assessed in relation to the amount of stress being experienced by the family or the social conditions in which they live. The various expectations we have about particular sections of the population come into play here.

The balancing of these two types of evidence results in the 'Rule of Optimism' being applied. This rule relies on two principles: cultural relativism and natural love. Cultural relativism is described as an agency justification, which acknowledges the deviance but allows the conduct because of the demands of the individuals' environment or culture. In other words, injuries to a child are assessed and a diagnosis reached by considering the external and internal pressures as well as perceived cultural norms as they are thought to apply to a particular family. Therefore professionals may expect less in the way of child care standards where there are external factors making high standards difficult to achieve. Our assessment of suspected cases of child abuse is often based on our assumptions about families, both in general and specifically. A social worker taking part in the study illustrates that point: 'In a sense, what I'm saying is that perhaps our set of values becomes consistent with the area in which we work, but becomes very much at variance with the sort of external set of standards' (Dingwall *et al.*, 1983, p. 90).

Natural love, the second principle, assumes that there is a natural bond between a parent and child based on love. Many assumptions are based on this principle, including the belief that children need their biological parents to get the best chance in life, and that so long as we can show that natural love exists, the parent cannot be a child abuser. Correspondingly, if we conclude that child abuse has taken place, it is often as a result of the moral view that the parent has violated that principle, and does not have a 'natural love' for the child. Moral character is, therefore, central to decision-making in child abuse and neglect, as with any other type of deviance (Dingwall *et al.*, 1983, p. 80).

These principles of cultural relativism and natural love are not handy escape clauses, but are based on deeply held beliefs and political imperatives about the role of the family in rearing children. These beliefs are given expression in the Irish Constitution—enshrined in Articles 41 and 42. Article 41 states:

> 1.1 The State recognises the Family as the natural primary and fundamental unit group of society, and as a moral institution possessing inalienable and imprescriptible rights, antecedent and superior to all positive law.
>
> 1.2 The State, therefore, guarantees to protect the Family in its constitution and authority, as the necessary basis of social order and as indispensable to the welfare of the Nation and the State. (*Bunreacht na hÉireann: Constitution of Ireland*, 1937)

Article 42.1 provides for the recognition by the state of the family as the primary and natural educator of children, and the state guarantees to protect the rights and duties of parents in that regard. Under Article 42.5 the state can remove the child from the family in exceptional circumstances but will always have regard for the natural and imprescriptible rights of the child.

The Constitution does not define the rights of children as distinct from those of the family. As such, the often conflicting needs of children and families are difficult to mediate. According to the Kilkenny incest investigation, a judgement by the Chief Justice, Mr Justice Finlay, means that it would not be proper to consider the rights of a child without first considering the constitutional rights of the family (McGuinness, 1993, pp. 30–1). Now this places the principle in the Child Care Act about the primacy of the welfare of the child in some confusion, except in so far as this assertion may be based on the general belief that the needs and rights of children are synonymous with those of their parents. For most children this position is probably acceptable, but for those who are the victims of abuse it may not be. The conflict that often arises between the rights of parents and family on the one hand and those of the child on the other is what throws professionals into the uncertain arena of child protection decision-making. Health boards must balance these sometimes conflicting rights. We have seen graphically how the uncertainty that arises whenever one tries to protect children has become manifest in painful and sometimes unhelpful inquiries in Britain.

The panel of inquiry set up following the death of Jasmine Beckford as a result of non-accidental injury criticised social workers for failing to recognise the risk to the child and take appropriate action (Beckford Report, 1985). Cyril Greenland, who was one of the expert witnesses at the inquiry, has written that prediction is possible in about 80 per cent of cases (Greenland, 1987). As a result, he helped shape the view expressed in the Beckford Report that the law is a central tenet of social work practice. This view is almost entirely reliant on the belief that we can accurately (and easily) predict and thus prevent child abuse. The view that we are capable of accurately predicting child abuse has been challenged by Robert Dingwall (1989). He points out that there would be too many 'false positives' identified, leading to an unacceptably high level of state intervention in the family. In the Beckford Report social workers were criticised for under-reacting, and failing to predict child abuse as they have been in other British inquiries. But what of the Cleveland Inquiry? Here much criticism was levelled at social workers for over-reacting and taking children into care unnecessarily, without having due regard to the consequences for the children or their families (Butler-Sloss, 1988). Arguably, however, the approach adopted in Cleveland, notwithstanding other failings, was consistent with the approach advocated by the Beckford Report. The law was used as a central tenet of the child protection service in Cleveland (Ferguson, 1991).

What is interesting about these reports is the public and media response. After the Beckford Report there was much public criticism and even humiliation of some professionals, especially social workers. This was because they were perceived to have failed in the protection of a child, and this failure was thought to have resulted in the tragic death of Jasmine Beckford. Similarly, there was much criticism of professionals after the Cleveland crisis in 1987–8. Here again, professionals were hounded by the public and the media to an intolerable level. But this time it was because the professionals were thought to have been too ambitious in their attempts to protect children brought to their notice. There was now a demand that a new balance be struck between the rights of parents and the protection of children. The view that the law was a central tenet of child protection practice as expressed in the Beckford Report was no longer acceptable to British society. The professional involved in child protection has therefore to make a huge personal investment in cases, attempting to weigh up often conflicting imperatives and social tensions. Referring to recent child abuse inquiries in Britain, Ferguson says:

> As the UK experience attests, for the professional involved, the personal and professional costs can be enormous. Jobs can be lost, careers can be ruined and personal lives deeply affected, as professionals are left feeling traumatised both by the guilt arising from knowledge of their involvement in the tragic consequences for children, and by the excessively critical reactions of the public, the media and other professionals to the individualised 'failures' attributed to them by the inquiry. (1993, p. 5)

These concerns weigh heavily on the minds of professionals trying to make decisions about children in Ireland, and have an impact on the way decisions are made about children. The Child Care Act 1991 must be considered in the context of a practice which has to take into account many factors that at first glance seem far removed from the public perception of child abuse as an easily identified problem. We are dealing with a practice of child protection which has not only to assess what may have been done to a child, but also to do so in a way that does not offend the privacy and primacy of the family and has regard to the cultural context in which the 'abuse' takes place. There is no doubt that this is a very difficult task.

Child Protection and the Child Care Act 1991

The sections of the Act dealing with child protection must be read in the light of the duties of the health board to provide appropriate family support services aimed at preventing the need to take children into care (*see* Section 3, which places the obligation on health boards to have regard to the principle that it is generally in the best interests of a child to be brought up by his or her own parents). Some difficulties associated with prevention programmes are discussed in a review of prevention programmes by David Gough (1993), who suggests that the effectiveness of prevention has traditionally been very hard to quantify in relation to the huge costs involved. For some children, however, the need to provide alternative care to that provided by the parents will arise.

Part III of the Act contains the provisions for the protection of children in emergencies. Section 12 allows for the removal by a garda of a child where it would not be sufficient for the protection of the child to await the making of an application for an emergency care order by a health board under Section 13. Any child so removed must be delivered up to the health board and may be retained in the custody of the health board for a maximum of three days, pending the hearing of an application for an emergency care order. When this happens during a weekend, health boards will have to ensure the availability of adequate resources for those dealing with such emergencies.

Section 13 allows a District Judge to make an emergency care order for a maximum of eight days, where there is reasonable cause to believe that there is an immediate and serious risk to a child's safety. Following this, application for an interim care order may be made. This lasts for a further eight days and is renewable.

The fairly strict time limits were imposed in an effort to safeguard the rights of parents not to have their children removed for long periods without good cause. However, the provision may actually work against parents, in so far as social workers and other professionals will have little time to consider all the relevant facts. One must bear in mind that social workers responsible for the investigation and assessment of suspected child abuse do so while managing full caseloads. Thus it may well be that a health board has to make a full case for a (long-term) care order in a very short time. Interim care orders can be extended beyond eight days with the parents' consent, regardless of what the Court thinks. It may well become more difficult for professionals to make decisions which amount to long-term care than it would be for them to decide on an interim solution pending counselling and treatment, something not really dealt with in this part of the Act.

This may well result in increased problems associated with making decisions about protecting children who have been or are being abused. For example, many professionals I am associated with do not wish to apply for long-term care orders, lest it discourage the parents. So fit person orders are often applied for in the (somewhat optimistic) hope that they will be a short-term measure and that the blow will not be as severe on the parents. The provision of longer-term interim care orders to allow for therapeutic interventions to be offered and carried out would have been more useful. But one result of this type of procedure under the present Act is that if counselling is not successful and it is finally decided that the child should remain in long-term care until he or she is sixteen, a whole new case has to be made. That is to say, the health board has to prove that the child is at risk at the particular time of the second application. This may work against some children. It remains to be seen whether the new Child Care Act can lead to more flexible use of the law in partnership with those charged with providing counselling and therapy. The Court could act as an independent arbitrator for the parents, and could also be a source of encouragement and motivation to parents to bring about much needed change for the benefit of their children. (For a more complete discussion of this aspect of child protection, *see* Dale *et al.*, 1986.)

Following the interim care order, and if the child still requires care, a health board can apply for a care order. Section 16 places a statutory duty on health boards to make application for a care order or a supervision order whenever it seems to the health board that the conditions required for the making of an order exist. This is very important, as it brings to the fore all the issues of child abuse definition already mentioned. The conditions for the making of a care order are contained in Section 18. The court must be satisfied that

(a) the child has been or is being assaulted, ill treated, neglected or sexually abused, or

(b) the child's health, development or welfare has been or is being avoidably impaired or neglected, or

(c) the child's health, development or welfare is likely to be avoidably impaired or neglected

and that the child requires care or protection which he or she is unlikely to receive

unless he or she is placed in the care of the health board.

The grounds for the making of a supervision order are the same as those for a care order, except that a supervision order can be granted on the less stringent basis that there are 'reasonable grounds for believing' that the conditions exist. The Court must then be satisfied that the child needs to be visited/supervised in the home to ensure that he or she is being properly cared for. While these sections appear clear, they are fraught with difficulties.

The Child Care Act makes it clear that in addition to the requirement that the relevant condition exists for the making of a care order, the child must require care or protection which he or she is unlikely to receive at home. This is crucial. It means that assessments will have to be made about the future ability of the parent or parents to prevent abuse occurring.

This is where the assessment of the commitment of the parents to engage in counselling and support will be of critical importance. It is at this stage that the dynamics described by Dingwall and his colleagues (1983) will surface. Up to now there has been much variation in practice from health board to health board. Indeed, there are wide variations in practice even within the same health board, as was shown earlier. These variations are probably due to the different practices and views of professionals working in child protection as to what constitutes child abuse and what should best be done about it. Whether these variations are acceptable is open to serious question. My own belief is that they are not. But in the absence of policy such differences are bound to emerge. As Brian Corby points out:

> If one takes a wide range of ill defined phenomena such as those that come under the heading of child abuse and asks a wide range of health, welfare and police officials to come together and agree on a course of action, then one can expect a certain lack of consistency in the decisions reached. (Corby, 1987, p. 80)

Decisions about child abuse and the children and families who experience it cannot be left to any group of professionals or individuals in health boards, no matter how large or wide the group. What professionals do, and how they respond to child abuse in relation to the protection of children, must be a reflection of agency policy. Policy in turn must reflect the wishes and aspirations of the society it seeks to serve. In a recent small-scale study, I found that only eight senior social workers out of a sample of 22 reported the existence of written local policies guiding child protection practice. Only three out of ten directors of community care reported such policies. Of the fourteen senior social workers who reported no policies, thirteen said there should be such policies (Kenny, 1991, p. 16). This situation should be rectified as a matter of urgency.

Conclusion

I have tried to discuss some of the Act's main implications for child protection from a 'social constructionist' perspective. The aim has been to draw attention to the varying nature of what is understood by child abuse and child protection. It is perhaps fair to say that many of the issues identified here have been taken up in the Kilkenny Report (McGuinness, 1993). That report, which managed to avoid some of the professional blaming of recent British child abuse inquiries, makes some fundamental recommendations (Ferguson, 1994). Among these are the recommendation that Articles 41 and 42 of the Constitution be amended to give specific recognition to the rights of children (p. 96). It is also recognised that the current Child Abuse Guidelines issued by the Department of Health are not uniformly implemented within the eight health boards. Therefore the report recommends that the guidelines be revised and given statutory effect in Sections 68 and 69 of the Child Care Act 1991.

We have seen how the difficulties associated with the definition of child abuse were central to the research by Dingwall and his colleagues (1983). The Kilkenny Report recommends that:

> precise and workable definitions of physical abuse, emotional abuse, sexual abuse or neglect are included in the revised guidelines; that professionals should be equipped to take case histories, apply indices of suspicion and standardised criteria for the clarification of outcome; that written protocols should be developed on inter-professional co-operation, as well as the maintenance of child abuse registers. (McGuinness, 1993)

The important point to make in relation to the Kilkenny Report is that the issues it so lucidly identified have been repeatedly experienced in other countries. In addition to the recommendations contained in the Kilkenny Report, we should not be afraid to learn from the experiences of our neighbours as well. Most people will remember the positive and constructive debate that took place following the Kilkenny case. It is now up to programme managers and the Minister for Health to initiate a debate about the development of a nationally acceptable policy and procedure for the protection of children in Ireland. Experience shows us that we are capable of pursuing that debate in a constructive and positive way.

References

Beckford Report (1985), *A Child in Trust: Report of the Panel of Inquiry Investigating the Circumstances Surrounding the Death of Jasmine Beckford*, London: London Borough of Brent.

Bunreacht na hÉireann: Constitution of Ireland (1937), Dublin: Stationery Office.

Butler-Sloss, Lord Justice E. (1988), *Report of the Inquiry into Child Abuse in Cleveland in 1987*, London: HMSO.

Corby, B. (1987), *Working with Child Abuse*, Milton Keynes: Open University Press.

Dale, P., Davies, M., Morrison, T. and Waters, J. (1986), *Dangerous Families: Assessment and Treatment of Child Abuse*, London: Tavistock.

Department of Health (1984–9), *Child Abuse Statistics*, Dublin.

Department of Health (1987), *Child Abuse Guidelines*, Dublin.

Department of Health (1991), *Survey of Children in the Care of Health Boards in 1991*, Dublin.

Dingwall, R. (1989), 'Some Problems about Predicting Child Abuse and Neglect', in O. Stevenson (ed.), *Child Abuse: Professional Practice and Public Policy*, London: Harvester Wheatsheaf.

Dingwall, R., Eekelar, J. and Murray, T. (1983), *The Protection of Children: State Intervention and Family Life*, Oxford: Blackwell.

Ferguson, H. (1991), 'The Power to Protect Abused Children: Reflections on Child Protection and the Cleveland Affair', *Irish Social Worker*, Vol. 10, No. 1.

Ferguson, H. (1993), 'The Latent and Manifest Implications of the Report of the Kilkenny Investigation for Social Work', *Irish Social Worker*, Vol. 11, No. 4.

Ferguson, H. (1994), 'Child Abuse Inquiries and the Report of the Kilkenny Incest Investigation: A Critical Analysis', *Administration*, Vol. 41, No. 4, pp. 385–410.

Gelles, R. J. (1975), 'The Social Construction of Child Abuse', *American Journal of Orthopsychiatry*, No. 44 (April), pp. 363–71.

Gough, D. (1993), 'The Case For and Against Prevention', in L. Waterhouse (ed.), *Child Abuse and Child Abusers*, London: Jessica Kingsley Publishers.

Greenland C. (1987), *Preventing C.A.N. Deaths: An International Study of Deaths Due to Child Abuse and Neglect*, London: Tavistock.

Kenny, P. (1991), 'Clinical Supervision of Social Workers in Child Protection Practice', unpublished paper.

McGuinness, C. (1993), *Report of the Kilkenny Incest Investigation*, Dublin: Stationery Office.

McKeown, K. and Gilligan, R. (1991), 'Child Sexual Abuse in the Eastern Health Board Region of Ireland in 1988: An Analysis of 512 Confirmed Cases', *Economic and Social Review*, Vol. 22, No. 2, pp. 101–34.

Chapter 4

FAMILY SUPPORT AND CHILD WELFARE: REALISING THE PROMISE OF THE CHILD CARE ACT 1991

Robbie Gilligan

A Parable of Good Works

Once upon a time there was a small village on the edge of a river. The people there were good and life in the village was good. One day a villager noticed a baby floating down the river. The villager quickly jumped into the river and swam out to save the baby from drowning. The next day this same villager was walking along the river bank and noticed two babies in the river. He called for help, and both babies were rescued from the swift waters. And the following day four babies were seen caught in the turbulent current. And then eight, then more, and still more. The villagers organised themselves quickly, setting up watch towers and training teams of swimmers who could resist the swift waters and rescue babies. Rescue squads were soon working twenty-four hours a day. And each day the numbers of helpless babies floating down the river increased. While not all the babies, now very numerous, could be saved, the villagers felt they were doing well to save as many as they could each day. Indeed the village priest blessed them in their good work. And life in the village continued on that basis. One day, however, someone raised the question: *'But where are all these babies coming from? Who is throwing them into the river? Why? Let's organize a team to go upstream and see who's doing it.'* The seeming logic of the elders countered: *'And if we go upstream, who will oper`ate the rescue operations? We need every concerned person here.'* 'But don't you see,' cried one lone voice, *'if we find out who is throwing them in, we can stop the problem and no babies will drown? By going upstream we can eliminate the cause of the problem.'* 'It is too risky.' And so the numbers of babies in the river increased daily. Those saved increased, but those who drown increase even more. (McCormack, 1989, pp. 29–30)

(60)

Introduction

The Child Care Act 1991 regulates the role of health boards in three major areas of child care: alternative care (fostering, residential care and accommodation for homeless children); child protection (the investigation, assessment and support of children in cases of known or suspected child abuse); and family support.

The Child Care Act 1991 is founded on the premise that it is generally best for children to grow up in their own family. While Section 3(3) imposes a general duty on health boards to 'provide child care and family support services', the Act (and indeed the Department of Health) does not specify the detail of what is envisaged in relation to family support. The purpose of family support, however, in the context of the Child Care Act 1991 is presumably to promote the welfare of children in vulnerable families and to minimise those circumstances where a child may have to be received into the care of a health board, or into accommodation under Section 5 of the Act, because of severe family problems or family breakdown. Family support also aims to prevent incidents of child abuse where these might be associated with identifiable psycho-social stress factors within the family. Family support can help make childhood a healthier, safer and more secure experience, even for those children growing up in high-risk conditions. Family support is not just about securing the safety of children in the face of immediate physical or sexual threat. It is also about promoting their welfare and normal development in the face of adversity. Family support activities seek to enhance the morale, supports and coping skills of all, but especially vulnerable, children and parents. Family support seeks to maximise the resilience of children and families in the face of stress, particularly by securing their integration into what hopefully prove supportive institutions such as the (extended) family, the school and the neighbourhood.

It is important to emphasise, however, that, despite its importance, family support provision within the child care system represents only one strand of what is required to secure the welfare of children and families.

Their welfare also depends on the value and status accorded to children and their carers, and the supports provided by society and the state through legislative and social provisions in relation to, for instance, incomes, jobs, housing for families, physical planning and 'parent-friendly' policies in areas such as childhood illness or maternity leave (Boushel, 1994, p. 182).

This chapter examines family support both as an instrument of child welfare policy and as a core element of the Child Care Act 1991. Some of the key concepts, principles and research evidence underpinning family support are explored, as are the mechanics of family support delivery, and its general policy prospects.

Key Conceptual Issues in Family Support

Family

Social change has increased the variety of family types in which children grow up in modern society. Children may live with their parents—married or not. They may live with a lone parent, whose status is the result of choice, desertion, death or separation/divorce. They may live with a parent who is married to or cohabiting with a step-parent. They may live with one or two parents who share the household with friends, relatives or lodgers. These various living arrangements may vary in terms of their stability. People may move in or out; families may move, whether by choice or not. Death, conflict or the demise of relationships may all alter the composition of a household, as may the arrival of new members through birth, new intimate relationships, or the accommodation of other adults on the basis of kinship, altruistic or financial ties.

The needs of each family are determined not only by its composition, structure or location. They are also influenced by the life cycle stage of its members, and by the psychological atmosphere of the family. They are influenced too by the family's physical, economic and social environment and by the degree of its integration into helping networks of kin and neighbourhood.

Parenting

While those involved in family support work may appreciate that parents—mothers and fathers—are key to child welfare, they must always remember that 'parenting is an onerous task' (McGuinness, 1993, p. 111), especially where supports are low and stresses are high. It is important that professionals in family support work do not see the word 'parent' as interchangeable with that of 'mother'. Fathers may often be rendered invisible by professionals who may ignore or even fear them (Milner, 1993), or indeed by mothers who see them as lacking the necessary qualities (Clarke, 1990). It is crucial to seek to involve men as fathers in family support work. Closer involvement in fathering may help to reduce the tendency of some men to engage in physical or sexual abuse of their children, and may serve to enhance the quality (and stability) of support available to a child growing up.

The Child

Family support is not just about working with parents on behalf of the child: it should also entail, where appropriate, direct work with the child through, for example, group work, counselling/therapy or activity programmes. Some research evidence suggests that such direct work may yield more positive results when compared with work with relevant adults (parents or teachers) (Kolvin *et al.*, 1987; McGuire and Earls, 1991, p. 300).

Family as Comfort: Family as Threat

Professionals and policy makers must be realistic about the qualities of the family. It can be a force for great good—and for great hurt. Adherents of family support must acknowledge frankly that family relationships can be the source and site of conflict, violence, abuse, injury and death. Romanticising the family is unhelpful, but so also is implying that the failings of some families characterise the nature of all.

Family Problems and Social Exclusion

Family problems or parenting difficulties cannot be seen as merely the failings of individuals. These problems arise in a context, and often out of a set of disabling conditions which are linked to public policies in the areas of housing, physical planning, (un)employment, income support, education and crime prevention. The victims of such processes become subject to social exclusion.

> Social exclusion is not just about lack of money, but may be about isolation, lack of work, lack of educational opportunities, even discrimination. The notion of social exclusion has a strong policy focus: it is often the result of the ineffectiveness of policies, of the perverse effects of policies. (Harvey, 1994, pp. 3–4)

In the view of one British educationalist, which has at least some relevance here, many families find themselves 'ring-fenced' in vulnerable run-down communities into which housing policy 'relocates single parents, rent-defaulters . . . alcoholics, the mentally ill and homeless' (Gleeson, 1994, pp. 16–17). From this perspective, a child's problem of, say, truancy cannot be seen as arising only from within the child, or the child's family, or even indeed the school, but must be understood within the ecology of the social and economic factors that shape the destiny of that locality and its inhabitants. From this perspective also parenting problems can be more correctly seen as the result not of character flaws in the parent, but of deficits in support available to them relative to the range and degree of stress that the hand of fate has dealt them over their lifetimes (Gilligan, 1991, pp. 8–10).

Support

Support has many facets, in terms of its sources, the forms it takes and the objectives it serves. Social support to families and children can occur in two ways—informally and formally (*see* Table 4.1). It may happen organically—that is informally—within the ties, relationships and resources of kin and neighbourhood. A neighbour may help mind the young children of a lone parent who is sick. A grandmother may have her grandchildren to stay with her for short stints, thus giving them a holiday and the parents a break. A next-door neighbour may have a ready ear and a cup of tea for a mother worn out by the relentless demands of toddlers.

Social support may occur on an organised or formal basis. A third party organises or provides help for a family, in response to a request, or where a need has become apparent. A public health nurse may arrange a babysitter to allow an isolated lone mother to join a women's group. A social worker may request a home maker to assist in a family where there are problems in day-to-day home management.

Table 4.1 Sources of social support

Informal (naturally occurring)	Formal (specially organised)
Family	Public health nurse
Friends	Doctor
Neighbours	Social worker
Church	Hospital
Social club	Health centre
Sports club	School
Residents' association etc.	Support group
	Playgroup etc.

The primary sources of support for most will be the informal sources encountered in normal daily living. In one study, inner-city Dublin mothers were found to value particularly the support of relatives and neighbours (Clarke, 1990). Where links to these informal supports are weak for some reason, or where the family experiences unusual degrees of stress, sources in the formal sector assume special importance. Families with low natural support and high stress are likely to be very vulnerable, and especially needy of support from formal sources. A key goal of formal support must always be to build up and sustain a family's network of informal supports (Gaudin *et al.*, 1993, p. 604).

Support from within the formal sector can take three main forms: (i) providing direct service, for example counselling, therapy, assessment, facilitation of a support group, etc.; (ii) identifying and mobilising existing resources in the person's network of informal social support, for example encouraging reliance on a neighbour as a babysitter or companion, or referral onwards to an appropriate service in the formal sector; (iii) helping create new resources by harnessing hitherto unrecognised potential resources in kin or neighbourhood networks, for example encouraging the establishment of a church-based social support group, or by instigating a new response to need within the formal sector.

Social support to parents and families—whether from formal or informal sources—can, it is suggested, be classified along six dimensions as set out in Table 4.2. Family support along any of these dimensions may, it is proposed, serve three separate functions: developmental, compensatory and protective.

Developmental family support seeks to strengthen the social supports and coping capacities of children and adults, in the context of their families and neighbourhood. Personal development groups, recreational projects, youth programmes, parent education or other adult education relevant to family living and relationships are examples of developmental family support. Developmental family support is not problem focused and is in principle open to anyone encountering the ordinary challenges of parenting and family living.

Compensatory family support seeks to compensate family members for the disabling effects of disadvantage or adversity in their present or earlier life. Examples of compensatory family support include high-quality day nursery programmes for pre-schoolers from very disadvantaged home circumstances, or special youth programmes for youth at risk in communities with high rates of truancy/early school leaving. Compensatory family support can serve as one important strand in the range of strategies necessary to counteract the toxic effects on personal, family and neighbourhood life of social exclusion (Harvey, 1994).

Protective family support seeks to strengthen the coping and resilience of children and adults in relation to identified risks or threats experienced within individual families. Examples of protective family support include day fostering for the children of drug abusing parents, refuges/support

Table 4.2 Dimensions of family support

Dimensions	Examples
Informational	Parenting and child development information
Emotional	Friendly, supportive listening ear
Material	Financial or other help in kind
Instrumental	Child care, babysitting, and other practical help
Educational	Day care with an explicitly educational focus
Crisis	Someone reliable to depend on in a crisis

Derived from:
Dunst and Trivette (1990), p. 329;
Sheppard (1994), pp. 287–310.

groups for women who are victims of domestic violence, support programmes in child behaviour management for parents encountering serious problems in this area, a discreetly presented 'club' aimed at raising the self-esteem and social skills of young victims of abuse or bullying, or the work of a home maker who seeks to enhance the home management and social networks of an isolated and poorly coping family newly arrived in an area. Protective family support will recognise the value of relationships, routine (bedtimes, etc.) and rituals (birthdays, Christmas, etc.) in giving greater structure and stability to home life for a child in stressful family circumstances (Sandler *et al.*, 1989). Family support in all its facets within the child care system seeks to strengthen and 'stress proof' the functioning of family members in relation to child rearing.

Why is Family Support Important?

The Developmental Implications of Childhood and Family Experience

Experiences in family relationships, from the earliest years onwards, shape the individual's development through childhood, adolescence and

(67)

adulthood. While family life is a positive experience for many children, it is also true that certain sustained incidents or processes in the interior of the family can induce enduring psychological trauma. Rejection, neglect or abuse by parent figures, prolonged separation from attachment figures in early childhood, parental loss (especially with poor replacement care), witnessing inter-parental conflict and violence, or erratic, unreliable or disrupted parental care can all seriously damage a child's development (Cicchetti and Lynch, 1993; Harris, 1993), especially in the absence of any countervailing protective factors, for example an excellent relationship with one parent or another key adult, or positive experiences in school (Jenkins and Smith, 1990; Rutter, 1991). The nature and quality of family experiences influence not only how a child copes with life growing up, but also help to determine the quality of that youngster's intimate relationships, parenting and mental health in adulthood. The child's destiny depends heavily on the balance sheet of risks and protective factors in the child's home life (Luthar and Zigler, 1991, pp. 15–17). Violence, conflict, illness or addiction in the home, sometimes combined with social isolation or rejection, may raise stress levels and diminish the range of possible protective factors. Family support may be especially valuable where it manages to reduce the number of risk factors (or buffer their effect), thereby improving the balance between risk and protective factors.

Support Improves Parenting

There is extensive evidence indicating the value of social support of the parent 'as a protective factor against both poor parenting and development of child behaviour problems' (Yoshikawa, 1994). Encouragingly, the positive effects of social support seem 'most potent under conditions of stress' (Bronfenbrenner, 1986, p. 730). The absence of social support for parents is also strongly implicated in the causation of child abuse and neglect (Cicchetti and Lynch, 1993). There are a number of Irish research reports which underline the value of family support.

A special child development programme, which supplemented routine public health nurse visiting with monthly visits from specially trained local 'community mothers', produced important gains for participating children and mothers, compared to those not receiving the additional support. This Eastern Health Board programme was directed at first-time mothers from disadvantaged areas in the first twelve months of the child's life. An evaluation showed that the children were more likely to have received all their primary immunisations, enjoyed more stimulation and interaction, were more likely to be breast fed until 26 weeks and to have a more appropriate diet. The mothers had a better diet too, and had much better morale than the women who had not received the extra support (Johnson *et al.*, 1993).

A follow-up study of a group of sixteen-year-olds who had attended a specially resourced inner-city pre-school showed that these young people were more likely to remain in school, get better qualifications and have fewer difficulties in school than their peers in the locality who had not attended the pre-school (Kellaghan and Greaney, 1993). (These findings echo impressive follow-up results on work, educational, family, income and law-abiding measures in a cohort of inner-city youngsters now aged 27 who had a high-quality pre-school experience in the USA (Schweinart *et al.*, 1993).) Studies of the effects of parent training courses on parental functioning and morale indicate clear gains for the mental health of participants (Mullin *et al.*, 1990; Dolan, 1993). In this context it is worth noting that children of depressed mothers are at greater risk of showing tendencies to educational and behavioural problems and to depression (Puckering, 1989).

The Difficulty of Replacing the Family

For all its limitations, the family is very difficult to replace—ask any child in care or who is homeless. Those who work closely with children cut off from living in their own family appreciate the enormous significance of the loss of one's family and the great problems in adequately replacing it. Issues about their family and their relationship to it seem to be the greatest concern preoccupying children in care (Whitaker *et al.*, 1984, pp. 10–11). The amount of social work time now devoted to facilitating access for children in care to their families may reflect a greater appreciation of the meaning of their family for these children (*see* Gallagher, this volume). Nevertheless, it is tempting to speculate, however unkindly, that, had the same level of effort gone into keeping the child in the family rather than *in touch with* the family, such family support might have obviated the need for admission to care.

Family Support Prevents Problems

Family support is preventive. It seeks to stop problems escalating and to minimise stigmatising or invasive measures. It aims to build up the positive resources of the family and empower its members (Wallerstein, 1993). Family support is to child care what vaccines, clean water, sanitation and food hygiene have been to health care. Just as hospitals and all the high-tech medicine in the world would be futile without this basic fabric of public health provisions, so too would be even the most elaborate child protection and alternative care, without the essential preventive fabric of family support. By building the self-esteem of parents and children, their sense of being able to influence events in their lives and the range of their social supports, family support work can open new positive alternatives for families. Working well, family support can blur the distinction between helping and being helped: empowering people to give and the recognition this entails can be very therapeutic. The Newpin Project in London, for instance, provides training opportunities for many of the parents receiving help from volunteers so that they in turn can play a helper role (Cox *et al.*, 1991). But, as with public health measures and illness, family support cannot claim to eradicate or prevent all serious child care problems.

The Political and Strategic Value of Family Support Work for Health Boards' Other Child Care Functions

While the Act strengthens the legal authority and responsibility of health boards in relation to the protection and welfare of children, the boards will depend heavily on the co-operation of both public and professionals in carrying out these functions. A legal mandate in principle is one thing. A mandate for its actions from local people and concerned professionals is quite another. Family support work offers an opportunity to present the compassionate and friendly face of a board as an institution. Goodwill earned in this way can yield a legitimacy and mandate for more contentious actions requiring legal or other coercive measures to protect children. If the public or professionals see only the 'heavy hand' of a board, they may begin to withhold trust in its actions, and more crucially withhold information about children known to the public or professionals to be 'in need of care and protection'. It also seems very likely that the courts, before granting child protection orders, will seek clear evidence that a board has made every reasonable effort to provide preventive support to the family concerned.

Key Principles of Family Support

Family support involves recognising and responding to the needs of families, especially when they are under stress. To be effective, family support must be responsive and accessible: above all, it must connect with the families who need the support when they need it. To be effective, family support must address the family's definition of the need or problem concerned (Dunst and Trivette, 1990, p. 327). Family support must be supportive: it must not be experienced as threatening, alienating or demeaning. Family support must be offered and available on terms that make sense within the lived reality of its target users. In practice, this will mean emphasising a low-key, local, non-clinical, unfussy 'user-friendly' approach. To be effective, it must generally be offered in or near the child's home, certainly within 'pram-pushing' distance. To succeed, family support must operate fundamentally on the principle of consent rather than coercion. It must be presented and perceived as enticing and attractive. Parents, guardians and children must be left with a clear sense of benefiting from their involvement with family support activities. Family support should aim to enhance rather than diminish the confidence of those being helped. It requires an orientation on the part of professionals which is one of respectful ally rather than patronising expert. It also needs to 'wrap around' the particular circumstances and child-rearing stage of the family (Whittaker, 1993, p. 9).

Family support services need to have the capacity not just to work in crises. They must also be available over the long haul. To use Harris' metaphor, 'milk-van support' (daily, low-key, routine) is likely to be more helpful than 'fire-brigade support' (once-off, emergency, dramatic) (1993, p. 99). While just 'being there' may be important at certain times, it is also sometimes important that family support work has a purposeful and focused quality. Where necessary, family support work, especially in its protective mode, should be focused: on a particular targeted problem or set of problems, for a specific time period, and with specific and measurable outcomes in mind. The work should be geared to searching for what works best in a particular set of circumstances, or across a set of cases belonging to a particular category of problem. This entails a strong evaluative component to the work, a clear obligation in a context of scarce resources and infinite need. Ultimately, however, support to families must be available on the basis of need rather than the prospect of success. While the work should be as effective as possible, the guarantee of success must not become a condition of help being offered. Family support should proceed from an ethic of care, the spirit of which is captured well in the fifteenth-century French adage, 'to cure sometimes, to relieve often, to comfort always' (Schneiderman *et al.*, 1994, p. 113).

The Mechanics of Family Support

Key Players in Family Support Work

The success of any initiative to expand family support services will depend on the interest and involvement of the relevant *health board* professionals. Social workers, psychologists, public health nurses, child care workers and doctors can: (i) help to identify patterns and concentrations of need; (ii) assist in the design and implementation of programmes, and of packages of support tailored to the needs of individual families; (iii) offer consultancy to other board staff (for example home helps, home makers, etc.) or volunteers as they undertake family support work; and (iv) help in the management of specific projects.

It is essential that family support work be regarded as a priority by the managers of these different professionals. Key to this is a clear message from the Department of Health about the central importance of family support for the implementation strategy of the Child Care Act. Just as there are Child Abuse Guidelines issued by the Department of Health (1987), there should also be Family Support Guidelines. Otherwise the risk is that child protection crises alone will drive the use of time by social workers and their professional colleagues. Family support work—with its emphasis on prevention, growth and change—can serve as an antidote to the often morale-sapping effect of child protection work and can reduce the demand for child protection services. A leavening of ongoing family support experience may help to strengthen the morale and effectiveness of those engaged in the important and demanding work of child protection. While some professional and para-professional posts should be earmarked for family support work, it is highly desirable that, as a matter of principle, all posts carry an explicit family support component in their duties.

There are strong arguments for promoting family support work by *lay helpers* in both the formal and informal systems. These relate, *inter alia*, to: (i) the demonstrated effectiveness of such help where well organised and supported (Cox, 1993); (ii) the protective value for vulnerable children of naturally occurring helping processes in communities (Sandler *et al.*, 1989), and for the self-efficacy and health of local adults (Rutter, 1990; Wallerstein, 1993); (iii) the value of such approaches in terms of generating client and community acceptance of the particular intervention and the broader work of the sponsoring health board; (iv) the potentially wide availability and low cost of such resources; and (v) the importance of lay helping in providing support to thinly dispersed populations in rural areas, where there is also limited professional cover.

Two Key Life Stages for Family Support Services

Where available, playgroups organised within the community or privately run are likely to be the dominant form of *early childhood* provision. Playgroups can offer valuable opportunities to young children for their social and psychological development and can also serve important protective and compensatory functions for children living in difficult home circumstances (Osborn and Milbank, 1987). Playgroups also offer valuable respite to parents, and are likely therefore to have a positive effect on parental morale, and thereby on the parent–child relationship. In rural areas particularly, the playgroup may constitute the only family support or child care presence in a community or its hinterland. The playgroup plays an important role in promoting contact between parents which may help stimulate mutual support between them and, perhaps, other initiatives for the benefit of parents, families and the community.

While the development of playgroups should be supported financially and otherwise, health boards' early childhood services should embrace a broader approach. In addition, of course, to the public health nursing service, parenting education, parent support groups, voluntary supportive visiting schemes, mother and toddler clubs and day nursery provision all have their place. Overall, the aim should be to provide early childhood services that are comprehensive and sustained, with a strong emphasis on parental and community involvement and good links with local schools. Early childhood intervention can make a difference in tackling disadvantage, according to a summary of American research. It must focus on both parents and child, last at least two years, have a strong educational emphasis in the day care or pre-school setting, and offer informational, health and emotional support to the parent, as well as vocational and educational counselling where necessary (Yoshikawa, 1994, p. 44).

One of the major effects of the Act will be to bring into much sharper focus the needs of *adolescents*—ten- to eighteen-year-olds. While some of the most challenging child care problems will be posed by this age group, it is essential that boards take a pro-active approach to preventing the escalation of personal or family problems in the lives of adolescents. Otherwise there is a real risk that, in a considerable number of instances, they will present for admission to the board's care or accommodation. Effective intervention with adolescents requires an appreciation—and conviction—that intervention can make a difference (Dryfoos, 1990) and dedicated provision to ensure acceptability to users and to ensure competence on the part of the professionals.

Neighbourhood youth projects (NYPs) can work on many relevant and pressing issues in the lives of adolescents: problems in relation to school; problems of family conflict; health education; social skills; enhancement of confidence and self-esteem; problems of substance abuse; problems of homelessness; problems of recovery from abuse. All these can be identified, addressed and monitored, uniquely, through the vehicle of the NYP.

It is recommended that each board build on the successful experience of the existing NYPs. Each should have secure staffing arrangements, a good-quality premises and adequate resources and supports. Each project should be encouraged to respond to local needs, but in line with certain broad principles: work at 'being there' for youngsters at risk; work with parents as part of the work with adolescents; work on a time-limited basis on specific issues, whether on a one-to-one or group basis; work substantially through groups; work closely with local services, especially schools; work with a strong evaluative approach, that is, to seek to assess and learn from the impact of each piece of work (Dolan, 1993).

The Three Key Sites of Family Support Work—Home, School and Neighbourhood

The home, as the family's own world, must be entered only with great tact and sensitivity, and following careful negotiation. Home helps can bale out parents worn down by ill health, depression or the relentless drain of rearing youngsters in poverty. Home makers and child care workers can work with parents to raise confidence and skills in the management of home and child. Voluntary visitors can offer companionship and non-judgemental support.

In the school, vulnerable children can gain greatly from engagement and attainment in the social and academic life of the school (Rutter, 1991; Gilligan, 1993). Well-run schools, alert to their potential contribution, can offer much to vulnerable children, families and communities. In addition to a supportive climate for the children, schools can become a focus for educational and development work with local adults, many of them parents of the pupils. Schools can be partners with health board personnel in the conduct of social skills and compensatory groups for vulnerable children, as well as in helping with support groups and courses for parents.

In the neighbourhood, a local resource centre can become the focus and catalyst for the fusion of local and professional energies to serve the needs of children and their families (Task Force on Child Care Services, 1981). These resource centres can host a variety of family support activities: day care for pre-school children, after-school care for at-risk youngsters, group work with adolescents, groups/courses for parents, etc. These centres are ideal for families living in high-stress vulnerable communities. There seems to be ample scope for each board to develop a network of such projects in partnership with other statutory bodies (VEC/Combat Poverty, etc.), with voluntary agencies, or with local communities themselves.

Premises may take a variety of forms: a disused portion of a local school, a hired pre-fab, a part of a local health centre and so on. What is more important is ensuring that there are at least two staff in each centre whose full-time attention is devoted to promoting its work and effective use.

The Family Support Role of Community Health and Specialist Services

Existing community health and specialist therapeutic services can contribute much to family support. The scope for expansion/development of courses/support groups for new parents seems considerable. Examinations at developmental clinics and school medicals can play a stronger role in identifying social need and in parent education and health promotion. Adoption of imaginative strategies may enhance take-up of services among groups with poor rates of service usage. Local research prompted Belfast health visitors to make their baby clinics more user-friendly, resulting in a threefold increase in attendance (Kilpatrick and Mooney, 1987). The special needs of particular groups of service users may repay special attention. Dedicated posts/services for the travelling community have been successful in the Eastern Health Board region and seem to warrant emulation in the other regions. Similarly, special attention to the health needs of teenage single parents and of adolescents generally is highly desirable (O'Sullivan, 1994). Many of these ideas lend themselves to productive collaboration with other board work (for example neighbourhood youth projects) or with external services (for example schools). The profound implications of maternal depression for child welfare call for a pro-active response by professionals in the boards' adult psychiatric services which is child and family focused and closely co-ordinated with the work of the child care services (Sheppard, 1994). In addition to specific health programmes, a number of specialist units offering a range of in-depth therapies to troubled families are also required.

The Prospects for Delivering on the Promise of Family Support

Will family support become the disowned orphan or the favoured child in terms of public policy in child care? Policy makers and policy analysts in other fields seem gradually to be growing more alert to the value of a family support approach in tackling a number of areas of difficulty in public policy, for example educational disadvantage and failure (Department of Education, 1992, pp. 46–8; Secretariat of the National Education Convention, 1994, pp. 114–15) and juvenile crime prevention (Dáil Éireann Select Committee on Crime, 1992, pp. 71–4; Interdepartmental Group on Urban Crime and Disorder, 1992, pp. 59–64). Despite the duty imposed in the Child Care Act and the recommendation supporting the development of family support in the Kilkenny Report (McGuinness, 1993), family support seems to be coming a poor third to child protection and alternative care in the battle for resources and professional time. Clearly, delivering family support in practice requires not just aspiration: it requires concerted action on a number of fronts.

Family support, therefore, must be given clear priority throughout the health services, from the Minister of Health and each health board chief executive officer down. There must be a clear message that work in child care is not to be framed narrowly and passively, nor is it to be driven exclusively by the last child abuse atrocity or the most recent child abuse referral. One of the most practical ways of signalling priority is by 'ring-fencing' resources—money and professional time—for family support work. All board services share a corporate responsibility to provide and promote family support. For that responsibility to be discharged, however, family support provision must become the responsibility of a named post-holder, who accounts annually for progress in promoting family support. Promoting family support means action on two key levels, by encouraging a 'family supportive' mentality among board personnel and stimulating a steady stream of family support initiatives within board services.

Health boards must also play a leading role in encouraging other statutory agencies and the voluntary sector in promoting family support activities within communities. In this way, the funding and status of family support work can be greatly enhanced. Resources for family support work should come from a share of 'new money' allocated by the Government for the implementation of the Child Care Act, from contributions through joint initiatives from other statutory organisations (for example VECs for adult education, the Combat Poverty Agency or housing authorities for community development work, the Department of Justice for work with young people at risk in their own communities), from collaboration with the board's other services, for example health promotion, mental health, etc., and through, where possible, some redeployment of existing staff and resources for children's services.

Conclusion

With leadership, with commitment to the values that must underpin family support, with the necessary guidance and resources from the Department of Health, and with the right level of priority, planning and evaluation on their own part, boards can deliver on the letter and the spirit of the Child Care Act 1991 in relation to family support. More importantly, they can make a positive difference to the lives of vulnerable children and their families. By the authority of their commitment and experience in this field, boards and their staff can also play an important part in fostering more family-sensitive and child-friendly policies in the spheres of work, physical and social planning, housing and income support.

References

Boushel, M. (1994), 'The Protective Environment of Children: Towards a Framework for Anti-oppressive, Cross-cultural and Cross-national Understanding', *British Journal of Social Work*, Vol. 24, pp. 173–90.

Bronfenbrenner, U. (1986), 'Ecology of the Family as a Context for Human Development: Research Perspectives', *Developmental Psychology*, Vol. 22, No. 6, pp. 723–42.

Cicchetti, D. and Lynch, M. (1993), 'Toward an Ecological/Transactional Model of Community Violence and Child Maltreatment: Consequences for Children's Development', *Psychiatry*, Vol. 56, pp. 96–118.

Clarke, J. (1990), 'Mothers' Perceptions of the Needs and Resources of the An Lár Community: A Qualitative Analysis', MSc thesis, University of Manchester Faculty of Medicine.

Cox, A. (1993), 'Befriending Young Mothers', *British Journal of Psychiatry*, Vol. 163, pp. 6–18.

Cox, A., Pound, A., Mills, M., Puckering, C. and Owen, A. (1991), 'Evaluation of a Home Visiting and Befriending Scheme for Young Mothers: Newpin', *Journal of the Royal Society of Medicine*, Vol. 84, pp. 217–20.

Dáil Éireann Select Committee on Crime (1992), *Juvenile Crime—Its Causes and Remedies—First Report of the Select Committee on Crime*, Dublin: Stationery Office.

Department of Education (1992), *Education for a Changing World—Green Paper*, Dublin: Stationery Office.

Department of Health (1987), *Child Abuse Guidelines*, Dublin: Department of Health.

Dolan, P. (1993), 'The Challenge of Family Life in the Westside—A Six Week Course for Parents of Young People Attending the Neighbourhood Youth Project', dissertation, Department of Social Studies, University of Dublin, Trinity College.

Dryfoos, J. (1990), *Adolescents at Risk*, New York: Oxford University Press.

Dunst, C. and Trivette, C. (1990), 'Therapeutic Aspects of the Assessment Process', in S. Meisels and J. Shonkoff (eds.), *Handbook of Early Childhood Intervention*, Cambridge: Cambridge University Press.

Gaudin, J., Polansky, N., Kilpatrick, A. and Shilton, P. (1993), 'Loneliness, Depression, Stress and Social Supports in Neglectful Families', *American Journal of Orthopsychiatry*, Vol. 63, No. 4, pp. 597–605.

Gilligan, R. (1991), *Irish Child Care Services—Policy, Practice and Provision*, Dublin: Institute of Public Administration.

Gilligan, R. (1993), 'Adversity in the Child's Home Life—The Protective Role of the Teacher and the School', *Studies in Education*, Vol. 9, No. 2 (Autumn), pp. 53–66.

Gleeson, D. (1994), 'Wagging, Bobbing and Bunking Off: An Alternative View', *Educational Review*, Vol. 46, No. 1, pp. 15–19.

Harris, T. (1993), 'Surviving Childhood Adversity: What Can we Learn from Naturalistic Studies?' in H. Ferguson, R. Gilligan and R. Torode (eds.), *Surviving Childhood Adversity: Issues for Policy and Practice*, Dublin: Social Studies Press.

Harvey, B. (1994), *Combating Exclusion: Lessons from the Third EU Poverty Programme in Ireland 1989–1994*, Dublin: Combat Poverty Agency (and associated agencies).

Interdepartmental Group on Urban Crime and Disorder (1992), *Urban Crime and Disorder—Report of the Interdepartmental Group*, Dublin: Stationery Office.

Jenkins, J. and Smith, M. (1990), 'Factors Protecting Children Living in Disharmonious Homes: Maternal Reports', *Journal of the American Academy of Child and Adolescent Psychiatry*, Vol. 29, No. 1, pp. 60–9.

Johnson, Z., Howell, F. and Molloy, B. (1993), 'Community Mothers'

Programme: Randomised Controlled Trial of Non-professional Intervention in Parenting', *British Medical Journal*, Vol. 306, pp. 1449–52, 29 May.

Kellaghan, T. and Greaney, B. (1993), *The Educational Development of Students Following Participation in a Pre-school Programme in a Disadvantaged Area of Ireland*, Studies and Evaluation Papers 12, The Hague: Bernard van Leer Foundation.

Kilpatrick, R. and Mooney, P. (1987), 'Tea and Sympathy: A Campaign to Improve Mothers' Involvement in a Local Baby Clinic', *Community Development Journal*, Vol. 22, No. 2, pp. 141–6.

Kolvin, I., Garside, R., Nicol, A., Macmillan, A., Wolfstenholme, S. and Leitch, I. (1987), *Help Starts Here: The Maladjusted Child in the Ordinary School*, London: Tavistock Social Science Paperback.

Luthar, S. and Zigler, E. (1991), 'Vulnerability and Competence: A Review of Research on Resilience in Childhood', *American Journal of Orthopsychiatry*, Vol. 61, No. 1, pp. 6–22.

McCormack, T. (1989), 'Approaches to Family and Community Education', in *Education for Family and Community Development*, Dublin: CMRS Education Office, pp. 27–50.

McGuinness, C. (1993), *Report of the Kilkenny Incest Investigation*, Dublin: Stationery Office.

McGuire, J. and Earls, F. (1991), 'Prevention of Psychiatric Disorders in Early Childhood', *Journal of Child Psychology and Psychiatry*, Vol. 32, pp. 129–54.

Milner, J. (1993), 'Avoiding Violent Men: The Gendered Nature of Child Protection Policy and Practice', in H. Ferguson, R. Gilligan and R. Torode (eds.), *Surviving Childhood Adversity: Issues for Policy and Practice*, Dublin: Social Studies Press.

Mullin, E., Proudfoot, R. and Glanville, B. (1990), 'Group Parent Training in the Eastern Health Board: Programme Description and Evaluation', *Irish Journal of Psychology*, Vol. 11, No. 4, pp. 342–53.

Osborn, A. and Milbank, J. (1987), *The Effects of Early Education—A Report from the Child Health and Education Study*, Oxford: Clarendon Press.

O'Sullivan, A. (1994), 'Adolescent Mothers: A Study of the First Year', unpublished dissertation submitted in partial fulfilment of the requirements for the Advanced Diploma in Child Protection and Welfare 1993–4, Department of Social Studies, University of Dublin, Trinity College.

Puckering, C. (1989), 'Annotation: Maternal Depression', *Journal of Child Psychology and Psychiatry*, Vol. 30, No. 6, pp. 807–17.

Rutter, M. (1990), 'Psychosocial Resilience and Protective Mechanisms', in J. Rolf, A. Masten, D. Cicchetti, K. Nuechperlein and S. Weintraub (eds.), *Risk and Protective Factors in the Development of Psychopathology*, Cambridge: Cambridge University Press, pp. 181–214.

Rutter, M. (1991), 'Pathways from Childhood to Adult Life', *Pastoral Care in Education*, Vol. 9, No. 3, pp. 3–10.

Sandler, I., Miller, P., Short, J. and Wolchik, S. (1989), 'Social Support as a Protective Factor for Children in Stress', in D. Belle (ed.), *Children's Social Networks and Social Supports*, New York: John Wiley, pp. 277–307.

Schneiderman, L., Faber-Langendonen, K. and Jecker, N. (1994), 'Beyond Futility to an Ethic of Care', *The American Journal of Medicine*, Vol. 96, pp. 110–14.

Schweinart, L., Barnes, H. and Weikart, D. (1993), *Significant Benefits: The High/Scope Perry Preschool Study Through Age 27*, Ypsilanti, Michigan: High/Scope Press.

Secretariat of the National Education Convention (1994), *Report of the National Education Convention*, Dublin: Stationery Office.

Sheppard, M. (1994), 'Childcare, Social Support and Maternal Depression: A Review and Application of Findings', *British Journal of Social Work*, Vol. 24, pp. 287–310.

Task Force on Child Care Services (1981), *Final Report*, Dublin: Stationery Office.

Wallerstein, N. (1993), 'Empowerment and Health: The Theory and Practice of Community Change', *Community Development Journal*, Vol. 28, No. 3 (July), pp. 218–27.

Whitaker, D. S., Cook, J., Dunne, C. and Rocliffe, S. (1984), *The Experience of Residential Care from the Perspectives of Children, Parents and Caregivers: SSRC Contract No. RB 33/12/7 Final Report*, York: Department of Social Policy and Social Work, University of York.

Whittaker, J. (1993), 'Changing Paradigms in Child and Family Services: Challenges for Practice, Policy and Research', in H. Ferguson, R. Gilligan and R. Torode (eds.), *Surviving Childhood Adversity: Issues for Policy and Practice*, Dublin: Social Studies Press.

Yoshikawa, H. (1994), 'Prevention as Cumulative Protection: Effects of Early Family Support and Education on Chronic Delinquency and its Risks', *Psychological Bulletin*, Vol. 115, No. 1, pp. 28–54.

Chapter 5

SECTION 5 OF THE CHILD CARE ACT 1991
AND YOUTH HOMELESSNESS

Eoin O'Sullivan

The enactment of the Child Care Act 1991 after a period of lengthy debate represents the single most important piece of legislation relating to the care of children since the foundation of the state. The Act deals with many areas of child care, but what is significant is that it is the first time that the needs of homeless young people are addressed in legislation, in that each health board is under statutory responsibility to provide reasonable, suitable and appropriate accommodation for homeless children under the terms of Section 5 of the Act.

The Child Care Act 1991 was over twenty years in the making. Section 5 was the first section implemented that imposed a clear new duty on health boards. Thus a critique of the experience and operationalisation of Section 5 serves as an indication of the commitment of the state to resource adequately sections of the Child Care Act 1991 as they are gradually implemented.

This chapter, while focusing on Section 5 of the Act, gives some pointers on other sections of the Act and their manner of implementation. It does not deal with the many sections that could prevent youth homelessness by improving child protection and providing foster and residential care, adequate after care, etc. This chapter outlines how Section 5 of the Act has been put into operation since its implementation on 1 October 1992. It looks at the response of the health boards once a child has become homeless, rather than at the preventive services operated by the health boards that can and do prevent youth homelessness from occurring. However, the scale of youth homelessness in recent years suggests that the preventive services are failing to deal adequately with significant numbers

(84)

of neglected children who subsequently become homeless.

Determinants of Youth Homelessness

Before examining the impact of Section 5 in providing services for the young homeless, the phenomenon of youth homelessness must first be understood. The young homeless are not members of a static community but are mobile, moving between their families, hostels, institutional care, prison and secure accommodation. There is sufficient evidence at this stage to confirm that it is a growing problem in Irish society. It must also be recognised that youth homelessness does not occur in a vacuum but rather is a manifestation of structural inequalities in Irish society and can only be alleviated by redressing these structural inequities. Equality of opportunity in the sphere of education, training, employment and housing policy needs to be implemented to prevent the flow of young people into homelessness. A high incidence of youth homelessness is likely to depend on a complex set of structural inequalities, including poor family relations, often exacerbated by poverty, illness and unemployment; lack of adequate after care for children leaving institutional care; poor educational opportunities leading to reduced employment prospects; and the lack of low-cost accommodation, either local authority or private rented, and the reluctance of landlords in the private rented sector to accept people on social welfare. Thus, responses to the causes of youth homelessness cannot be successfully developed in isolation from other child care services and wider issues of equality, in particular access to education that meets the needs of the child.

For example, according to the Department of Education's *School Attendance/Truancy Report* (1994), findings from various sources suggest that in Dublin schools one pupil in seven is affected to some degree by school attendance difficulties, the comparable figure for Cork being one in nine. More importantly, the report indicates that 8 per cent of primary school-leavers may not transfer to second-level schools at all. It is these young people who are most vulnerable to homelessness. This lack of successful transition to second-level education, along with high rates of school absence, has serious consequences for young people in terms of a lack of meaningful participation in society, and homelessness may be one of the consequences for many. As Hannon and O'Riain have pointed out:

> The large increase in unemployment over the past decade has led to a disproportionate increase in the unemployment rate for those without qualifications. These extremely damaging effects on employment chances have also reduced successful emigration chances and, as a consequence, have led to larger retention rates of the unqualified unemployed in the parental home: an increase not only in the social pressures and tensions on themselves but also on their families. (1993, p. xvii)

In terms of the *presenting* causes of youth homelessness in Ireland, the deterioration of relations within the family and a lack of adequate after care for those leaving institutional care figure most prominently in the existing research in Ireland. However, it is clear that the background causes of youth homelessness are more firmly rooted in the inegalitarian nature of Irish society. Homelessness should be viewed as a result not of individual pathology, but as a consequence of deteriorating social conditions such as high unemployment, poverty, marital breakdown and other family problems (NESC, 1993, p. 468).

The factors that can precipitate youth homelessness are, therefore, multi-dimensional, and responsibility for the alleviation of youth homelessness lies with government departments, not just the Department of Health and the health boards. However, once a child becomes homeless, the responsibility for protecting the child from the damaging effects of homelessness lies with the health boards. Although health boards by themselves cannot compensate for the ill effects of unemployment and poverty, the complex division of responsibility between the Departments of Health, Education and Justice in regard to homeless young people seriously undermines the provision of an effective and co-ordinated service for these children.

Youth Homelessness in Ireland—A Review of Some Recent Evidence

Since the Streetwise National Coalition conducted its national survey of the extent of youth homelessness in Ireland in 1987, all the available evidence points to an increase in the rate of youth homelessness (McCarthy and Conlon, 1988). Surveys conducted in Dublin (Focus Point and the Eastern Health Board, 1989; Tallaght Homeless Advice Unit, 1994), Louth (Dillon *et al.*, 1990), Limerick (Keane and Crowley, 1990; Keane 1992), Clare (Dillon, 1992) and Waterford (Homeless Youth in Waterford Study Group, 1992) all show high numbers of young homeless children in their area and have highlighted the lack of suitable accommodation for children once they become homeless. The most comprehensive research into youth homelessness to date in Ireland is the joint Eastern Health Board/voluntary sector research into the extent of youth homelessness in the Eastern Health Board region in 1993 (Eastern Health Board/Voluntary sector, 1994). This research shows that there were 427 new cases of youth homelessness in the Eastern Health Board region in 1993, that is 427 unique individuals who were out-of-home in 1993.

Fig. 5.1 (page 88) shows the number of new cases encountered per month and the number of children already known to the notifying agencies from previous months who were encountered as homeless a further time. This gives a clearer picture of the number of homeless children overall who were encountered each month. While the rate of youth homelessness reported was 429, that is 429 unique individuals were encountered as homeless in 1993, the *incidence* of youth homelessness was 916. By incidence of youth homelessness, I mean the number of times a child was encountered as homeless by a notifying agency. As Fig. 5.2 (page 89) shows, many young homeless had more than one incidence of homelessness. There were 856 episodes of homelessness for the 429 unique individuals.

It is clear from the numbers placed in bed and breakfast accommodation, hospitals and garda stations that the current service provisions in the Eastern Health Board region are unable to cope with the numbers of homeless children in need of care.

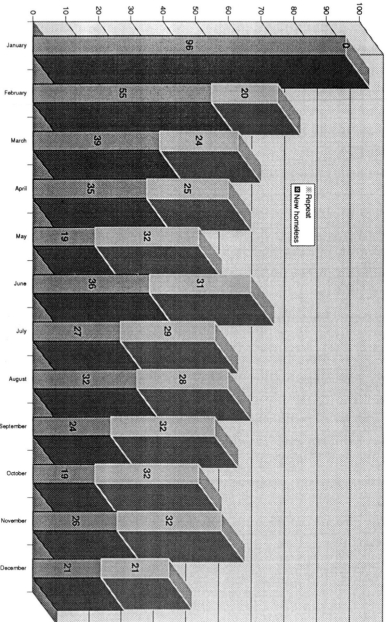

Figure 5.1: New and repeat incidences of homelessness (Eastern Health Board, 1993)

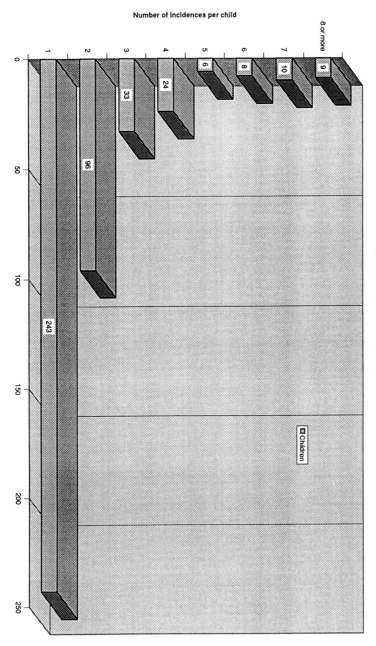

Figure 5.2: Multiple incidences of homelessness
(Eastern Health Board, 1993)

In terms of ascertaining the level of services for homeless children and the demand for these services, the Section 8 reports produced by the health boards are illuminating. Under the terms of Section 8 of the Child Care Act 1991, each health board is under statutory obligation to produce a report on the adequacy of the child care and family support services available in its area on an annual basis. In particular, the report should have regard to the needs of children who are not receiving adequate care and protection and, in particular, under Subsection (d) children who are homeless and under Subsection (e) children who are at risk of being neglected or ill-treated. The first such reports were to be completed by each health board on 1 December 1993, and they provide valuable information on how health boards are dealing with their new responsibilities under Section 5.

The Mid-Western Health Board admits that homeless boys are offered overnight accommodation in an adult hostel because of a lack of suitable accommodation and that this is not a proper environment for impressionable young people and that the experience in the Board would suggest that the 'position of homeless boys has gone underground in Limerick with the boys and agencies making repeated informal arrangements of a temporary nature as they see that no formal service exists' (1993, p. 113). The Board also admits that it cannot fulfil its statutory obligations under Section 5 to meet the needs of homeless people under the age of sixteen and has only a limited number of beds for those aged sixteen to eighteen.

The South Eastern Health Board acknowledges that a substantial number of children become homeless in its area and promises that

> in 1994 the Health Board will examine the need to establish hostels for homeless young people. The facilities may be augmented by foster care, supervised flats, accommodation in family digs, and a register will be commenced. Further proposals and more accurate statistics for the delineation of youth homelessness in each area are presently being developed. (1993, p. 30)

The Western Health Board is currently the only board that does not place homeless children in bed and breakfast accommodation. At the time of writing (late 1994) there were 23 beds for homeless children in its area, 8 for boys and 15 for girls, with a budget of £284,000 per annum. The level of services in the area is deemed satisfactory by the Board. The Board is also in the process of piloting an outreach service for homeless children in Galway City. The opening of the Edmund Rice Home for homeless girls and the eventual adequate funding of Cyrene House for boys has improved the situation in the Western Health Board area dramatically. A second hostel for boys is currently being established in Galway under the management of a voluntary organisation, Boys' Hope—Ireland.

The report from the Midland Health Board simply states that a hostel for homeless children was opened in 1991 and that a hostel for homeless girls operates in Tullamore. It does not state how many beds are available, the numbers of homeless children in the area, or whether the existing services can cope. It acknowledges the use of bed and breakfast accommodation for homeless children. The Board promises to assess the situation of youth homelessness in 1994.

The report of the Southern Health Board reveals that 22 homeless children under the age of sixteen and 29 homeless children aged sixteen to eighteen were encountered during the year ending 31 December 1992. The majority of these homeless children were encountered in Cork City. While the report states that 'The Board meets its obligations under Section 5 of the Child Care Act,' it goes on to state that 'homeless girls may be accommodated in a hostel provided for homeless women' and that 'there is as yet no such facility for homeless boys. Two emergency foster homes in Cork city funded by the board, can be accessed by the Board. The Community Welfare Service plays an active role regarding the payment of overnight accommodation for 16 to 18 year olds' (1993, p. 34). It is difficult to understand how the Southern Health Board can meet its obligations under Section 5 of the Act with no suitable accommodation for homeless boys and when the only facility available for homeless girls is an adult hostel.

The report of the North Eastern Health Board highlights the lack of services for homeless children in its area and its dependence on bed and breakfast. It states:

The health board is now responsible for providing accommodation for homeless children up to 18 years of age. It is particularly difficult to arrange foster care for these children. To date ad hoc bed and breakfast arrangements have been made. A hostel facility for boys and girls is urgently required in the region. If emergency admissions are to be made an option it will be necessary to have a 24 hour social work service. (1993, p. 7)

The report of the North Western Health Board notes that the Board has 'virtually no residential care facilities' (1993, p. 8), and that only in Sligo is there any adequate provision for homeless children. It is significant that, after the Eastern Health Board, the North Western Health Board had the highest rate of placement in bed and breakfast accommodation during 1993, testimony to the lack of residential placements and over-reliance on foster care.

Scope of Section 5

Until the passing of the Child Care Act 1991 there was no specific statutory provision for homeless children in Ireland. Health boards had responsibility for children up to the age of sixteen while other statutory bodies had responsibility once the young person became eighteen. There was thus a gap in services for the sixteen- and seventeen-year-olds. The Child Care Act 1991 remedied this situation by defining a child as someone up to the age of eighteen and by placing a clear obligation on the health boards via Section 5 of the Act to provide accommodation for homeless children. In theory, homeless children now have a right to suitable accommodation in Ireland. Unlike the Housing Act 1988, a definition of youth homelessness is not articulated in the legislation. However, in Section 2 of the Act the homeless child is defined as under eighteen years of age. This is a significant and progressive development in light of the previous age of health board responsibility of sixteen. In practice, a common definition of youth homelessness has been agreed by both the voluntary and statutory bodies. Youth homelessness is defined as those under the age of eighteen who are:

- sleeping rough

- squatting

- in insecure accommodation, with friends or relatives, and intermittently homeless

- in a flat without a parent or guardian and unable to cope

- in an adult emergency hostel

- in an adolescent emergency hostel

- in bed and breakfast, or a commercial hotel

- with emergency carers

- without accommodation

Origins of Section 5

Section 5 of the Child Care Act was only introduced at the Special Committee stage of deliberations on the Child Care Bill on 12 December 1989 as Amendment No. 27. The draft amendment read:

> Where it appears to a health board that a child in its area is homeless, the board shall enquire into the child's circumstances, and if the board is satisfied that (i) there is no accommodation available to him which he can reasonably occupy, and (ii) he is unable to provide or arrange accommodation for himself, then, unless the child is received into the care of the board under the provisions of this Act, the board shall take such steps as are reasonable to make available suitable accommodation for him.

In light of the lack of guidelines on this section to date, it is instructive to examine in detail what was said regarding Section 5 during the various debates in the Dáil, Seanad and Special Committee. In announcing the new Amendment, the Minister of State at the Department of Health, Noel Treacey, introduced Section 5 as follows:

> The purpose of this amendment is to make specific statutory provision for the problem of homeless children. It places a duty on health boards to respond to genuine cases of children who have no home . . . The type of assistance that a health board will give in any case will depend on the circumstances. In the case of younger children who are not yet ready to live independently, clearly direct care by a health board would be the appropriate response. There may, on the other hand, be older people who do not need or want to be taken into care but who need assistance. In such cases a health board, rather than receiving these children into care, would have the option of making available accommodation for them. I am leaving open the type of accommodation which health boards may make available so as to ensure sufficient flexibility to deal with every contingency. (Dàil Eireann, 1990, cols. 90–1)

The introduction of this section was welcomed by the majority of the Special Committee, with one member even going so far as to describe it as a milestone in the history of social legislation in Ireland. Nevertheless, other members were less than impressed. In particular, Brendan Howlin TD suggested that the amendment was creating a new category of homeless people. Furthermore, he asked:

> Why create a separate category of homelessness for children who are to be treated in a different way from other children who require care? The Minister has created a separate category for homeless young people, separate and above the normal category of young people who require care and protection under Section 4. After the enactment of the Bill every child who is not receiving adequate care and protection will be the responsibility of the health board but we have created a separate category for homeless young people and the comprehensiveness of the Bill does not seem to apply to them. For this category, uniquely, all the health boards have to do is take such steps as are reasonable to make accommodation available for them. (cols. 98–9)

Minister Treacey replied that the section was being introduced

> to give the health boards an option to deal with adolescents as distinct from infants or older children. We are talking about the strong fifteen-year-olds and children up to eighteen years of age. I expect that . . . this provision will in the

main be used to cater for older children, perhaps for fifteen-year-olds and upwards, who need bed and breakfast accommodation as distinct from a more permanent form of accommodation. Obviously the first efforts of the health boards will be directed towards returning the homeless child to its family, if that is possible. Where that is not possible the health board would have a choice. They could take the child into care either on a voluntary basis or through the courts, or provide the child with accommodation under the terms of the new section. (col. 101)

This comment was much criticised by those working with the young homeless and it is worth noting that in introducing the Bill to the Seanad and outlining the purpose of the new section, the Minister was far more circumspect in his description of the aims of the section. He stated that

Section 5 is an entirely new provision which was inserted at the special committee. It aims to deal with the problem of children and young people sleeping rough on the streets of our cities and towns. It requires a health board to provide accommodation for homeless children who have no accommodation they can reasonably occupy.

When questioned on the implications of this section by Senator Brendan Ryan, Minister Treacey replied:

The form of words we are proposing here 'that if there is accommodation available to him which he can reasonably occupy' is wide enough to include children who have a family home, but whose circumstances are intolerable. I am leaving open the type of accommodation which health boards may make available so as to ensure sufficient flexibility to deal with every contingency . . . I would expect that where it is reported to a health board that a child appears to be homeless, the board would investigate the matter as soon as possible to establish the facts and to make services available if this is necessary. (*Seanad Debates*, 1991, col. 495)

He further added:

I accept that some of the accommodation in which young people have been placed has not been entirely suitable. This has been due to the shortage of places available for the young homeless. I expect this problem to diminish as

the new places . . . begin to come on stream. When we are talking about children here, we are dealing with people who are single up to the age of 18 years of age. While most homeless children are likely to be confused and upset and in need of care as well as accommodation, this may not always be so, particularly in the case of older children. If the child needs continuous care, then it is open to the board to take the child into its care either on a voluntary basis under Section 4 or to seek a care order under Section 18. If, however, the child's needs are not such as to require that he be in care, the board can provide accommodation under this section. All of these provisions taken together provide sufficient flexibility to enable the boards to provide the level and type of service that best meets the needs of the individual child. (*Seanad Debates*, 1991, cols. 500–1)

However, due to pressure from the Seanad, in particular Senator Ryan, the Government introduced an amendment to Section 5 (Government Amendment No. 2), which substituted an entirely new section for the original Section 5 of the Bill. The essential change was the deletion of the precondition of paragraph (ii) of the original draft, that a health board must be satisfied that a homeless child is unable to provide accommodation for himself. In addition, Government Amendment No. 3 included into Section 8 of the Act, Review of Services, the requirement that a health board, in preparing its annual report on the adequacy of child care and family support services in its area, should have particular regard for children who are homeless.

The Final Composition of Section 5 and its Provisions

The final version of Section 5, which became Part II, Section 5 of the Child Care Act 1991, came into effect on 1 October 1992 and read as follows:

Where it appears to a health board that a child in its area is homeless, the board shall enquire into the child's circumstances, and if the board is satisfied that there is no accommodation available to him which he can reasonably occupy, then, unless the child is received into the care of the board under the provisions of this Act, the board shall take such steps as are reasonable to make available suitable accommodation for him.

In announcing the implementation of this section of the Act, the Minister for Health, Dr John O'Connell TD, stated that:

> The commencement of Section 5 will be welcomed by the various voluntary organisations dealing with homeless youngsters. This will impose for the first time ever a statutory duty on the health boards to provide accommodation for children up to the age of 18 years . . . The problem of youth homelessness has been targeted by the Government for particular attention. We have initiated a wide ranging programme of developments to improve the availability of services and accommodation to these unfortunate children. Additional hostel and other residential places have been developed around the country. Many of these new services are already in place and others are about to come on stream. (Department of Health, 1992)

While it is accepted that the Minister was genuine in his efforts to assist the young homeless via Section 5 of the Act, a number of concerns remain, in particular:

- From the information available in the Section 8 reports, it is clear that insufficient facilities for homeless children exist in Ireland. In particular, many health boards are becoming increasingly reliant on bed and breakfast accommodation in attempting to meet the needs of homeless children. It is evident that the spirit in which Section 5 was introduced has not been realised on the ground. Reasonable, suitable and appropriate accommodation for homeless children is not being provided by the majority of health boards. There has been much optimism about the implementation of the Child Care Act 1991 from those concerned with child welfare in Ireland, yet the example of the implementation of Section 5 gives rise to concern regarding the commitment of the state to promoting the welfare of homeless children.

- Under Section 69 of the Act, the Minister may give general directions to a health board in relation to the performance of the functions assigned to it by or under this Act and the health board shall comply with any such direction. To date, no directions have been issued by the Minister regarding the use of Section 5. To do so would clarify the purpose of Section 5, in particular the usage of Section 5 *vis-à-vis* Section 4, and the relationship of Section 5 to the general principle of the Act of promoting the welfare of the child. It would appear from the debates on Section 5 that no specifics will be given with regard to this section, supposedly to give the health boards greater flexibility, although in practice this has simply led to confusion and a poor service.

- When Section 4 is implemented in due course, what criteria will be used to determine whether to place a child in care under that section, or simply to provide the child with accommodation under Section 5, and who will make this decision—front-line workers, referral agencies, child care development officers or programme managers? And, indeed, is a child placed under Section 5 deemed to be in the care of the board?

- For children catered for under Section 5 as opposed to Section 4, will the principle of Section 3 that the health boards 'regard the welfare of the child as the first and paramount consideration, and in so far as is practicable, give due consideration having regard to his age and understanding, to the wishes of the child' be applicable? If the child is simply accommodated under Section 5, will he or she be considered to be in the care of the health board? If not, will the child lose out on a range of benefits, in particular the provision of after care as envisaged under Section 45 of the Act? The situation currently appears to be that those children provided with accommodation under Section 5 are not subject to the other sections of the Act. It is as though Section 5 has no relationship with the remainder of the Act, and its operationalisation is a cynical manoeuvre on the part of some health boards to divest themselves of the responsibility for adequately promoting the welfare of the homeless child. The use of Section 5 is, in effect, placing homeless children outside the mainstream of child care services.

- Placing homeless children in bed and breakfast accommodation leaves them with few or no structured activities during the day. Once the children have had their breakfast, they are forced to spend the rest of the day wandering the streets until the bed and breakfast admits them again that night. In particular, the fact that they receive only £5 a day to purchase food, clothes and other necessities means that they are highly susceptible to becoming engaged in minor acts of delinquency to supplement their income, including prostitution in some cases. An emerging trend is the criminalisation of homeless children in order to secure them accommodation within the Department of Education Special School system.

- Health boards have the authority to provide care for homeless children under Section 36 or under Section 19 to get a supervision order in respect of the child in order to promote the welfare of the child 'whose health, development or welfare is likely to be avoidably impaired or neglected'. The welfare of the homeless child, in particular the physical and social welfare of the child, is surely being avoidably neglected and impaired if the child is placed in unsuitable accommodation, particularly an unsupervised bed and breakfast or adult hostel even if in practice such accommodation is viewed as reasonable. Again, it appears that the overriding philosophy of the Act does not apply to those children catered for under Section 5. In other words, Section 5 of the Child Care Act 1991 appears not to conform to the overriding philosophy of the Act, which views the welfare of the child as paramount.

At the Streetwise National Coalition/Resident Managers' Association 'Counting the Cost' conference held on 28 October 1992, the Minister of State in the Department of Health, Chris Flood TD, stated that

I particularly want to assure you that in bringing this section [Section 5] into operation, it has been made clear to health boards that the placement of homeless children in bed and breakfast accommodation or in adult hostels is not an acceptable solution to the problem of youth homelessness and that appropriate hostel, residential or family placements must be sought. I intend to ensure, personally, that this directive is adhered to.

This was a welcome departure from what Noel Treacey suggested it would entail during the Special Committee stage of the Bill. Unfortunately, even as the Minister was delivering his speech homeless children were being placed in bed and breakfast accommodation and in adult hostels. Despite the provision of some additional places for them, homeless children are increasingly being placed in bed and breakfast and adult hostel accommodation. In practice all health boards, with the exception of the Western Health Board, use bed and breakfast accommodation for home- less children. Table 5.1 gives a breakdown of the use of bed and breakfast accommodation for homeless children under Section 5 of the Act. In addition, during 1993, 29 children were placed in hospitals and 3 children were placed in garda stations.

It is evident that children placed in bed and breakfast accommodation are spending longer periods of time in this type of accommodation, as the cost of placing children in bed and breakfast has risen rapidly since 1991. For example, in 1991 the Eastern Health Board spent £6,800 on providing bed and breakfast accommodation for 39 homeless children while in 1993 over £40,000 was spent on 76 children. Based on the average cost per night of £15 in 1991, the average length of stay for homeless children in bed and breakfast was 11.6 nights, while in 1993 the average length of stay was 35.1 nights. The official position with regard to the use of bed and breakfast accommodation as articulated by the then Minister for State at the Department of Health, Willie O'Dea TD, was that:

> It must be recognised that sometimes there is no other alternative to the use of bed and breakfast accommodation, particularly in an emergency or in cases where the homeless youngster refuses the health board's offer of a place in a hostel or other residential setting. In such a situation the youngster may opt to

stay on the streets unless the health board provides him with bed and breakfast accommodation. (*Dáil Debates*, 1994, col. 474)

Table 5.1 Use of bed and breakfast accommodation for homeless children under Section 5 of the Child Care Act in 1993

Health board	No. in B&B	Male	Female	Age range	Length of stay (no. of nights)	No. of cases
Eastern	76	54	22	13–17	1–10	39
					11–20	10
					21–30	8
					30+	19
Midland	8	1	7	<18	1–3	6
					30+	2
Mid-Western	3	3	–	<18	1	1
					14	1
					21	1
North Eastern	7	5	2	<18	7	2
					28	2
					40+	3
North Western	23	18	5	<18	1–2	23
South Eastern	5	2	3	16–17	1	1
					3	2
					21	2
Southern	9	4	5	15–18	1	3
					1–5	4
					28	2
Western	none	–	–	–	–	–

However, the scale of bed and breakfast usage suggests that not all the children placed in bed and breakfast were emergency cases, and if this is the case it points to the utmost urgency in providing alternative emergency accommodation that is reasonable, suitable and appropriate.

Despite the fact that the majority of health boards make use of bed and breakfast accommodation according to their own reviews of the adequacy of child care and family support services, compiled under the terms of Section 8, the Minister nevertheless claimed that 'The practice of placing homeless children in bed and breakfast accommodation is not widespread. It is mainly confined to the Eastern Health Board, where the incidence of youth homelessness is highest' (*Dáil Debates*, 1994, col. 475). As Section 5 was one of the first sections implemented, it is clear from reviews of child care services and other available data on youth homelessness that much of the optimism about the impending full implementation of the Child Care Act is unfounded. It is hoped that the experience of Section 5 will not be replicated as further sections are implemented. It is clear, based on the experience of Section 5, that there is much that needs to be done to translate the lofty ideals of the Child Care Act 1991 into a reality that ensures that the welfare of homeless children is promoted in a positive manner.

References

Dáil Debates (1994), 25 May, Dublin: Stationery Office.

Dáil Eireann (1990), Child Care Bill 1988, *Special Committee Report*, Dublin: Stationery Office.

Department of Education (1994), *School Attendance/Truancy Report*, Dublin.

Department of Health (1992), press release, 23 October.

Dillon, B., Murphy-Lawless, J. and Redmond, D. (1990), *Homelessness in Co. Louth: A Research Report*, SUS Research for Dundalk, Simon Community and Drogheda Homeless Aid, Dublin.

Dillon, C. (1992), *A Survey of Youth Homelessness in Co. Clare*, Clare Youth Centre.

Eastern Health Board (1989), *Report on the Adequacy of Child Care and Family Support Service*, Dublin.

Eastern Health Board/Voluntary sector (1994), Unpublished survey of the extent of youth homelessness in the EHB region in 1993.

Flood, C. (1992), Speech given by Chris Flood TD at the opening of the Streetwise National Coalition/Resident Managers' Association Conference 'Counting the Costs' in the Gresham Hotel, 28 October 1992.

Focus Point and the Eastern Health Board (1989), *Forgotten Children— Research on Young People who are Homeless in Dublin*. Dublin.

Hannon, D. F. and O'Riain, S. (1993), *Pathways to Adulthood in Ireland. Causes and Consequences of Success and Failure in Transitions amongst Irish Youth*, Economic and Social Research Institute, Paper No. 161, Dublin.

Homeless Youth in Waterford Study Group (1992), *Where will I Sleep Tonight?* Waterford.

Keane, C. (1992), *Youth Homelessness in Limerick 1990/1991*, Limerick: Mid-Western Health Board/Limerick Social Service Council.

Keane, C. and Crowley, G. (1990), *On My Own. Report on Youth Homelessness in Limerick City*, Mid-Western Health Board and Limerick Social Service Centre.

McCarthy, P. *et al.* (1991), *At What Cost? A Research Study on Residential Care for Children and Adolescents in Ireland*, Streetwise National Coalition in collaboration with the Resident Managers' Association, Dublin: Focus Point.

McCarthy, P. and Conlon, E. (1988), *A National Survey on Young People Out of Home in Ireland*, Dublin: Streetwise National Coalition.

Mid-Western Health Board (1993), *Report on the Adequacy of Child Care and Family Support Services*.

Midland Health Board (1993), *Report on the Adequacy of Child Care and Family Support Services*.

NESC (National Economic and Social Council) (1993), *A Strategy for Competitiveness, Growth and Employment*, Report No. 96, Dublin: National Economic and Social Forum.

Nolan, B. and Farrell, B. (1990), *Child Poverty in Ireland*, Dublin: Combat Poverty Agency.

North Eastern Health Board (1993), *Report on the Adequacy of Child Care and Family Support Services*.

North Western Health Board (1993), *Report on the Adequacy of Child Care and Family Support Services*.

O'Sullivan, E. (1993), 'Irish Child Care Law—The Origins, Aims and Development of the 1991 Child Care Act', *Childright*, June, No. 97.

Seanad Debates (1991), 30 May, Dublin: Stationery Office.

South Eastern Health Board (1993), *Report on the Adequacy of Child Care and Family Support Services.*

Southern Health Board (1993), *Report on the Adequacy of Child Care and Family Support Services.*

Tallaght Homeless Advice Unit (1994), *'Out of the Gaff': A Report on Homelessness in Tallaght,* Dublin.

Western Health Board (1993), *Report on the Adequacy of Child Care and Family Support Services.*

Chapter 6

THE IMPLICATIONS OF THE CHILD CARE ACT 1991 FOR WORKING WITH CHILDREN IN CARE

Helen Gogarty

This chapter considers the Child Care Act from the point of view of children and young people in care. Children are recipients of services within a legal and agency context, and therefore their viewpoint has to be understood in that way. In most cases, it can take many years before a child or young person is able to look back on the years in care and have a real sense of understanding of what has happened and why. This chapter is an attempt to look at issues that arise in this area of work, how they have been dealt with by one small treatment team, and the implications that may arise for this work with children under the Child Care Act 1991.

Agency Context

The Donegal treatment team was set up in 1989 in response to a crisis in the fostering service, when it was found that a number of children in care were presenting with major disruptions and fostering breakdowns. The social work department divided into a number of specialist teams, including the treatment team, which consisted of three people, and was given the task of working with approximately 30 per cent of the children in care who needed a more in-depth service than could be offered in a general fostering context.

New cases requiring investigation were referred to a separate child protection team, and the remaining fostering cases were allocated to the fostering team. Although the treatment team had some very difficult cases to deal with, the size of the caseload was protected and limited. This made possible both planned and long-term work. Each member of the team took on a small caseload of eight or nine children, each of whom was seen approximately every two weeks. A group was also set up for teenagers in care.

Because of the fact that the child is in a network of family of origin and foster family, much work is also done with these systems which are so much a part of the child's life.

Values

A number of values underpin the work of the treatment team.

1) The work is child-centred. This means that the child is the main focus, along with whatever he or she chooses to bring to the sessions.

2) Every effort is made to ensure confidentiality for the child, because at times a trusted outside adult is an important ally, and can even act as an advocate if this is what the child wishes.

3) A balance is sought between directive and non-directive work based on the child's level of trust. This means that the pace of work is directed by the child.

4) We have tried to find ways to help the child on his or her inner journey, using work with the senses, play therapy, stories, painting and working with water and clay.

5) The treatment team does not usually become involved in investigations because this may prejudice the trust between child and worker.

6) The focus on problems/issues rests on what the child brings rather than what is known about the family. This leads to a very different insight.

Theoretical Perspectives

One of the most important theoretical perspectives in the area of treatment relates to the area of attachment and bonding. We need to know when the first and subsequent separations occurred, what the child's understanding is of what has happened, and how these gaps can be bridged and repaired for the child. The work of Neumann (1973), Bowlby (1979) and Fahlberg (1988) has been of particular relevance here in leading towards a deeper understanding of the effect of separations on the child, as well as the relationship between the attachment process and the stages of development in the child.

In helping to repair attachment problems we are indebted to Nessie Bayley and the methods she has developed in the 'In Touch with Children' programme (Batty and Bayley, 1985). Using this programme as a base, we have been able to develop both an attachment profile and an attachment programme to analyse and help repair difficulties for children in this area. Neumann's theory of childhood emotional development, which includes a progression from the mother/child unity to an experience of a matriarchal and then a patriarchal stage of development in the child, has enabled a greater understanding of this process (1973).

The grief process is perhaps the reverse side of attachment. Having been separated from parents and other family, most children in care are experiencing some of the stages of grief. Sometimes because of unresolved difficulties grief does not come to a natural end for children and young people in care. It is therefore necessary to be aware of these stages in working with a particular child in order to assess what stage the child has reached in resolving grief and loss.

Coming into care, with all its attendant burdens on the child, can cause gaps in the developmental process, either socially, emotionally, physically or educationally. One of the very important tools in working with the child in care is a model of normality in the above areas. While it needs to be flexible, it also needs to have some boundaries which are objective and which can be measured.

Assessing the needs of children and how they are coping with their environment is very necessary. The Mulberry Bush Therapeutic School Needs Assessment (Dockar Drysdale, 1993) has become a very important part of our work. It does not claim to be objective. Nevertheless, it enables the families and workers involved with the child to map out the child's strengths and difficulties, leading to an assessment of needs. In her book *Therapy in Child Care*, Barbara Dockar Drysdale (1968) refers to islets of functioning ego. Her work has helped us to see how much easier it is for the child to move from positive areas, whether it be relationships that still function well, or memories to be treasured, or places of meaning from the past which can still be visited and loved. There has been a tendency to focus on the trauma and pain that the child may be suffering. The Mulberry Bush experience has helped us to turn away from this with positive effects. The differentiation in their needs assessment between integrated and unintegrated children has also helped us on the rare occasions we have worked with such children to understand their behaviour, and to see their behaviour as a language conveying meaning to the adults around.

Two other papers have had considerable influence on treatment work with children in Donegal. 'Child Mistreatment: Possible Reasons for its Transgenerational Transmission' is the work of Professor Philip Ney (1989). In this paper he suggests a triangle or triquetra of abuse where the roles of victim, observer and perpetrator rotate according to time, place and circumstances. This theory has been found to be enormously helpful in dealing with the emotional consequences of abuse, particularly in relation to the mother/child relationship in families where abuse occurs. It is also helpful because it accommodates itself to trauma theory, systems theory and psychoanalysis. In terms of treatment, the relationship of the victim with the perpetrator is often more clear-cut than that with the observer. At this stage in the process it becomes important for victims of abuse, whether in care or not, to get some help in disentangling these strands of emotion and relationship. This is never a clear-cut process, and a model such as Professor Ney's provides a useful framework for understanding.

In the area of identity with teenagers in care a second very useful framework has been provided by Paul Brinich in his article 'Adoption, Ambivalence, and Mourning' (1989). In this paper Brinich helps us to understand how children who have been adopted reach a stage of understanding about their parents, both birth parents and adoptive parents, by sifting through both negative and positive feelings. This helps towards a successful outcome in the teenage identity crisis. The experience of young people in care suggests that the higher the number of parents and parental figures one has to deal with in this process by sifting and reintegrating, the more complicated the procedure becomes emotionally. This is further suggested by the high number of care breakdowns at the stage of identity. Nevertheless, the model offered by Brinich helps us to understand the ambivalence, which is often of pathological proportions, and which young people in care need to contain within themselves in their struggle to build up an identity. Sometimes this has to be done in a context of lack of security and containment in their lives.

These then are the cornerstones of our work in treatment and the theories that provide a framework within which we are able to proceed.

The Perspective of Children in Care

While I cannot refer to specific cases, I can say that, having worked with children and young people experiencing the care system for the past four years, the view does look quite different when we try to experience it from a child's perspective. Children often have a surprising perspective on the events leading up to and following what we call care. They see things from an absolutely unique point of view and it is one of which little has been heard to date. To those on the outside some things that happen in families may seem to be quite appalling. However, to the child they may seem normal. On the other hand, something that seems trivial to the adult, such as the loss of a pet, may assume enormous proportions to the child, and this may well be the issue that the child will bring up in treatment later on.

It seems to me that the care process itself is like that. It is invested with many positive expressions, yet to the child it may not seem like a caring experience at all. Many children in care have experienced physical or sexual abuse and the loss of their families through the care process. The adult perspective, and certainly one I shared while working mainly with adults, was that the abuse must be the most traumatic experience. From the child's point of view this is often not the case. They tend to see the separation from their families as being the most difficult thing to recover from. Recovery from physical or sexual abuse, if handled at the child's pace, tends to come up in different ways according to their stage of development. It may show itself as a lack of trust in friends during the teenage years, or a difficulty with a teacher who perhaps reminds the child of the person who abused them in the past. Yet the loss of family is a continuing deep pain that the child carries always. We as professionals have not always understood this well enough.

In their 1984 research Rowe *et al.* found that 28 per cent of children in long-term care had no information on their family of origin. This posed a number of problems for children when they reached the stage of identity during their teenage years. In Donegal, although there have been a few situations in which one or both parents have disappeared for a time, this is extremely rare. Consequently, most children can be given some concrete information about their families of origin and the circumstances of coming into care. I believe that this has been helpful for them.

According to available research the pattern of access appears to be more frequent in Ireland than it is in Britain. In recent years, because of the work of Millham and Bullock and others, social workers have been devoting more time and effort to making access a more meaningful experience for both child and parent (Millham *et al.*, 1986). In Donegal the frequency of access has also increased over the past few years because of a growing awareness of the needs of the child in this area (see Gallagher, this volume).

At the stage of identity young people need to know their story as experienced by various members of their family, especially their parents. In the treatment team we have found the taking and passing on of the stories of the child's parents to be one of the most important tools in our work. While parents may have difficulty in understanding some of the procedures of the social work role, they have no difficulty accepting their own child's need to know their story. The taking of a story is different from the taking of a history. Its structure is taken from the story-giver rather than the history-taker; this allows a surprising degree of flexibility and necessitates a very open attitude in the listener. Almost by definition, therefore, some surprising things emerge, and their significance may even be surprising to the person telling the story. This can lead to a new understanding of the relationship between the child and the parents, and also between the family and the agency. Once given, these stories are kept in a safe place until the child asks for them. This indicates a readiness in the child to receive the information and make sense of it.

June Thoburn (1993) has stated that there are two essential elements in enhancing the well-being of children in care. These are a sense of continuity in belonging to a family to which the child feels himself or herself fully attached and a sense of identity which is best achieved by continued contact with important people from the past.

The experience of working directly with children in care leads to an appreciation of the importance of these two concepts for the child, yet at times they can appear to contradict one another. It is especially so at the stage of identity which has also been highlighted by Rowe *et al.* (1994) as the most difficult period for many children in care. As the child seeks equilibrium in the face of conflicting positive and negative feelings about parents, foster parents, the agency and the care process itself, the most important thing the professional can do is to stay still and provide a secure space within which the child can explore, symbolise and safely project feelings and emotions. Echoing what June Thoburn has said, the agency must develop modes and methods to facilitate both the measurement and repair of the attachment process. The agency must also allow, through its access arrangements and direct work with the child and parents, the development of a sense of identity for children in care. When there has been a great deal of physical and sexual trauma for the child, it is tempting to foster the idea of rescue, where the child is removed and can forget what has happened or perhaps work through it and get on with life. The experience of direct work with children, however, lends weight to the research which shows that in the long term identity issues will tend to cause disruption, and that contact with important people from the past—

while it may cause some disruption for the child in the short term—leads to a greater likelihood that the placement will not break down in an unplanned way (Rowe *et al.*, 1984; Fanshel and Shinn, 1978).

There are some other important insights from children and young people in care. Many feel that the adults around them do not listen enough, and that even if explanations are given for the changes in their lives, these explanations are given in a language they do not understand. It is important for adults both to listen to children and to find a language that has meaning for them.

In Donegal, because of the geography of the area, many children have to be separated from siblings through the care process. It has proved to be difficult to assess adequately attachment between siblings, especially if the care application is hurried. Many children feel the separation from siblings most acutely, and it is the cause of enormous grief. It is important, however, when care is being considered to look at this issue if possible.

The extended family is also a very important part of the life of the child in care. In some countries models of intervention based on the extended family taking responsibility for the care of children are being developed. Jane Rowe (1984) looked at this option and found that it worked very successfully. Children were more secure, had less sense of stigma, and breakdown rates were lower. The experience in Donegal echoes these findings, as indeed do the comments of young people themselves, who often have deep and meaningful attachments towards people in their extended family which are not taken sufficiently into account in the initial assessment, when care is being considered. One of the problems here is that perhaps the tools for measuring extended attachments are not easily available. This, I think, is the measure of the lack of awareness of the importance of these issues for children.

Finally, the area of prevention and help for parents is often referred to in retrospect by children in care. They wish that something could have been done and wonder whether their removal from their family was really necessary. Very often in teenage years, when young people in care are working through identity issues, they need to go home and experience life with their original family. At this stage resentment is often expressed towards the agency that removed them from home. Parents move into a pedestal position and sometimes foster parents are rejected. Yet, when some young people go home it does not work out the way they wish, and they need care again. Sometimes neither the system itself nor the emotional resources of foster parents are sufficiently flexible to allow this. It is important, therefore, to work closely with the child, the foster parents and the birth parents in order to prepare them for this time when the areas of attachment and identity usually come together.

Implications of the Child Care Act for Working with Children in Care

There are a number of important provisions in the new Child Care Act which will change or have the potential to change both the experience of care itself and the wider field of prevention and care of families in the community.

The definition of a child in Section 2 as 'any person up to 18 years' has the very positive effect of extending the length of time available to young people to make decisions about their future. Many young people struggle at this stage in their decisions about whether to return home or not. Some have very ambivalent feelings because of the processes so well articulated by Brinich (1989). Sometimes young people do return home. Others do so only to come back into care again. The fact that the decision rests on their shoulders at that early stage of sixteen, when there may also be developmental gaps to be coped with, has placed a large burden on the shoulders of young people. They feel that the decision is up to them, yet at times they are unable to make it. That extension of two years can make a positive difference.

The change will also have huge implications in terms of resources, not least because some young people may need to be taken into care between the ages of sixteen and eighteen. At this stage ordinary fostering is not usually an option. Young people have made their attachments and there may also be control issues involved. Caring for this group of young people will place a heavy burden on the health boards because consideration will have to be given to providing residential placements for them.

Part II, Section 3 of the Act requires health boards to promote the welfare of children who are not receiving adequate care and protection, and gives the power to provide child care and family support services to the health boards. It also requires that health boards have regard to the principle that it is generally in the best interests of a child to be brought up in his or her own family.

This is a very important provision because, while it is necessary to receive children into care, and some children have very positive experiences in care, the research both here and in Britain shows a pattern of high levels of breakdown and disruption, especially during the teenage years when identity is an issue. If young people fall out of the care net and have lost their birth families, it can be devastating for them, leading to homelessness, early pregnancy, lack of social and educational skills, lack of support, and many other problems.

Young people in care often express a wish that difficulties in their lives such as parental abuse or neglect could have been dealt with in some way other than separation from their families. While sometimes this path is inevitable, I believe a great deal more could be done in terms of direct intervention in the parent–child relationship. Two examples are the use of play therapy with both parents and child to enhance the positive aspects of the relationship and skilled intervention in the area of attachment to help parents not to misread the signals a child is sending. This is sometimes related to physical abuse or neglect of children.

In some ways many of our prevention services are too broadly based and do not direct themselves clearly enough at specific families where care proceedings are a possibility. In particular, our tools of intervention are not subtle enough to analyse and help to repair difficulties in the attachment process between parents and children. This often has to be done in the treatment area anyway between foster children and foster parents to help prevent a breakdown. It may often be more helpful to direct these interventions at an earlier stage in the process to repair difficulties in the child's own family of origin.

In Part II, Section 5 of the Act, health boards are required to make available accommodation for children who are homeless and have no accommodation they can reasonably occupy. Some of the children we have worked with have found themselves homeless in the post-care situation, and accommodation has had to be found for them. However, because of the profound nature of their problems they have been unable to cope on their own, and need a much more supportive environment than is presently available. It is hoped that resources will be provided under the Act to give such support and accommodation to young people, especially those who have been in care and for whom family support is minimal or non-existent.

Part III, Section 13 of the Act enables a District Judge to make an emergency care order placing a child in the care of a health board for up to eight days where there is an immediate risk to his or her safety. While there is further provision in the Act for the District Judge to make an interim care order if necessary, there are possible grounds for concern that the time limit of eight days may be insufficient to do an extensive assessment of the difficulties in the family. Given the enormous implications of the decision for or against a care order for the child, it is very important that all aspects be given due consideration. We need to consider not just the circumstances and difficulties within the immediate family, but also the views of the child or children, the help which may or may not be available in the extended family, and the patterns of attachment within the family.

Part V, Sections 24 and 25 express the very important principle of placing the welfare of the child in the primary position in relation to care and protection, and making legal provision for this. However, there may be a difficulty in the area of legal representation for children, because children and young people who are the subject of care proceedings may not easily trust a solicitor sent to represent them. They may refuse to speak or they may have very ambivalent views about wanting to come into care and not wanting to. Sometimes it has taken many months for children to trust enough to reveal their true feelings and opinions, and these are usually ambivalent when they are revealed. Consideration needs to be given as to how this problem can be addressed.

Part IV, Section 37 of the Act deals with access arrangements and requires the health board to facilitate reasonable access for parents and other persons who have a bona fide interest in the child. Access is often a problem area for children in care. Many children express very strong feelings of wanting more access. Sometimes children do not want access at all. Where parents have disappeared for a time the yearning a child feels is often very acute, yet some children express a wish never to see a parent again. Usually this happens when children feel very let down and neglected. Sometimes the ambivalence and polarity of feelings are such that parents who have not contacted a child for a very long time are invested with positive feelings, and foster parents who have devoted years of caring for a child are seen in a negative light by that child. These emotions of ambivalence and polarity need to be understood clearly by everyone involved in working with children in care.

Access is the point at which the three corners of a triangle meet—the child, the foster parents or residential worker, and the birth family. It is the point where the child bridges the need for security and attachment on the one hand, and meaningful relationships from the past and perhaps the future on the other. It is the responsibility of the social worker to build a relationship with the child to the point where he or she is sensitively aware of the child's need for and response to access, and how this can be met. Young people in care often report that their social worker did not know them well enough to be aware of difficulties in the area of access. Young people also very often express a wish to have more access with their siblings, cousins, extended family and friends. Again, knowledge of the child will help the social worker to become more aware of these networks of attachment.

Because access is by definition triangular in arrangement it is often fraught with enormous tensions. Foster parents sometimes feel that it is not good for a child because the child reacts negatively afterwards. Parents often feel resentful if their child shows more attachment to their foster parents than to them. The child may need to have more contact with the birth parents at difficult stages of development and is often caught between these two realities. The social worker should try to be a bridge to all three sides of this tense triangle, understanding the frustration of the foster parents, the anger of the parents, and the child's need to release feelings of grief and anxiety after an access session. The foster parents' sincere wish to protect the child from this, and the social worker's understanding of what Thoburn (1993) calls the need for meaningful contact from the past, can also be an area of tension around the child.

The area of access needs all the resources of imagination and understanding that the social worker and the health board can provide. An appeal can be made to the Court where the arrangement is considered unsatisfactory. Within that framework, however, a great deal remains to be done. In Donegal, because of the wishes of children and parents and a greater understanding of this whole area, the frequency of access has increased in recent years. We need, however, to make the access experience more meaningful and enjoyable for all concerned, especially for the child in care.

Part VI, Section 41 requires the Minister to make regulations in relation to the placement of children with relatives. Some children we have worked with have expressed a wish that this option had been better explored. Some have eventually ended up living with relatives anyway. It is apparent that some relatives would have been willing to help during a crisis, but did not feel justified in coming forward because they were not directly approached. There may well be an issue of confidentiality here, but given the strength of the extended family in Ireland, a model of intervention based on the extended kinship networks (such as operates in New Zealand) involving the placement of children in the extended family seems to reduce the risk of an identity crisis leading to breakdown.

Kilkenny Report Recommendations Regarding Treatment

In the Kilkenny Report (McGuinness, 1993) the investigating team points out that while there have been improvements in the provision of validation and assessment for victims of child sexual abuse, there has been no significant development of treatment provision. I concur with this view and hope that the implementation of the Child Care Act will move this development forward, and that health boards will be enabled to set up treatment facilities for all members of the family where child abuse has occurred. This is an area where there are huge gaps at present. While we have attempted to bridge this gap in Donegal by providing treatment within the care service, there is an urgent need to extend this service to families where care has not been the outcome, especially for the traumatised child. Having worked also with victims of physical and sexual abuse where the child remained at home, I believe that in this situation the child is able to deal with the issue of abuse more directly. This is because when children are able to remain at home they do not have the added grief of separation from their parents and family.

The Kilkenny Report also recommends the introduction of the Child Abuse Prevention Programme in all classes of primary school level. From a treatment point of view I have a number of concerns about this recommendation. There is a relationship between the abuse itself and the attachment process, between child and parents and other caregivers. If a child is attached in the normal positive sense and abuse occurs from outside, it is more likely to be experienced as a 'no' or 'bad' feeling. However, as children are going to become attached to those who care for them in any case, abuse occurring within a caring context, even one that may later become more overtly abusive, is much more problematic. There are complications that emerge later on in treatment that can be difficult to disentangle. I am concerned that simplistic ideas of good and bad touch may make this more difficult for the child.

Given the fact that children are egocentric and tend to blame themselves for what happened, we may find them also blaming themselves for not making the right assessment of the touch dilemma. Disclosure in the school setting may cause additional problems for the child. At the later stage of treatment children need to move on and leave traumatic events behind. In my experience the place of disclosure is significant for the child and may become associated with feelings connected with the abuse.

Conclusion

Working with children and young people in care over the past five years has presented me with a complex picture of the child's view of the care process. There are two main aspects to the child's world: the relationship and the care they receive from their foster parents or residential child care workers and their relationship with their own birth family. The health board, operating in a legal context and through the professionals involved and the foster parents, also has many points of connection to the child. The picture is further complicated by the developmental process itself; for example, at certain stages of development the children need to feel a strong sense of security with one set of parents, at other stages they need to make strong connections to the past. Perhaps it is a feature of human survival that, once initial danger or stress is over, we tend to concentrate on present conditions, or perhaps it is the case that grief over the loss of family and familiar surroundings eventually takes up the space once occupied by other traumas and difficulties.

One of the insights which has emerged from working in treatment with children in care is that, no matter how traumatic their previous experiences have been, children often feel the loss of family as extremely painful. This experience of separation makes it more difficult for them to deal with the trauma of physical or sexual abuse. By contrast, children who have not been received into care, and who have managed to retain the security of home, are able to work through their experiences of abuse more easily.

This is not to suggest that children do not need to be removed from their families if this is required to ensure their protection. It is to say, however, that the experience of care is not universally positive for children, especially in the long term.

References

Batty, P. and Bailey, N. (1985), *In Touch with Children*, London: British Association of Adoption and Fostering.

Bowlby, J. (1979), *The Making and Breaking of Affectional Bonds*, London: Tavistock Publications.

Brinich, P. (1989), 'Adoption, Ambivalence, and Mourning', *Adoption and Fostering*, Vol. 1.

Dockar Drysdale, B. (1968), *Therapy in Child Care*, London: Longman.

Dockar Drysdale, B. (1993) *Therapy and Consultation in Child Care*, London: Free Association Press.

Fahlberg, V. (1988), *Fitting the Pieces Together*, London: British Association of Adoption and Fostering.

Fanshel, D. (1975), 'Parental Failure and Consequences for Children— The Drug-abusing Mother whose Children are in Foster Care', *American Journal of Public Health*, Vol. 65, No. 6, pp. 604–12.

Fanshel, D. and Shinn, E. (1978), *Children in Foster Care—A Longitudinal Investigation*, New York: Columbia University Press.

McGuinness, C. (1993), *Report of the Kilkenny Incest Investigation*, Dublin: Stationery Office.

Millan, N. (1992), *Story-telling and the Art of the Imagination*, Element Books.

Millham, S., Bullock, R., Hosie, K. and Little, M. (1986), *Lost in Care: The Problem of Maintaining Links between Children in Care and their Families*, Aldershot: Gower.

Neumann, E. (1973), *The Child*, London: Maresfield Library.

Ney, P. (1989), 'Child Mistreatment: Possible Reasons for its Trans-generational Transmission', *Canadian Journal of Psychiatry*, Vol. 34.

Rowe, J., Cain, H., Hindley, M. and Keane, A. (1984), *Long-term Fostering and the Children Act*, Research Series 3, London: British Association of Adoption and Fostering.

Thoburn, J. (1993), 'Negotiating Foster Placement Agreements', Workshop delivered at the Eighth International Foster Care Conference, Dublin (July).

Chapter 7

PARENTS, FAMILIES AND ACCESS TO CHILDREN IN CARE: THE IMPLICATIONS OF THE CHILD CARE ACT 1991

Sile Gallagher

Introduction

This chapter presents the findings of a study on access for children in care carried out in late 1993 in Co. Donegal. 'Access' is the term used to describe contact between children in care and their families. This topic is of interest for a number of reasons, both personal and general. My impression from working in the area was that access provisions were given quite a high priority by the social workers, myself included, for the children in care in Co. Donegal. There seemed to be a high level of contact between children in care and their natural parents, but we wanted to find out how accurate this impression might be.

Second, it seemed likely that the level of access contact might be increasing prior to the implementation of Section 37 of the Child Care Act 1991. This section requires health boards to facilitate reasonable access between a child in care and his or her parents or any other person who has a bona fide interest in the child. Full implementation of Section 37 will give parents increased rights to apply to the courts if they are not satisfied with the access arrangements made by the health board. Obviously, it would be important to have a baseline of the current levels of access for children in care if any significant increase is to be expected in the future. I was also interested in establishing the general picture and pattern of access arrangements.

A third strand of interest came from research studies which emphasise the importance of access contacts for children in care. The key findings from previous research can be summarised as follows:

1) Regular access during care is the best indicator that a child will leave care rapidly (Millham *et al.*, 1986).

2) Access contact is crucial for the child's ongoing emotional self identity (Fanshel and Shin, 1978).

3) Fostering tends to be more successful, with fewer breakdowns, where contact with the natural family is maintained (Berridge and Cleaver, 1987).

4) When children leave care, a majority return to their natural families and the community from which they came (Department of Health, 1990).

A fourth motivation for this study came from concepts within a total quality management (TQM) approach to our work and the encouragement of quality assurance and our own service evaluation. Within the fostering section of the Co. Donegal social work department we were aware that a significant proportion of our time was taken up in providing access arrangements and that a high value was put on this work by both the department and our client group. So it seemed logical to examine this aspect of our work in reasonable detail by measuring baseline social work activity rates and evaluating the quantity, content and quality of access from the perspective of both children in care and their families.

Methodology

This study examined all the access activity in the Donegal Community Care Area for a one-month period from 17 November to 17 December 1993. In this 'slice of time' method, each social worker responsible for foster care placements was requested to

1) record the amount of time and involvement spent on access-related activities for this month period

2) complete a questionnaire for each access contact that a child in care

had during this period

The following information for each child was elicited by the questionnaire:

- identification number

- date of birth

- sex

- age during study period

- date of reception into care

- length of time in care

- the number of access visits the child had in this period

In relation to each access visit the following data were collected:

- who the access was with (for example parents only, parents and siblings or siblings only)

- the time spent on the access visit

- who the organiser was and who supervised the access contact

- the place of access (for example natural home, health centre)

- the means of transport used by parents and children to reach the access venue

- the distances the parents and children travelled to reach the access venue

- what happened during the access visits

- an evaluation of the quality of the access visit for the child and for the access recipients (usually the parents) by the social workers; a Lickert scale was used for this purpose (*see* p.138).

Social workers were also given a form to complete detailing the time they spent in access-related activity and each received a copy of the questionnaire. The questionnaire was completed either in direct interviews with

(123)

social workers or over the telephone. The data were analysed with the use of the EPI-Info Statistics Package, which speeded up and facilitated calculation of the frequencies and percentages of all variables, and permitted the analysis of differences between means (ANOVA) or chi-squares where appropriate.

Social Work Time and Involvement

Social workers were asked to provide information on how much time they spent in access-related activity for this one month. They were asked to account for time spent in:

- organisational and administrative tasks related to access visits, discussion, phone calls and writing case records

- direct contact, that is time spent accompanying or supervising access participants

- travel time, that is time spent by social workers travelling to and from access venues or the parents' or children's homes

- other access-related activity, for example tracing a natural parent or attending a court hearing regarding access rights

Donegal has nineteen social workers in total; most work in smaller 'specialist groups'. There are four social workers (two of whom job-share) specialising in fostering work, this being equivalent to three social work posts. The majority of the access visits (77 per cent) were undertaken by these four workers. The remaining access visits (23 per cent) were covered by six other social workers. Most of the latter group of workers devoted only 5 per cent of their work time to access activity. The statistics which follow are based on my estimate that within this one-month period the average full-time social worker worked a total of 140 hours (4 weeks at 35 hours a week). The total amount of time spent by all the social workers when they were involved in access-related work was 178 hours.

This rate of social work involvement in access alone is equivalent to 1.25 social workers whose only role and function would be to cover access-related work. The following is an estimate of how social workers' time is divided between tasks relating to the provision of access for children in care: organisation and administration 25–30 per cent; direct contact 35–55 per cent; travel 25–30 per cent. Roughly 25–30 per cent of social work time is spent in organisational and administrative tasks, summarised as follows:

- telephone calls or visits to foster parents and natural parents to discuss and arrange times and venues for visits

- discussions with natural parents to keep them informed of the child's progress and to ensure their attendance at access

- writing case notes and reports

- attending review meetings to consider a child's progress in care, and issues related to access arrangements

- during this study period, two social workers attended a court hearing where a child's contact and access with the natural family were agreed on

This latter court attendance task for social workers may well increase with the introduction of the new regulations governing access arrangements outlined in the Child Care Act 1991.

Roughly 35–55 per cent of social work time was spent in direct contact and supervision of visits. This involves being present when a child and parent meet, being available to discuss any issues that may arise for the child or the parent, mediating between all the participants to the access or accompanying children on an outing to see their brothers or sisters. Over a quarter of social workers' time is spent in travel. This reflects the geography of Donegal—a large rural county. The distances are recorded below in the sections on miles travelled by children and parents.

It is clear that the tasks involved in arranging access are wide and varied, requiring planning and organising, and making substantial demands on social work time.

Findings

Frequency of Access Visits

By way of introduction to the more detailed analysis of the data, Table 7.1 shows the frequency of access contacts that the 79 children in care had during the period from 17 November to 17 December 1993.

Table 7.1 Frequency of access visits

No. of contacts	No. of children	Per cent of children
No contact at all	17	21
One access visit	15	19
Two access visits	32	40
Three access visits	10	13
Four or more access visits	5	7
Total	79	100

Perhaps the most striking finding from Table 7.1 is that 60 per cent of the children had two or more access contacts during this one-month period.

Characteristics of the Sample of Children in Care

Table 7.2 Age categories of study children

Age category (years)	Children	Per cent
0–4.9	13	16
5–9.9	19	24
10–14.9	26	33
15 and over	21	27
Total	79	100

In this period there were 79 children in care (31 boys and 48 girls). At January 1994, the youngest child was aged eight months and the oldest was aged 20.5 years. Table 7.2 shows the breakdown by different age categories. Thirty-two children were under ten years, 58 children were less than fifteen years old. A surprisingly high number were aged fifteen years and over. Four young people in the latter group were being supported in a higher education course.

Length of Time in Care

In this population of 79 children, the mean length of time in care was 5.8 years. The shortest period was one month. The longest period in care (until January 1994) was 18 years, the child having been placed at birth.

Placements

The Donegal Community Care Area is totally dependent on foster care for children needing care, as no residential care facility exists in the county. These 79 children were cared for in 35 different foster families. The category 'foster parent relative' describes a placement where children were placed with relatives who were approved as foster parents. There were four such placements in this study. Two of these foster parent relatives also care for other non-related foster children.

Average Length of Access Visit

Table 7.3 Length of access visits

Length (hours)	No. of visits	Per cent
Less than 2	83	65.0
2–4	25	19.5
Over 4	20	15.5
Total	128	100.0

For each access visit social workers were asked how long the child spent with his or her natural family. Eighty-three access visits (65 per cent) lasted less than two hours; 25 access visits (19.5 per cent) lasted between two and four hours; 20 access visits (15.5 per cent) were over four hours long. The latter visits included a number of overnight visits, mainly where siblings visited each other in their respective foster homes (see Table 7.3).

Of the 79 children in care during this one-month period, 62 (78 per cent) had one or more access contacts with their natural families during the period under study.

Children without Access

A total of 17 children had no access in this period. This figure accounts for 21 per cent of the care population. In this group 12 children (70 per cent) were aged over ten and a half years. Information from the social workers involved indicated that in nine of the cases parents had abandoned or refused contact. Some of these parents had no fixed abode, while some could not be traced despite efforts being made. Two children refused contact themselves or did not want to maintain contact with their parents. These two did have contact with their siblings, however. Two other children had infrequent contact, whilst three other children had contact more regularly, but none in the period under study.

Evidence from the social work records indicated that a total of 12 children (15 per cent) had little or no contact with their parents throughout the year of 1993. In the first comprehensive study of children in care in the Republic of Ireland, undertaken in the Mid-Western Health Board area by the Economic and Social Research Institute (O'Higgins, 1993), it was found that, of a total population of 392 children, 44 per cent had no visits from parents or else very poor contacts in 1989. Although the population of children in care in Co. Donegal was five times smaller than that of the Mid-Western Health Board area, it seems to be a significant finding that only 15 per cent of the Donegal children had little or no access with natural family, whereas 44 per cent of the Mid-Western sample had little or no access for the twelve-month period covering 1989. This may be a reflection of changing trends in access provision over time and of regional policy differences.

Children with Access

In this section I examine the characteristics of the access visits that occurred during this thirty-day period. Table 7.4 lists the number of visits by each category of relative.

Table 7.4 Access by relative category

Relative category	No. of visits
Mother only	16
Father only	11
Both parents only	9
Parents and siblings	24
Parents, grandparents and siblings	36
Parents and grandparents	13
Siblings only	18
Grandparents only	1
Total	128
Total no. of children who had access = 62	

It can be seen that 85 per cent of all access contacts involved the children's parents. This is to be expected. One would expect natural parents to have the most access contacts with their children in care. Sixty-one per cent of all access contacts involved the children's siblings. In most cases children saw their siblings in the company of the parents and other relatives—this combination accounted for 47 per cent of all access contacts. But in 14 per cent of all access contacts, children were seeing their siblings only.

A number of research studies in the area of sibling contact comment on the special relationship that siblings have with each other. Their importance endures when all other relationships, except with parents, may diminish or be forgotten. Obviously, great effort is needed to maintain these links between siblings, and the high proportion of siblings involved in access visits is a very good reflection of this practice by social workers. In the sample of 79 children, there were 60 children who were part of a sibling set, i.e. 76 per cent of all the children in care consisted of sibling sets. Of these 60 sibling set children, 31 (52 per cent) were in a foster care placement together with one or more siblings. The other 29 children (48 per cent) had become separated within foster care. The latter group tended to have four or more siblings in the sibling set. It tends to be more difficult to find a placement that can accommodate a whole family of four or more children.

Thirty-nine per cent of access contacts involved the children's grandparents. This is a significant and surprising finding, and a positive one for this group of children in care. Other research studies have found that extended family can often be excluded and contact lost when children enter a care system (Millham *et al.*, 1986). Rowe *et al.* (1984), in a longitudinal study of foster care placements, commented that contact with grandparents is extremely beneficial for children in care, even if contact with the natural parents has ceased.

Contact Time according to Relative Category

Table 7.5 Time spent at access meetings by relative category (1)		
Relative category	*No. of visits*	*Mean contact time (hours)*
Mother only	16	4.0
Father only	11	3.2
Both parents only	9	4.1
Parents and siblings	24	1.4
Parents, grandparents and siblings	36	1.5
Siblings only	18	9.4
Parents and grandparents	13	2.9
Grandparents only	1	2.0
Total	128	

Social workers were asked what length of time a child spent with his or her natural family. Table 7.5 shows the average time spent at access meetings.

In this study period, when a child met with one parent only, the visits lasted on average 3.7 hours. When a child met with his or her siblings only, there was a dramatic increase in the time spent, an average 9.4 hours. Venue seems to be the key determinant here, because when siblings met each other only, they often met at each other's foster homes, sometimes for an overnight stay. I amalgamated the categories above and looked at the average contact time from the point of view of who was involved (see Table 7.6).

Table 7.6 Time spent at access meetings by relative category (2)

Relative category	No. of visits	Mean contact time (hours)
Parents	109	2.9
Siblings	78	4.1
Grandparents	50	2.1

It must be noted that these categories of contact time do overlap; for example, when the child in care meets with parents and siblings at the same time. On average, when siblings are involved in the access contact, the visit lasts over an hour longer than any other combination of family members. It is quite clear from the data presented in this section that both siblings and grandparents are very significant and active participants in access for children in care. These findings are consistent with my own and colleagues' impressions, from working with children in care, that it is important for children to retain links with a wide variety of family relatives.

Organiser and Supervisor of Access Visits

For every access contact the social workers were requested to differentiate between who was the organiser of the visit, and who was the supervisor. The organiser was defined as the person who made all or most of the arrangements for an access visit such as time, means of transport and venue, whereas the supervisor was defined as the responsible party (usually a social worker or foster parent) who was present for some or all of the access and generally supervised it.

Table 7.7 Organiser of access visits

Organiser	No. of visits	Per cent
Social worker	93	73
Foster parent or foster parent relative	26	20
Original parent	3	2
Child in care	6	5
Total	128	100

As Table 7.7 shows, social workers organised a majority of all visits (73 per cent). Foster parents and foster parent relatives were also involved in organising a further 20 per cent of visits.

Table 7.8 Supervisor of access visits

Supervisor	No. of visits	Per cent
Social worker	84	66
Foster parent or foster parent relative	14	11
Unsupervised	30	23
Total	128	100

Again, Table 7.8 shows the significant role of social workers in the supervision of access visits. The figure of 23 per cent of 'unsupervised' access visits would typically consist of older children visiting their natural parents in the natural home. In a high proportion (65.5 per cent), the social worker was both the organiser and supervisor of an access visit.

Child and Parent Transport

Foster parents were responsible for transporting children for 83 (65 per cent) of access visits during the period under study (see Table 7.9). This is a very large amount of time and involvement devoted by foster parents to the children in their care. The categories of foster parent, foster parent relative, social worker and North Western Health Board taxi together account for transporting children for 111 access visits (87 per cent). Given that the NWHB provides foster parents with a travel allowance for the purpose of facilitating access, this means that the NWHB provides funding directly or indirectly for 87 per cent of access visits. Again, this represents a commitment to the policy of maintaining links between children and their natural families.

Table 7.9 Child transport

Child transported by	No. of visits	Per cent
Foster parent or foster parent relative	83	64.5
Social worker or NWHB taxi	28	22.0
Original parent or public transport	11	8.5
Child did not travel	6	5.0
Total	128	100.0

Table 7.10 Parent transport

Parent transported	No. of visits	Per cent
Natural parent organised own transport	66	51.5
Parents did not travel	27	21.0
NWHB taxi	28	22.0
Social worker, foster parent or foster parent relative	7	5.5
Total	128	100.0

In 66 (51.5 per cent) access contacts, the parents organised their own transport. Parents did not travel for 27 (21 per cent) access contacts because children were visiting the parental home. In 35 (28 per cent) of access contacts, transport was provided by the social worker or by a taxi funded by the NWHB. This may seem to be a very high proportion of funding or assistance for natural parents, but many parents with children in care often have personal difficulties such as mental health problems or learning difficulties. In other research studies it has been found that parents face numerous restrictions in maintaining contact with their children: transport availability is one of them (Millham *et al.*, 1986). Public transport in Co. Donegal is not easily available and many parents do not have their own transport and could not afford to travel if assistance was not provided.

Therefore the availability of funded transport enables and facilitates parents in maintaining contact with their children (see Table 7.10).

Miles Travelled by the Children

For each access contact a child had during the period 17 November to 17 December 1993 the distance travelled by the child was recorded. The total distance travelled by children for all access visits during the period was 6,238 miles. It must be noted that in a significant proportion of access visits, two or more siblings shared the same transport, so the actual mileage of vehicles would be less than the figure above. Nevertheless, over 6,000 miles is an enormous figure for the travel of 62 children during a 30-day period. The average return journey travelled by a child per access contact was 48 miles.

Miles Travelled by the Parents

The total distance travelled by parents for all access contacts during this one-month period was 3,088 miles. The average return journey travelled by a parent per access contact was 24 miles. These great distances reflect the geography of Co. Donegal. Children travelled on average twice as many miles as parents because visits usually occurred nearer to the parents' homes. Children were brought to these venues by foster parents, social workers or by NWHB-funded taxis. This again reflects the importance with which parental contact is regarded.

Activities during Access

It was found that the activities engaged in or time spent during access fell into four or five natural categories, and the distribution of these is shown in Table 7.11. This gives a general picture of what happens for a child during access visits. There were 11 access contacts involving overnight stays and these involved seven children (siblings) spending time at each other's foster families, and one visit of a child going to her brother's home. A total of 104

Table 7.11 Activities during access

Activity	Number	Per cent
One or more overnights	11	8.9
Tea, talk and outing	36	28.0
Tea, talk, maybe games	68	53.0
Brief visit	11	8.9
Other	2	1.0
Total	128	100.00

access contacts (81 per cent) involved children and their natural parents having tea and a chat. When younger children were in attendance they would also play games. In 36 out of 128 access contacts (28 per cent) the children and parents had an outing in addition to the usual tea and chat. Outings usually consisted of a visit to shops in town or to a café/restaurant. Interestingly, when siblings met each other it was for an overnight stay or an outing. Eleven access contacts (8.9 per cent) were described as brief visits, and were usually visits where there was quite a bit of tension or anxiety on the part of the child. This was either as a result of the child not feeling comfortable seeing a parent or where parents were unpredictably upset or angry.

Access Venues

The Family Resource Centre was the place in which 44 out of 128 access contacts (35 per cent) happened. Fifty per cent of the latter visits involved access with grandparents, parents and siblings. Sixty-six of all access contacts (52 per cent) took place on health board property such as a health centre or the Family Resource Centre (see Table 7.12). Good use is made of the existing facilities within the health board when one considers that over half of all access contacts took place either at the Family Resource Centre or a health centre. The Family Resource Centre is a popular venue as there is a large comfortable sitting room with kitchen facilities to make tea. This venue facilitated parents, grandparents and siblings all meeting together in 21 access contacts.

Table 7.12 Venues used for access visits		
Venue	*No. of contacts*	*Per cent contact*
Family Resource Centre	44	35
Health centres	22	17
Foster home or foster relatives	9	7
Original home	26	20
Outing or other venues	27	21
Total	128	100

From the information collected, a pattern emerges where, in the majority of access visits, foster parents take the child(ren) to the access venue and remain with the children during access visits. So even though visits to the foster home happened in only nine contacts, foster parents were present and involved at other access venues. Of those visits which did take place at the foster home, all involved siblings visiting each other, except for one access contact where parents and siblings visited together. A number of research studies have found that parents find it very painful and difficult visiting their children in care. Visiting children in the place where they are cared for (whether a foster home or a residential setting) heightens parents' already strong sense of failure and guilt about being unable to provide the care their children require (Aldgate *et al.*, 1977, McAdams, 1972). Therefore the use of neutral venues such as the resource or health centres or outings may well be less daunting venues for natural parents.

Twenty-six access contacts (20 per cent) took place in the parents' home. There can be considerable advantages to such visits because children are able to see their families in their normal everyday routine. Visits home mean that children can watch TV, go for a walk or have a family meal. Access contacts in formal settings tend not to allow parents a parenting role. This can increase their anxiety and feelings of inadequacy (Berridge, 1985).

Visits home can also mean that children can visit friends and neighbours. This is a good opportunity for children where there is no risk to their safety or well being. This practice of allowing children to visit home recognises the importance of maintaining strong links with the family, the extended family and the local community. It also recognises the reality that the majority of children who leave care actually return to their natural home (Department of Health, 1990).

Contact Time and Venue

There were significant differences in the length of contact time between the children in care and their families according to the venue of access (see Table 7.13).

Table 7.13 Length of contact time

Venue	No. of contacts	Mean contact time (hours)
Family Resource or health centre	66	1.3
Outing or other neutral venue	27	3.1
Natural home	26	6.1
Foster home or foster relative's home	9	12.8
Total	128	

When visits took place at the Resource Centre or a health centre or any other neutral venue outside a home setting, the duration of the contact time was much less than when the visit was in a home setting. Transport arrangements and limits on professionals' time would be two reasons for this. Obviously it is easier and more natural to stay for longer periods in a family home setting. On average children spent 6.1 hours visiting their families when the venue was the natural home. It must be noted that 61.5 per cent of these children were aged over 11 years, and their access did not need to be supervised by a social worker. When access visits occurred at foster parents' homes the visits lasted much longer, 12.7 hours on average, but this was a small sample, mainly of siblings visiting each other, and is probably not representative of the general picture. Overnight stays of siblings at the foster home increased the average in that category during the period under study. Nevertheless, it would be worth exploring whether more access visits could take place within the foster home setting. These visits obviously make more demands on foster carers and would only be possible with their agreement and co-operation.

Quality of Access Experience

For every access contact the social workers were requested to evaluate the quality of the access experience (1) for the child, and (2) for the access recipient(s), usually the parents. The Lickert scale shown below was used.

Very negative experience				Mixed experience		Positive experience
-3	-2	-1	0	+1	+2	+3

Child's Experience of Access Visits

Out of the total of 128 access contacts, 95 contacts (74 per cent) were rated as positive experiences for the children; 23 of the access contacts (18 per cent) were evaluated as being mixed experiences for the children concerned. Social workers rated only 10 access contacts (8 per cent) as being a negative experience for the child. The high percentage of positive rated experiences of access contact for the child indicates the value attached to access by social workers, both in the particular and the general.

Parents' Experience of Access Visits

When evaluating the access recipients' (usually the parents) experience of access visits the social workers rated the recipients as having positive experiences in 117 (91 per cent) access contacts. In 11 cases (9 per cent) the access recipients' experience was rated as being mixed or negative. As stated above, 74 per cent of children's access contacts were experienced as positive, whereas 91 per cent of recipients experienced their contacts as positive, as rated by social workers. This seems to indicate that on the whole access is experienced as very positive by nearly all concerned but somewhat more so by the parents.

Contact Time and the Child's Experience

I examined whether the amount of time spent in access visits related in any way to the child's experience of the access. Table 7.14 indicates the positive relationship which exists between these two variables.

Table 7.14 Contact time and child's rated experience		
No. of visits	Mean contact time (hours)	Child's rated experience
10	1	-3 or -2 or -1
23	1.2	0
29	2.7	+1
45	4.1	+2
21	6.8	+3

The above analysis indicates that the more positive the child's experience, the more contact time there is. In the vast majority of access contacts between children in care and their families social workers evaluated the quality of the access experience as positive for both parties. This is a significant finding and reflects the opinion of many workers in this area about the importance of the biological link between children and their parents even where children have been physically separated from their families. This finding supports the reasoning that access and contact with the child's natural family should be promoted and continued by social work practitioners.

Conclusion

The most striking general conclusion from this survey is that there is a high degree of access contact and activity among our population of children in care in Co. Donegal. This is reflected in the tables covering frequency of access, distance travelled, venues and activities for access, as well as more globally in terms of social workers' time and involvement in access-related activities.

We have strong grounds for believing that this one-month time sample is quite representative for the whole year: the period under study avoided special times of the year such as Christmas, Easter and summer holidays, and social workers' impressions were that this was a period of normal access activity. What is not so clear is whether the Co. Donegal population of children in care could be typical in having more access involvement than other health board areas in Ireland. Certainly there is a positive outlook on the importance of access for the child and family in this area.

The rates of access involvement in this study of practice in 1993 were found to be much higher than for the Mid-Western Health Board population of children in care in 1989 (O'Higgins, 1993). This difference may be partly explained by regional policy differences, and perhaps also by differences in facilities and provisions for access. But it is tempting to conclude that there has been a significant and general increase in access activity over time, and that this anticipates the requirements of Section 37 of the Child Care Act 1991 whilst reflecting the spirit of this Act. For our own NWHB region we propose to carry out a follow-up study in three to five years' time in order to ascertain whether there will be any change in access activity rates as a result of full implementation of the new Act. From this study, though, it seems we are already starting from a fairly high baseline of access involvement.

References

Aldgate, J., Maluccio, A. and Reeves, C. (1989), *Adolescents in Foster Families*, London: British Association of Adoption and Fostering.

Berridge, D. (1985), *Children's Homes*, Oxford: Basil Blackwell.

Berridge, D. and Cleaver, H. (1987), *Foster Home Breakdown*, London: Blackwell.

Department of Health (1990), *Survey of Children in Care 1990*, Vol. 11, Dublin.

Fanshel, D. and Shin, E. (1978), *Children in Foster Care*, New York: Columbia University Press.

Foord, H. (1987), *Access: Children in Care and their Families*, Bristol Papers in Applied Social Studies No. 5, University of Bristol.

Gilligan, R. (1990), *Foster Care for Children in Ireland: Issues and Challenges for the 1990's*, Dublin: University of Dublin.

McAdams, P.T. (1972), 'The Parent in the Shadows', *Child Welfare*, Vol. 11, No. 1, pp. 51–5.

Millham, S., Bullock, R., Hosie, K. and Little, M. (1986), *Lost in Care: The Problems of Maintaining Links between Children in Care and their Families*, Aldershot: Gower.

O'Higgins, K. (1993), *Family Problems and Substitute Care*, Paper No. 28, Broadsheet Series, Dublin: Economic and Social Research Institute.

Rowe, J., Cain, H., Hundleby, M. and Keane A. (1984), *Long Term Foster Care*, London: Batsford, British Association of Adoption and Fostering.

Ryburn, Murray (1993), 'Open Practice in Child Care, Policy and Planning', paper delivered at the Eighth International Foster Care Conference, Dublin (July).

PART II: *Practice Perspectives*

A PROGRAMME MANAGER'S PERSPECTIVE

Michael McGinley

As a programme manager (community care) with the North Western Health Board (NWHB), a key part of my role is to manage the implementation of the Child Care Act 1991 and to monitor policy and practice development in the health board region. The Act sets out functions, duties and obligations of health boards.

The Organisation of Health Boards

The eight health boards were established under Section 4 of the Health Act 1970. This Act outlined some of the broad provisions relating to the composition of the health boards and also made provision for the making of regulations to deal in more detail with defining the functional areas of health boards and specifying the membership of each health board. The North Western Health Board consists of 27 members—fourteen elected local authority members, six medical practitioners, one general nurse, one psychiatric nurse, one dentist, one pharmacist, and three ministerial nominees. Elected local authority representatives have a majority; this is a statutory requirement in the composition of all health boards. The Board meets once a month with the exception of August and its main function is to decide on policy in relation to service provision, service priorities, allocation of resources, etc. Health boards, including the NWHB, have delegated responsibilities for management functions to the chief executive officers. Under the Health Act 1970 responsibility for all personnel matters and all questions relating to the eligibility of persons for health board services are functions of the chief executive officer of the board.

Programmes of Services, Organisation and Responsibilities of Management

The management structure in health boards is organised in such a way that a chief executive officer has overall executive and management responsibility. Services are managed in the context of programmes of services. Smaller health boards such as the NWHB have two programmes of services—a programme of community services and a programme of hospital services. Larger boards have three programmes of services—a programme of community services, a programme of general hospital services and a programme of special hospital services. The special hospital services include geriatric hospitals, psychiatric hospitals and services and usually institutions for the mentally handicapped.

A programme manager is responsible for managing each of these programmes of services under the general direction and supervision of the chief executive officer. In the NWHB the programme of community services is divided into two community care areas—Sligo/Leitrim and Donegal—and each area has a director of community care/medical officer of health (see Fig 8.1). Each professional group in a community care area is managed by a senior superintendent or principal grade within that profession and these senior professional personnel report to the director of community care/medical officer of health. A recent working party report recommended significant changes in the management structure at community care area level which will involve abolition of the post of director of community care/medical officer of health and the replacement of that structure with the establishment of a department of public health within health boards. At the time of writing, negotiations to achieve these changes were at an advanced stage between the Department of Health and the Irish Medical Organisation. The structure is already modified to an extent in the Sligo/Leitrim area of the NWHB (see Fig. 8.1).

From what has been outlined above, it is clear that the duties and

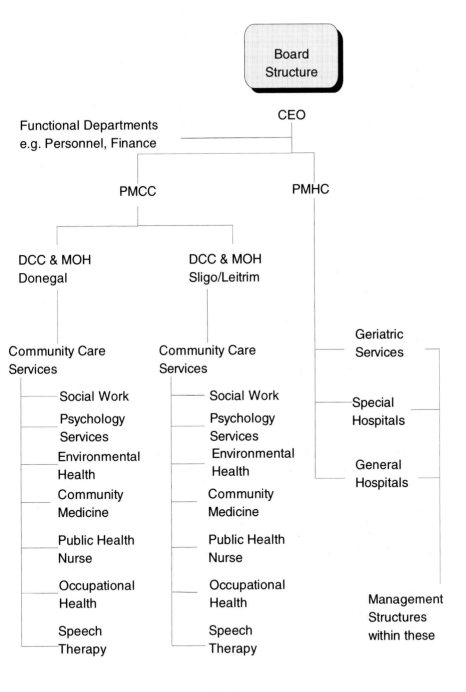

obligations provided for in the Child Care Act 1991 are the direct responsibility of the board and of the board's most senior managers, namely, the chief executive officer and the programme managers. The programme manager for community services has responsibility for ensuring that the board's obligations under the Act in community settings are met. The programme manager for hospital services has responsibility for ensuring that the obligations of the board under the Act in relation to hospitals are met. The programme managers of community services have a direct managerial obligation to ensure that health boards have policies and procedures approved which will enable their staff to provide adequate child welfare and protection services. It is particularly important to emphasise that services provided by board staff must be in accordance with approved health board policy.

It is important to stress this because in many situations professional staff seem to believe that the services they provide should be determined more by other factors such as the advice given by professional bodies. It is clear from an examination of the Child Care Act 1991 that the duties and obligations to implement the requirements of the Act are placed on health boards and not on any particular persons or professional groups who may be employed by health boards. The only person whose duties are specified in the Act are those of the chief executive officer. Indeed, it should be noted that the Act provides that health boards act in accordance with any directions given by the Minister for Health. This clearly requires, therefore, not only that services provided to protect and promote the welfare of children be in accordance with board policy but also that board policy comply with any directions given by the Minister.

Policy Formulation

An explanation of the way in which health board policy is approved may be helpful at this stage. Board policies for all services, including those concerned with the care and protection of children, are usually approved as a result of reports placed before the board by the chief executive officer and programme managers. Many factors are taken into account in the formulation of proposals for board policy which are recommended to the board. National policy communicated to the board's chief executive officer from the Department of Health is a most important factor, as are the recommendations from various national and international reports (for example McGuinness, 1993). Amongst the most important factors influencing the formulation of board policy are the recommendations from, and the results of discussion with, the various professional staff employed by health boards in providing child care services.

Also of importance are the recommendations from voluntary organisations involved in child welfare and protection work. Unfortunately, programme managers do not always inform professional staff that their comments and recommendations were influential in formulating policy, with the result that staff frequently believe their comments and views are ignored and have no influence. As a programme manager, I believe this is one area of my work which requires more attention in future. There ought to be communication with staff, if at all possible, regarding their influence in formulating board policies which directly affect their work. Naturally, the availability or otherwise of resources has a major influence on board policies in that it would be irresponsible of any senior manager to recommend proposals to the board without regard to the financial implications of such proposals if they are approved as policy. It is obvious, therefore, that many factors influence the formulation of board policy and ongoing reviews of policy.

The Child Care Act and the Adequacy and Evaluation of Services

In accordance with Section 8 of the Child Care Act, the health board is required to have a report prepared annually on the adequacy of the child care and family support services available in its area. Particularly valuable in preparing this report are the work and recommendations of the Child Care Advisory Committee established under Section 7 of the Act. Professional personnel from the health board, the gardaí, the schools, the Probation Service and many of the voluntary organisations providing child care services, in addition to board members, are represented on the Child Care Advisory Committee in the NWHB area. The work and recommendations from a committee composed of personnel with this vast range of knowledge and skills will continue to be most valuable in all aspects of child care policy.

In reviewing the adequacy of child care services an obvious weakness is the lack of any agreed criteria for determining the adequacy of services. For example, what level of family support service would be deemed adequate in relation to families with particularly identified levels of need? In the health services generally we have been particularly poor in evaluating the effectiveness or outcomes of service provision. We have tended in the past to examine the adequacy of services by reference to input; for example, the number of particular staff employed. For child care services we have not set out criteria of adequacy even by reference to resource input, let alone by attempting to determine the adequacy of services by reference to the required outcomes of service delivery (*see also* Ward, 1993; Whittaker, 1993).

I suggest that any successful attempt to determine the adequacy of child care services requires that senior health board managers immediately set about establishing appropriate criteria against which future adequacy of services can be evaluated. This will be a most complex and difficult task but the difficulty associated with the task is no reason for avoiding it. There are at present many very wide variations relating to all aspects of child care services. There are variations between health boards and even wide variations of practice between different community care areas in the same health board. Such wide variations of practice are probably related to different opinions and practices within professional groups and obviously this is not a situation which can or should continue.

Promoting the Welfare of Children

It is clear from the Act that health board policy will have to provide for the promotion of the welfare of children; this requires taking such steps as are necessary to identify children who are not receiving adequate care and protection. Board policy and procedures will require all appropriate board staff to become more aware of and alert to the need to identify such children. The roles of general practitioners (GPs), public health nurses, home help staff and all other professional staff who are regularly in close contact with families are of great importance. The GP and the public health nurse are particularly involved with families and children at such critical times as the ante-natal period and the immediate post-natal period. They are also very closely involved with families because of the full range of child health services that are provided in the early years of life.

Hospital-based staff, especially those who work in accident and emergency departments and those who work in paediatric departments, are also particularly well placed to identify those children who are not receiving adequate care and protection and to identify the early signs of non-accidental injury.

To ensure the greatest degree of success in identifying early signs of abuse or neglect and families requiring particular support, staff must work closely together and make sure that their efforts are co-ordinated. At present, the co-ordination of services to support families and protect children at community care level is a responsibility delegated to the director of community care/medical officer of health, who liaises closely with hospital-based personnel in relation to child care services. Discussions are well advanced which may see this particular position replaced by other grades of staff. There will need to be one manager at community care level who will continue to have a delegated responsibility for co-ordinating all child care services, including those that are hospital-based. The important role of GPs in identifying children who are not receiving adequate care and protection must be acknowledged because, although they are not employees of the health boards, they do provide services to them and work very closely with health board staff in hospitals and in the community. Health boards have staff who are regularly in contact with families and children; the essential requirement is that such staff be trained to be alert to the indications of abuse or neglect and be prepared to take on their responsibility of identifying children whom they believe are being neglected or abused.

Co-ordinating Service Provision

Having identified families in which children are believed to be at risk, board policy will require that a range of family support services be made available. There will be an obligation on the board to ensure proper co-ordination of the family support services provided by voluntary organisations and board staff. The vital contribution of home-making services, home help services, counselling services, etc. to families cannot be over-emphasised. It is clear that a major effort will be required by boards to provide the type of family support and preventive services which will, if at all possible, enable children to remain in their own homes with their own families. Ensuring co-ordination of family support services at district level will be most important.

In the NWHB area the public health nursing district is an aggregate of district electoral divisions; the Board has on average one public health nurse per population of approximately 2,000 persons. The public health nurse, with her intimate knowledge of the families in her district, is well placed to co-ordinate family support services and to ensure that service delivery is targeted to support those families most in need. The co-ordination of work relating to the investigation of individual cases of suspected abuse and the action, if any, to be taken is a matter which requires to be further clarified in the drawing up of new policies and procedures. The same is true of all aspects of work relating to case conferences.

Taking the next largest district, with a population of approximately 25,000, it will be necessary to put in place arrangements for co-ordinating the efforts of GPs, public health nurses, home help staff, social workers, psychologists, hospital-based staff, personnel from the gardaí, schools, voluntary organisations and individual voluntary workers. The families in which children are at risk in such a district are probably well known to the GP, public health nurse, community psychiatric nurses, counsellors on alcoholism, etc. What is required from a management point of view is a mechanism for targeting the required support to the families who need it.

The district with a population of 25,000 has a senior public health nurse, area medical officer, psychologist, social worker, home help organiser and other staff. A small core team led by a senior public health nurse or area medical officer is required to take on the co-ordination and organisation of child care services and ensure that proper inter-agency arrangements are made. Co-ordination of services at community care area level is the responsibility of the director of community care/medical officer of health and the appropriate senior health professional staff. The management and co-ordinating structure suggested provide for proper co-ordination at the smallest district level by the public health nurse; at a district level of approximately 25,000 population by a small core team; at community care level by the director of community care and the appropriate senior professional staff. The programme manager, community care, is responsible for ensuring that management and co-ordinating arrangements are in place at these various levels.

The Need for Public Confidence

A health board can successfully carry out its child protection role and child care and family support work only if there is public confidence in the board, its staff and its work. Policies, procedures and mechanisms must, therefore, allow community leaders, voluntary organisations and those from other agencies to make their views, comments and observations known to board staff involved in child welfare and child protection work. Views expressed from these sources must be taken fully into account and be seen to have been taken into account.

The Need for Policies and Procedures

Health board policies and procedures must enable the board to carry out its obligations to make the necessary applications to the courts to take children into board care when necessary. As these sections of the Act are implemented, health boards will need to set out their initial policy position. But as the courts will interpret these various sections, boards will need to constantly review their policies and procedures in relation to this work. Care proceedings are one of the most difficult areas of board work. It is essential that boards act effectively and without hesitation or reservation to make applications to the courts for the care of children when it is considered appropriate to do so to protect the welfare of the children concerned. It is important to note that in accordance with Section 72 of the Act any function with respect to legal proceedings in relation to the care and protection of a child is specified as a function of the chief executive officer of the health board. There is provision in the Health Act 1970 for chief executive officers to delegate any of their duties or functions, but, if this particular function is not delegated in accordance with the provisions of the Health Act 1970, approval from the chief executive officer of the health board is necessary in each case involving legal proceedings.

Supporting the Child's Family

During the times of legal proceedings there will be serious stress and trauma to the family as a whole, and the board must be sensitive to this and do what is possible to provide the necessary support for all family members. Health board staff and counsellors will probably be involved in counselling and treating parents or family members who were involved in perpetrating the abuse of children and will certainly be involved in counselling and supporting family members who have been affected by the removal of a child from the family. The best possible way to reduce the amount of subsequent work which will be necessary and to lay a good foundation for future work is to provide the maximum support for these family members at the time of their greatest stress and trauma. Working effectively and decisively to ensure that the child victim of abuse gets the necessary support and protection is of paramount importance and is not incompatible with providing adequate support for other family members.

If, during care proceedings, the board is unable to assign a particular support person to the family members other than the child or if an offer of a support person is not accepted then board staff should accept that family members are entitled to personal representation and should co-operate fully with such a personal representative, whoever may be selected by the family. This appears to be a matter of great difficulty for some professional staff who put forward the issue of confidentiality. If a parent, parents, or a family member clearly confirm that a person wishes to accompany them on certain visits to health board staff and that a particular person is regarded as a personal representative of the family then the question of confidentiality need not be such a major issue. A health board professional worker assigned to support the parents, who may include the perpetrator of abuse, or a personal representative of the parents can in fact be of considerable assistance, as such a person will be able to take a much more objective view than the parents or perpetrator themselves and can be of invaluable assistance in preparing the way for subsequent treatment, counselling or rehabilitation work.

The Health Boards' Care of Children

The Act places an obligation on health boards to provide adequate care for those children who have been taken into health board care. In the case of the NWHB over 90 per cent of children in the Board's care are in foster homes. Although this is considered a highly desirable position, further research may be needed to determine the most appropriate role for health boards in their work of supporting foster parents. The effect of moving children to a number of foster parents within a small number of years should be more closely examined. It will be particularly important for the programme manager to ensure that adequate arrangements are in place for appropriate access for natural parents to their children in health board care. Under Section 37 of the Act, board service personnel are required to make a genuine effort to facilitate natural parents in access arrangements; access will have to be provided in appropriate settings. This is a time-consuming and expensive aspect of service provision, but an important one. It is also an area of service provision wherein it may be possible to use less skilled staff and support arrangements to enable access visits to take place. Although in some situations the presence of a social worker is essential, social workers who are highly skilled and expensive may be devoting time to access arrangements which could be adequately catered for by less skilled and less expensive personnel.

Inter-agency Co-operation

In all of the boards' work under the Act it will be necessary for health board senior managers, particularly programme managers, to ensure that adequate arrangements are in place for inter-agency co-operation. It is particularly important that policies and procedures are in place to ensure close co-operation and working between health board staff, the gardaí and those working in schools. The question of inter-agency co-operation cannot be left dependent upon whether local personnel are co-operative. Co-operation between these agencies is absolutely essential for successful child protection work and arrangements for co-operation must be put in place and made known at all levels in these organisations (McGuinness, 1993).

Conclusion

The obligation of the programme manager is to ensure that appropriate policies and procedures are in place to allow services to be effective and efficient. Services must meet the stated objectives of approved policy and the best possible value for money must be obtained in service delivery. Evaluation mechanisms must be put in place and the results of the evaluation analysed and utilised to enable ongoing reviews of policy and service delivery. Criteria of quality must be determined in child care work and quality systems put in place. The process to achieve this should begin immediately. Policy formulation and reviews, resource allocation, monitoring and evaluation mechanisms, particularly regarding quality and effectiveness of services and efficiency, are particular obligations of senior health board managers.

References

McGuinness, C. (1993), *Report of the Kilkenny Incest Investigation*, Dublin: Stationery Office.

Ward, H. (1993), 'Assessment and the Children Act 1989: The Looking After Children Project', in H. Ferguson, R. Gilligan and R. Torode (eds.), *Surviving Childhood Adversity: Issues for Policy and Practice*, Dublin: Social Studies Press.

Whittaker, J. (1993), 'Changing Paradigms in Child and Family Services: Challenges for Practice, Policy and Research', in H. Ferguson, R. Gilligan and R. Torode (eds.), *Surviving Childhood Adversity: Issues for Policy and Practice*, Dublin: Social Studies Press.

Chapter 9

A PERSPECTIVE FROM THE COURTS

Judge Liam O. McMenamin

It is unfortunate that this very important piece of legislation is being introduced in such a haphazard manner, but the long shadow of the Department of Finance hangs over it. It was only through the process of preparing this chapter that I was made fully aware of the sections in being, and the sections in limbo. To avoid any further confusion, I would suggest that the remaining sections of the Act are brought into being in one omnibus Ministerial Order, rather than a tortuous procedure of a series of individual Orders. Certainly, in all court cases it would be necessary for the applicants to show that an actual section was in force, and this could lead to some unnecessarily embarrassing moments. It must also be remembered that extensive new powers are given to the gardaí, who must be protected from legal challenges on technical grounds.

There has been a delay of many years in updating the Children Act of 1908, but one must quote the proverb that 'It is an ill wind that blows no good.' The courts now have statutory and Supreme Court signal guidelines—the interest of the child is paramount. All the cases under the Act are emotionally charged, and the application of this principle can ease the burden of duty on a court in arriving at a reasonable conclusion in these very difficult cases. It must be remembered that all the recent family law legislation was tacked on to the already rickety system of the courts without any training or specialised back-up. There was a lot of heady talk about the establishment of special Family Law Courts, with counsellors and qualified assistance, but this was another chimera. However, if the forthcoming divorce referendum obtains a majority vote in favour, then all the courts in the land will have to be reorganised. These courts have not been re-cast since early Victorian times and cannot carry their present burden, let alone a new deluge of divorce and family cases. I heard a recent estimate of 25,000 cases to come into the court lists if the law is changed.

Another important basic principle is established: that a care order should be made only as a last resort. This should afford an opportunity to parents (or a parent) to show good intent to ensure a reasonable future for the child or children. If all the proposed back-up services are in fact supplied, then the number of children leaving parental control should be kept to a minimum. May I also add here that I have nothing but praise for the foster parents who have taken on some very difficult cases with outstanding results, and who have become psychological parents in the place of the natural parents.

I note with interest the establishment of child care advisory committees in each health board area. However, the committee acts only in an advisory capacity. It would be my intention to utilise the powers given under Section 27 (calling for reports etc.) to request a report from this committee on an individual case. The members are drawn from the locality and would have essential background knowledge of a case. All cases come within a very rough rule of thumb—either badness, madness or sadness. Local knowledge can help in this regard.

Section 12 gives powers to the gardaí to enter without warrant to remove a child to safety where 'there is an immediate and serious risk to the health and welfare of the child'. This provision will eventually give rise to some controversy in some highly publicised case. In my opinion the Oireachtas should have gone further and indemnified the gardaí against any claims taken against them when they have acted in good faith under the terms of the section. This is a provision affecting the 'inviolability of the home' and the Supreme Court has indicated in many cases that such inviolability must be maintained.

The next provision is an application for an emergency care order, to be applied for within three days. If no sitting of the Court is within that time, a special sitting is to be arranged. On the one hand the Act says the application is to be taken at a sitting scheduled within the three days.

However, Section 29 (3) provides that

> the District Court . . . shall sit to hear and determine proceedings under Part III, IV, or VI at a different place or at different times or on different days from those at or on which the ordinary sittings of the Court are held.

Great care must be taken in respect of this latter provision. It has the good intention of keeping the cases out of the ordinary lists and preventing mixing with litigants and defendants in an ordinary sitting, but the hearing would have to be a special and distinct arrangement.

Section 18 sets out the criteria for making a care order. In the past number of years the issue of child sexual abuse has come to the fore, and is again another very difficult area for judicial decision. The medical evidence is very important, but the evidence of children of a tender age is difficult to assess, and the more corroboration available the better.

Section 19 is very useful. The supervision order can be an effective half-way house between refusing an application and making a care order. I am not suggesting that it become known as the 'Pontius Pilate' section for the judiciary, but certainly errant parents cannot complain if there is supervision. Again, the interest of the child is paramount, and the parents can suppress their indignation. The onus of proof under this section is not as onerous as an application for a care order, and this would cover many cases.

I will be only too happy to utilise the statutory powers given under Section 25 and appoint a solicitor to represent the child. Again this will be a local input. Evidence can be adduced to assist the Court in arriving at a proper conclusion. We should not be left playing hunches or tossing mental coins—the consequences are much too grave. This also applies to Section 26—provision for a guardian *ad litem*.

Section 37 deals with access. Any such order cannot be made without a detailed knowledge of the case, and the assistance mentioned above could be crucial. We arrive at judicial decisions in best conscience, but we are entitled to have the full facts and the best back-up available. There is no point in the Oireachtas promulgating essential laws if the financial resources are not made available. If alleged mistakes are made, then the proper parties must take the blame. However, said proper parties are quite adept at keeping their heads well down when a controversy arises, and leave it to others to bear the public criticism.

Court proceedings are kept as informal as possible, with due regard to the possibility of emotions and tensions overflowing. No wigs or gowns are allowed and proceedings are held in the judge's chambers or suitable room. However, in too many towns and villages (and even cities) the courtroom facilities range from poor to appalling. No steps are taken for the upkeep of the actual courthouses themselves, let alone providing family law facilities. Many women are hindered or even stopped from going to court by the fact that they must parade to some run-down wreck of a building supposed to pass as a courthouse in the centre of their town or village for all the population to observe. This would be bad enough, but a child care case would be telegraphed, a fact contrary to the spirit of the sections of the Act already mentioned. Families often prefer to have their cases heard in an alternative court district. Many District Judges have complained about their accommodation, but any activity regarded by the authorities as 'non-productive' will not get funds. I fear that the Child Care Act is also regarded as 'non-productive' and will always be starved of funds to implement the necessary and laudable provision.

Chapter 10

A CHILD PSYCHIATRY PERSPECTIVE

Don C. McDwyer

Introduction

Child psychiatry is a young speciality. It emerged, following a prolonged labour extending over the last sixty years, from the mixed parentage of general psychiatry and paediatrics. It was nurtured firstly by the development of child guidance clinics from the 1920s onward, and more recently by the growth of hospital-based departments, which are now the dominant and preferred service design (Black, 1993). Some have felt that this works against the current ideal of community-oriented services, but the experience of community-based child guidance clinics was often one of professional isolation, poor inter-agency communication and under-resourcing. Hospital-based services enjoy more ease of liaison, and the disadvantage of greater distances for patients and families to travel may be offset by the provision of multi-disciplinary children's centres, in which paediatrics, child psychiatry, physiotherapy, speech therapy and other related therapies may be found in close relation to each other and are able to communicate with greater regularity and ease. This is as yet not a common pattern, but one which should be built into future planning of new hospital developments.

Other child psychiatrists work in inpatient units, specialising in the intensive treatment of severely disturbed young people (Department of Health, 1993). Beds are rarely needed for prepubertal children, but there is a serious underprovision of inpatient adolescent units in Ireland, and nothing at all for young people who need secure therapeutic accommodation. The 1993 Yorkshire Television programme on the unfortunate life and death of Philip Knight, who committed suicide aged fifteen in Swansea Prison because no suitable secure placement was available for him, shows how tragic the results of such a failure of appropriate provision can be.

Some child psychiatrists specialise in the validation of child sexual abuse and treatment of associated problems. The majority, however, particularly in rural areas, are generalists. They see the full range of child psychiatric problems: conduct and emotional disorders; developmental problems; formal mental illnesses; psychosomatic disorders; and the broad range of clinical problems associated with dysfunctional or abusive families.

Child psychiatrists are a rare breed, and it is only in recent years that they have begun to crop up in rural areas. At the time of writing, there are 35 consultants in the state, 22 of whom work in the Eastern Health Board area. The North Western Health Board has one consultant, although the long-term aim would be to appoint a second. Even with the help of an excellent multi-disciplinary team, this seems hopelessly inadequate when compared with even conservative estimates of the prevalence of emotional and behavioural disturbance among children and adolescents in the community. A typical figure would lie between 10 and 15 per cent, giving total figures of 8,000–12,000 in the region as a whole. Kolvin (1973) has calculated that the average child psychiatry service sees about 1 per cent of the children in its area. This means that our direct impact on the total scale of the problems is very small, and that over 90 per cent of children in difficulties will never be seen by us. This carries two implications: (i) we must ensure that the 10 per cent we do see are the ones most in need of our special skills; and (ii) the other 90 per cent are being managed by the best efforts of families, schools, GPs, voluntary agencies and health service professionals, all of whom need and deserve our support, advice and training to assist them in their task.

These people, who are in daily contact with the children and families at risk of psychiatric disorder, do a great deal of preventive and therapeutic work, as well as identifying and referring on the more seriously disturbed clients who need more specialised help (Sussenwein and Treseder, 1985).

While not wishing to understate the importance of direct clinical work, child psychiatrists will readily admit that much of their most effective work involves liaison, consultation and training with all professionals who are regularly involved in work with children and families. In particular, our position, bridging, as it does, the gap between the medical and psychosocial fields, gives us a key role in managing the care of children and families whose problems are multiple, severe, or not fitting neatly into any distinct category. These will also be the ones for whom the Child Care Act 1991 comes most prominently into play. Child psychiatrists will therefore often be at the centre of its workings, whether in clinic, case conference or courtroom (Black *et al.*, 1991).

The Act

I do not wish to get bogged down in specifics here: space does not allow it, and neither is my legal expertise sufficient to examine the sections critically and comment on whether they will achieve their objectives. The Explanatory Memorandum (Department of Health, 1992) states succinctly that 'the purpose of the legislation is to update the law in relation to the care of children', and this is precisely what it appears to do. It brings us from the horse-and-cart era of the Children Act 1908 to the internal combustion age of the present. Space Age it is not, however. It takes no account of the fact that society in general, and the roles and functions of the family in particular, are changing faster now than they have ever done before. Child psychiatrists are used to taking a developmental perspective: what is right for a child of nine will not meet the needs of the adolescent a few years later. Flexibility and the ability to review and adapt must be built in.

The new Child Care Act is certainly a great improvement on what went before, but failure of imagination has given us a structure which will in all likelihood be out of date and requiring review in five to ten years' time. The Act is full of good ideas which have not been thought through in terms of how they will be implemented and how the different agencies involved will interact. This is not so much the function of the legislation itself, but of the detailed guidance which the Act requires and which should have followed it. I do not suggest anything like the eight ponderous volumes of horrendous complexity which accompanied the UK Children Act 1989. It would, however, have helped greatly to have had the principles outlined in the introduction to the Explanatory Memorandum expanded into detailed statements of the philosophy behind the Act, and the structures envisaged. As it stands, these matters have been left very much to the interpretation of the various health boards and courts. This lack of a unifying vision may lead to a level of confusion, disagreement and inconsistency which could undermine the innovative principles of the Act. In those circumstances, professionals and courts will tend to fall back on the old and familiar pathways, and the significant resources which are being made available will be wasted on patching up the 'old banger' rather than putting a more efficient new model on the road.

I have selected a few sections of the Act which I feel illustrate its good points and failings, and these are outlined below.

Child Care Advisory Committees (Section 7)

I believe that these committees are potentially a powerful force for the identification of need and the promotion of good practice in all areas of child care. Given the right constitution and support from health boards, their reports should carry significant authority. Equally, their membership needs to be of sufficient calibre and seniority to justify such authority. I see their main functions as:

1) to encourage inter-agency co-operation and joint planning
2) to promote a broad multi-agency approach to training on relevant topics
3) to commission research on specific questions related to child care and family support
4) to co-operate in these matters with similar committees in other health board areas
5) to report regularly and in a meaningful way to the health board

As things stand, it will be very difficult for any child care advisory committee to establish an effective role for itself, because of the vagueness of the committees' functions as specified in the Act, and the lack of any national co-ordination. What happens, for instance, if all the different committees start collecting information on child care issues in their own areas without any prior standardisation of methodology? I understand that moves are under way to ensure this standardisation, but only because of the foresight and motivation of certain academics. Nothing is in place yet to ensure rational and comprehensive provision of services across different health board areas.

The child care advisory committees could become redundant talking shops, but I am convinced that they have the potential to be a powerful and progressive force for improvement and innovation in child care practice. To achieve this they will need to do much more than react sluggishly and predictably to the latest report, legislation or crisis. They will need to inform themselves about the latest research and patterns of practice across the world, discuss these intelligently and come up with practical applications in the special situation of Ireland. They will have to address complex issues such as measurement of need (as opposed to demand), prioritisation of needs and services in the setting of limited resources, and accurate evaluation of both the quality of service and the outcome. This is analogous to the concept, now well accepted in the medical world, of clinical audit (Grath, 1992). This function is equally valid in all branches of public service, and placing it within the remit of the child care advisory committees would have the great advantage of entrusting it to a mixed body of professionals and informed lay people who are near to the services on the ground, rather than instituting some grey bureaucratic review procedure within the Department.

Certain organisational structures would be necessary to make these functions possible:

1) A national conference of child care advisory committees, with a standing committee to arrange meetings and organise the work detailed above.

2) A facility for audit committees to be drawn from different child care advisory committees, so that child care advisory committees are not in the position of auditing their own local services.

3) Resources for a central office with secretarial and scientific support to enable the work to be done.

4) Resources to enable members to take leave from their normal duties to attend meetings and carry out audits.

Child Protection (Parts III and IV) and Jurisdiction and Procedure (Part V)

Once again, the Act lays out with clarity and brevity the bare bones of a child protection policy. The health board must apply for an order, if it appears that there are good grounds for one. The Court may make a care order if it is 'satisfied' that grounds of abuse, avoidable impairment or neglect are met; or a supervision order if it finds 'reasonable grounds' (a lesser degree of proof) to accept them. If a care order is made, the health board has the authority, among other things, to decide the type of care the child should have, and to give consent to any necessary medical or psychiatric examination, treatment or assessment. A supervision order compels the parents to allow the board access to the child, and may direct them to submit him or her to medical or psychiatric assessment or treatment.

To counterbalance these stark prescriptions, the Act is permeated by three philosophical principles exhorting wisdom, moderation and regard (both for the wishes of the child and for the integrity of the family). To quote precisely:

A health board shall
(i) regard the welfare of the child as the first and paramount consideration, and
(ii) ... give due consideration ... to the wishes of the child, and
(iii) have regard to the principle that it is generally in the best interests of a child to be brought up in his own family.

The Act presumably also intends that courts should abide by these principles, since in that setting they will frequently be invoked and tested, particularly in those cases where two or more of them may conflict, or their interpretation may be open to question. To help the Court decide, the Act specifies that it may procure reports, make the child a party to the proceedings, or appoint a guardian *ad litem*.

Reports

According to the Act, the Court may procure a report from any person it wishes (professional or lay), on any question affecting the welfare of the child, and may call the person making the report as a witness. I do not know how this will work in practice, but I assume that courts will have mechanisms to prevent a proliferation of contradictory reports bringing confusion and discredit on itself and all those involved in the case, not least the report-writers. In some cases the existence of a report favouring one side merely stimulates the other side to search for another expert, preferably with more imposing credentials, who will take the opposing view. This can become a small but thriving industry, with certain experts becoming known among lawyers for the positions they hold on certain child care issues, and for how they perform in the witness stand. I have seen, in another jurisdiction, a dubious practice build up in which a small number of expert witnesses are kept extremely busy travelling from court to court pronouncing on what is best for children they may never have seen, in cases they have had no direct involvement with.

While this type of thing is clearly an abuse to be avoided, genuine, well-considered reports can be of great benefit in finding the way forward in complex and difficult cases. Many professionals dread the ordeal of court appearance, but in good practice the two systems should work in a complementary fashion. If the professionals present a coherent and convincing case indicating the best outcome for the child, the Court has the power to make it happen. A good court decision can provide the essential stability without which therapeutic goals cannot be achieved. Things are often not this simple, and many cases drag on hopelessly from court to court, with increasing polarisation of the parties and distress of the child, and with the chances of a workable resolution diminishing all the time. Some of these can be traced back to the effects of a hasty and incomplete first hearing. These things cannot be rushed; it is better to set aside a week for the first hearing (except where emergency or interim orders are needed), making sure all the complexities are examined, reports are received and points of view are heard, so that a fair and rational decision can be made, which is then more likely to be accepted by all parties.

Child as Party and Guardian *ad litem*

The Act states that the Court may, in order to ensure that the interests of the child are adequately represented, make the child a party to the proceedings, with his or her own legal representation if required. Alternatively, the Court may appoint a guardian *ad litem*. The Act is not specific about the duties of the guardian *ad litem*, and I am working on the assumption that these will be similar to those already existing in different jurisdictions. If that is the case, the guardian would be a child care professional, usually a social worker, who is independent of the health board, the Court and all the other parties in the case. The guardian interviews the child, usually several times, in order to get the full picture of the child's experiences, understanding, fears and wishes. He or she gets to know all the important people in the child's life and has discussions with the key professionals involved, including those who are preparing reports. He or she then prepares for the Court a report examining all aspects of the case from the child's point of view, looking at the impact that the options in front of the Court may have on the child, and making recommendations about the course of action required to obtain the best outcome for the welfare of the child.

This is a very important and progressive provision in the Act, and it clearly fits very well with its primary principle to regard the welfare of the child as the first and paramount consideration. Similarly, the provision to make the child a party to the case is clearly in line with the second principle: 'to give due consideration, having regard to his age and understanding, to the wishes of the child'. It is a clear and strong statement about the importance of those wishes to give them full legal representation in court. What baffles me is why, given the inherent logic in these provisions and their consistency with the underlying principles of the Act, the Act then appears to make them mutually exclusive. If a child who has a guardian *ad litem* becomes a party to the proceedings, the guardian is discharged. Perhaps this is an attempt to keep costs under control by avoiding duplication, but if so it is seriously misguided for a number of reasons:

1) The functions of a child's solicitor and a guardian *ad litem* are not the same at all. One represents the child's wishes, while the other writes a report about the child's welfare. In many cases the two do not coincide.

2) The functions of each can be complementary. For example, the presence of a child's solicitor will ensure that the guardian gives due weight to the child's expressed wishes in putting forward recommendations about his or her welfare. Conversely, the guardian can help the solicitor in those cases, particularly those involving younger children, in which the child is unable to express clearly what he or she wants, or may say things he or she does not really mean because of pressure or confused loyalties.

3) By the nature of the work, the guardian *ad litem* often spends a lot of time with the child and builds up a close and trusting relationship. If this is brought to a sudden end by the discharge of the guardian, the abrupt disappearance can be distressing and emotionally damaging for the child. At the very least, there needs to be provision for the guardian to prepare the child for his or her departure, and where appropriate to have a limited number of 'follow-up' sessions.

Promotion of Welfare of Children (Part II)

I have already visited this part in discussing child care advisory committees and identification of need, and now I return to look at the provision of child care and family support services. Once again, the Act presents us with a paradox: the third fundamental principle states that 'it is generally in the best interests of a child to be brought up in his own family', and yet practically all of this important part of the Act is concerned with children who are not in their own families. Special mention is made of orphans and children who are abandoned, homeless, neglected, ill-treated or uncared for; while no reference is made to the much larger number of children who are at risk of emotional, physical or educational damage through living in dysfunctional families. There are huge numbers of children whose development is blighted by failure of parenting and education, bad family and personal relationships and resulting low self-esteem; all of this leading inexorably to the same cycle of deprivation being visited on their own families in turn. A brief mention of the need to 'provide child care and family support services' does not do justice to the scale and importance of this problem, and avoids completely the issue of the very substantial resources necessary to make any impact on it.

What does family support mean? This varies enormously with the problems of the family concerned. To some, it may mean practical help in sorting out benefits, transporting a handicapped child to school, or paying for building alterations to make the house negotiable in a wheelchair. To young, inexperienced parents it may be parenting or home-making classes at a Family Resource Centre (Cox, 1993). Other families are too disabled emotionally to benefit from practical measures alone, and these are also the ones at highest risk of having children who suffer from psychiatric disorder, emotional, physical and sexual abuse, educational failure, delinquency, physical illness and developmental delay. They make high demands on all services, which in turn have a high level of failure and frustration in dealing with them.

For example, a certain family may be so chaotic that they find it impossible to get the children dressed, fed and ready for school in time. The health board employs a home help to assist them, but she soon finds that the parents take advantage of this to stay in bed in the morning, leaving all the work to her. More and more is demanded of her as the weeks progress, and she increasingly becomes the butt of verbal abuse from both the children and the parents. Sooner or later she decides it is not worth it and resigns: the family cannot regain the level of functioning they had before she started, the children's school attendance declines, and they are in a worse position than ever. This is not the home help's fault: she has not been trained for the very difficult and specialised task of supporting a dysfunctional family without undermining the little skill and confidence they already have. A similar outcome can ensue with a family going through a crisis of control. The parents are unable to cope with the behaviour of one or more of their children. Anxiety and tension rise, with increasing levels of conflict and confrontation at home. They ask for one of the children to go into care for a few weeks for things to cool down, and this is granted. When the time comes for the child to go back, his or her behaviour towards the parents has worsened because of anger at their rejection. They cannot face the thought of a return to the previous level of conflict, or worse, and so the child stays in care, the feelings of anger and rejection increasing and expressing themselves through disturbed behaviour.

Child psychiatry teams spend much of their time with families such as these, trying to understand their many predicaments and help them function better within their limited emotional and physical resources. But we are a scarce resource, given that Kolvin (1973) has calculated that only 10 per cent of children with child psychiatric problems ever receive specialist professional treatment. This is why so much of our time is spent linking with and supporting other agencies who are in regular contact with children and families in need. These include social work, education, paediatrics, primary care, mental handicap and voluntary agencies.

Family support is a very intensive and demanding area of work. In many cases, a great deal of professional time and expertise are devoted to a family for little visible result. They continue to have problems, and perhaps the only positive outcome that can be pointed to is that they have not fallen apart. The value of the work is unproven, because the necessary scientific studies are not yet complete. In any case, it is difficult to prove a negative: that is, that something awful would have happened but for the work that was done. Whatever the result, the work will need to continue. In a civilised society, we cannot witness the amount of distress and damage caused by these problems without acknowledging the need to intervene. It is the type of intervention which needs to be critically examined, and more creative and effective methods found.

For example, at present health board staff and voluntary agencies in the community largely work along parallel lines. They are dealing with the same families, but each carves out a specialist niche and concentrates on its own area of work, having little contact or co-ordination with other agencies seeing the family, unless some crisis pulls them all together at a case conference. In parts of Britain and America, an attempt has been made to combine the best of what professional agencies and voluntary workers have to offer in co-operative befriending schemes. The key concept is that these families do not benefit from receiving advice or information on how to solve their problems. The very nature of their problems makes it impossible for them to take advantage of this type of help. Indeed, the inevitable failure which results leads to them feeling even more demoralised and alienated from the helping services. What they do need is someone who can spend a much greater amount of time with them, listening to their problems and slowly building a relationship of trust and confidence. This can then be used to suggest, model and encourage better ways of coping, which are accepted because the worker is seen as a friend and equal, rather than a disapproving outsider. The voluntary worker has the time and commitment to do this, but not the specialist expertise or professional backup to ensure effectiveness or avoid pitfalls. This is where the health board professionals come in: each voluntary worker meets regularly with a professional therapist to discuss the work, usually in a group setting which ensures peer support as well. The befrienders would also be assessed for suitability before starting, and receive formal training before and at regular intervals during the work. Early results from these programmes are encouraging, with both befrienders and families reporting high levels of satisfaction.

Conclusion

From the child psychiatrist's viewpoint, the Act is a mixed blessing. The principles it contains, and the new measures for child protection and court orders, seem be an improvement on those of the 1908 Act. Time will tell how they function when they are fully activated. The welcome stress placed on identifying children in need, and promoting family support, is infuriatingly not followed through with any guidelines on how they should be achieved. This leaves it entirely up to the health boards and child care advisory committees, and so far they have not been quick off the mark. Finally, placing the limit of childhood at eighteen years of age has caused great practical problems for existing child psychiatry services whose upper limit was sixteen. They are faced with a 12 per cent increase in workload without any corresponding increase in resources, and many are sceptical about their ability to contribute to a new deal for the nation's children unless appropriate resources are in place to back up fine words.

References

Black, D. (1993), 'A Brief History of Child and Adolescent Psychiatry', in D. Black and D. Cottrell (eds.), *Seminars in Child and Adolescent Psychiatry*, London: Gaskell.

Black, D., Wolkind, S. and Harris-Hendriks, J. (eds.) (1991), *Child Psychiatry and the Law* (2nd edn), London: Gaskell.

Brunel Institute of Organisation and Social Studies (1976), *Working Paper HS/1—Future Organisation in Child Guidance and Allied Work*, London: Brunel University.

Children Act—England and Wales (1989), London: HMSO.

Cox, A.D. (1993), 'Befriending Young Mothers', *British Journal of Psychiatry*, No. 163, pp. 6–18.

Department of Health (1992), *Child Care Act 1991: Explanatory Memorandum*, Dublin.

Department of Health (1993), *Medical Manpower in Acute Hospitals: A Discussion Document* (The Tierney Report), Dublin.

Gath, A. (1992), 'Audit', in D. Bhugra and A. Burus (eds.), *Management Training for Psychiatrists*, London: Gaskell.

Kolvin, I. (1973), 'Evaluation of Psychiatric Services for Children in England and Wales', in J. K. Wing and J. Hafner (eds.), *Roots of Evaluation*, Oxford: Oxford University Press.

Sussenwein, F. and Treseder, J. (1985), 'Psychiatric Social Work', in M. Rutter and L. Hersov (eds.), *Child and Adolescent Psychiatry: Modern Approaches*, Oxford: Blackwell.

UK Department of Health (1991), *An Introduction to the Children Act 1989*, London: HMSO.

Chapter 11

A PAEDIATRIC PERSPECTIVE

Catherine M. Ryan

Introduction

Consultant paediatricians are by definition based in hospitals dealing with general paediatric patients, both acute and chronic, on an inpatient and outpatient basis. Neonatal care is an important part of the workload. This varies from neonatal intensive care to care of the neonatal newborn. Outside the cities, paediatricians are on call on a one in two basis which means every second night and every second weekend.

The population of the North Western Health Board (NWHB) is around 208,000. About 30 per cent are aged fifteen or under. While paediatric care is normally given up to the age of fifteen, the 1991 Child Care Act defines a child as being under eighteen. The ramifications of this for paediatricians remain to be seen. There are about 3,000 deliveries a year in the NWHB area, ensuring a continuing supply of patients, even though the birth rate has declined over the last ten years.

In the Letterkenny Hospital catchment area there are about 120,000 people with about 1,600 deliveries annually. Inpatient and outpatient care, including peripheral clinics, is delivered by two consultant paediatricians with backup from five non-consultant hospital doctors. As well as normal paediatric problems, such as asthma, epilepsy or kidney infections, the work involves social and domestic problems which form an integral part of family life. In paediatrics, not only the child is treated—the parents and indeed the whole family have to be taken into consideration. This is particularly true for handicapped children. Care of long-term patients is quite difficult and can be very tricky when the child, with epilepsy or diabetes, for instance, becomes a teenager, and starts reacting against the treatment. As with other problems, a multidisciplinary approach is best in these cases.

The general health of the childhood population has improved considerably over the last twenty years. The emphasis has changed from dealing with issues such as acute dehydration from gastroenteritis, which used to be such a problem in the past, to social problems.

As in other areas, evaluation of child abuse is performed by paediatricians. This includes medical examinations for child sexual abuse of both boys and girls, identification and diagnosis of non-accidental injury and cases of neglect. The prevalence of child abuse in this health board has not been noticeably different from other areas. Relatively few cases of child abuse present directly to the hospital. The majority are referred for medical examination through the social worker service, while a smaller number are referred from general practitioners.

Most general paediatricians in the country see less than five new cases of child sexual abuse per year. Some see and examine between five and ten cases per year. The initial examination may take an hour or more, usually as an unscheduled appointment in a busy week. The follow-up case conference may take one to three hours. There are also other case conferences about children who have been seen before. Medical examination is only part of the necessary investigation pattern. There is no clear-cut diagnostic test for child sexual abuse. In many cases, abuse may leave no physical signs even though it may have been going on over a prolonged period. Many physical signs are capable of wide interpretation. One example of this is anal dilatation. Minor anal dilatation is not an infrequent finding in normal children. It has been made quite clear from the proceedings of the Cleveland enquiry that child sexual abuse must never be diagnosed from physical evidence alone (Butler-Sloss, 1988). Obvious exceptions to this are findings of pregnancy, venereal disease or seminal products.

In nearly all cases of sexual abuse, suspicions have been raised or disclosure made before the child reaches the paediatrician. However, the diagnosis must also be considered in relation to symptoms which present routinely to paediatric clinics, such as behaviour change, bed wetting and vaginal discharge, as well as sleep disturbance or inappropriate and unusual behaviour in small children.

In cases where there is a suspicion that 'there may be something going on' doctors, as well as other health care workers and non-health care workers such as teachers to whom there may be disclosure, may be ambivalent about pursuing the matter further. This is based on their own personal experience or on the perceived 'normality' of the family involved (within the wider boundaries of normality). Some sources quote the incidence of some sort of child sexual abuse in females to be as much as 20 per cent and in males to be up to 10 per cent. Perhaps abuse may be considered 'normal' in some families as the history can go back two or even three generations.

Child abuse in all forms, including child sexual abuse, has always been present in society (Mrazek and Kempe, 1981). Kempe and Kempe (1978) suggest that society must go through six stages before child abuse is eliminated. Firstly, denial that either physical or sexual abuse exists to a significant extent. Secondly, the community pays attention to the more lurid forms of abuse, such as the battered child, and begins to find ways of preventing and coping more effectively with these. Thirdly, physical abuse is better managed and attention is paid to more subtle forms of abuse such as poisoning or the infant who fails to thrive. In stage four, the community recognises emotional abuse, deprivation and patterns of severe rejection. In stage five, the community acknowledges the existence of the sexually abused child. Finally, in stage six, the community guarantees that each child is truly wanted and provided with loving care, decent shelter and food as well as first-class preventative and curative health care.

Increased awareness of child physical abuse has led to public outcry and enquiry when children die. The Colwell case in Britain (Colwell Report, 1974) led to a public outcry in the mid-1970s and also raised public awareness. Maria Colwell was returned to her mother and stepfather by social services after several years in a foster family. She became the family drudge and scapegoat. Bruising and cruel treatment were not reported by shopkeepers, school teachers, neighbours and others until after she was killed by her stepfather. Professionals involved were blamed for Maria's death. The Kilkenny case bears some resemblance to this, as it had been going on for so long and those involved seemed powerless to stop it (*see* Ferguson, 1994).

Following the Colwell enquiry the Department of Health and Social Services (DHSS) recommended that area review committees be set up to oversee the management of all child abuse cases, to review the machinery for referral and to set up procedures to ensure that suspected cases of child abuse were correctly notified and dealt with. This kind of impetus happened in Ireland subsequent to the Kilkenny incest case. Much work had been done prior to this case and the Kilkenny investigation (McGuinness, 1993), but the whole scenario of child abuse, especially child sexual abuse, has come to the fore. Again the insinuation has been that professionals have been somehow to blame. Having carefully read the report, I consider that the tissue of cover-up, denial and lies instigated by the perpetrator over the years in the Kilkenny case were sufficient to cloud the issue considerably, for professionals and members of the public alike.

Management

The most recent Department of Health guidelines on the investigation and management of child abuse were published in July 1987. From my perspective, they are very reasonable, except that there is no mandatory requirement for professionals to report suspected child abuse. The structures contained in the guidelines should work well and have been in place in this area for many years. The Child Care Act 1991 will in some ways tighten up procedures. I agree with the recommendation of the Kilkenny Report that there should be a mandatory system of reporting, a standardised notification system and precise definitions of the different forms of abuse. I am not sure that every case needs to be reported to the gardaí. The gardaí are obliged to make a separate investigation if they are informed. Many cases never get to court and some are resolved by the family with the help of the social workers and other health board professionals. Training and collaboration are key elements in the management of cases.

The question of mandatory reporting raises many dilemmas. In my practice, I have always reported reasonable suspicions which may or may not have been validated. However, a teacher in a rural area may feel very threatened and vulnerable if he or she reports their suspicions. There must be backup and support for such people as well as training.

The Implications of the Child Care Act 1991 for the Practices of Consultant Paediatricians

All consultant paediatricians in general paediatric practice are involved in the management of child abuse. In Dublin, Cork and Waterford there are child sexual abuse assessment clinics run and staffed by the community care services as well as investigations and management of child sexual abuse. Hospital and social services deal with cases of non-accidental injury and neglect.

It is not known whether the Child Care Act will result in more referrals, but there will certainly be an increased workload in relation to supervision orders, as the monitoring of such cases is likely to require more case conferences on an ongoing basis and more clinic follow-up for these children as part of the general paediatric services. As part of an evaluation of the likely impact of the Child Care Act from a paediatric perspective I surveyed 28 consultant paediatricians outside Dublin in order to ascertain if the amount and content of work were the same elsewhere as in this region. There were sixteen replies. Outside the cities, all consultant paediatricians are involved in the management of child sexual abuse. This mainly involves medical examination of girls and boys. In some cases examination of girls is in conjunction with a gynaecologist. The number of referrals is similar around the country. About half the paediatricians questioned expressed a preference for further involvement in the management of child sexual abuse if time permitted. About two-thirds would like further involvement (time permitting) in the management of child care issues other than child sexual abuse. The concept of community paediatrics, which is a joint hospital/community care appointment, has been much discussed recently. Community paediatrics has been in place in the UK for some years. The NWHB has approved of the concept, but no further progress has been made in this regard to date.

Child Care Act 1991

Part 1.2 (1) defines a 'child' as any person under the age of eighteen years other than a person who is or has been married. This has particular implications in the case of an underage girl who has had a child (or more than one). It remains to be defined who has the legal responsibility for the child of the child. Who, for instance, can give permission for hospital treatment?

Part 11, Promotion of the Welfare of Children: The Act places new duties on health boards to promote the welfare of children in their area. This includes identifying children who are not receiving adequate care and protection and co-ordinating relevant information about them from a variety of sources. This implies that doctors are required to take a pro-active stance in identifying children at risk. Also, in co-ordinating information about such children, a multi-disciplinary approach is crucial and this is likely to be effected through attendance at case conferences, the development of protocols between professional groups for communicating information, and so on.

The Child Care Advisory Committee which was established in this area under the Act must report and keep under constant review the availability and adequacy of services in this area. The chairman of the committee is a consultant paediatrician. In one of the nearby health board areas there is no consultant paediatrician on the committee.

Part 111, Section 12 (1) refers to the powers given to the gardaí to remove a child to safety. The emergency care order (ECO) replaces the place of safety order. The gardaí will not need a warrant from the District Court to enter a dwelling and remove a child to safety. The use of this kind of power could be challenged constitutionally, especially if there was insufficient evidence (*Bunreacht na hÉireann: Constitution of Ireland* (1937), Articles 40–5). If the emergency action is taken by the gardaí, a decision has to be made by the health board to apply for an emergency care order within three days, which is a short time, especially over a weekend.

Difficulties may arise during out of hours activity. Social workers would need to be 'on call'. Hospitals are always open and could receive small children on a temporary basis, but general paediatric wards, which are the norm around the country, would not be able to cope with older children who may be unruly. In practice, the majority of applications for emergency care orders (like place of safety orders currently) will result from action taken by health board social workers to protect children at risk. Social workers have no powers under the Act to remove a child without first applying for an emergency care order. Judges are given the new power to order medical or psychiatric examination, treatment or assessment of a child. In cases of acute assault or rape of a young person, this would have to be done immediately. The ECO lasts for a maximum of eight days after which, if it still wishes to proceed with the case and go for care proceedings, the health board must apply for an interim care order.

The interim care order (ICO)—a new provision under the Act—may be granted by the District Judge and lasts for eight days. There is, however, scope for extending these orders if necessary (Section 17 (2)). Unlike under previous legislation, parents will now have the right to challenge the power of the board to keep the child in care on an emergency basis by opposing the board's application for an ICO.

At present there are no suitable residential centres available in this area. The only centres are hospitals, either general hospitals or residential centres for the mentally handicapped. Suitable foster homes which could be used in emergency situations will have to be found.

Supervision Orders

Section 19 of the Act introduces the supervision order. The order lasts for one year and will give health boards a statutory power to supervise children in their own homes or at some other place designated by the Court (such as a family centre). There is no way of knowing how this system will work until it is tried. In the UK, there have been well-publicised cases of a child being returned to his or her parents and subsequently found to be neglected or ill-treated or killed. Nobody can be supervised all the time. Decisions about supervision versus care orders will at times be very difficult and may be proved right or wrong only with hindsight.

Part V: Jurisdiction and Procedure. Section 24 emphasises that within the legal framework of the Act: (i) the welfare of the child must be regarded as the first and foremost consideration; and (ii) due consideration must be given to the wishes of the child. Children, however, may have very mixed feelings. The breakup of the family may, in many cases, seem to them to be a worse option than the continuation of abuse. Threats by the perpetrator, if he or she is a family member, and mistaken loyalty may occur. When the abuse is extra-familial it is usually easier to sort things out after disclosure, which again may be delayed for a long time due to threats or enforced secrecy.

In any event, due deliberation and consideration have to be given to the concept of what is best for the child, especially if the health board in question wishes to take the child into care and the parents or other parties object. The balance of evidence will come from health board professionals, usually social workers. The highest standards of professional integrity must be upheld at all times.

Family Support Services

Many voluntary agencies and parochial workers contribute to family support in various ways. The work of all agencies, whether state (through health boards or social welfare) or voluntary, should be co-ordinated. The Kilkenny Report (McGuinness, 1993) recommends the extension of available family support services such as family resource centres and home maker schemes. Even where the children are healthy and there are two parents in the home normal parenting is a difficult task. Where there is one parent it is obviously more difficult, especially where she (as it is nearly always the mother) lives alone with the child. Where poor social circumstances prevail, with perhaps the addition of a child with sickness or handicap, everything is made much more difficult.

Greater co-operation between community care and hospital would be more helpful in identifying 'families at risk'. In itself, and with the provision of necessary help and support, this may be instrumental in promoting the welfare of children and reducing the incidence of child abuse, especially physical abuse and neglect. The greater availability of social workers in rural areas to whom people, either the general public or those in authority such as teachers or clergy, could go and discuss a particular family or problem could also help in averting problems before they arise. Preventive programmes are most important. The 'Stay Safe' programme for schools and the intense media coverage of child abuse must make nearly all children aware of the existence of child abuse and give them at least a preliminary concept of how to avoid it and perhaps how to tell somebody about it.

As mentioned in the Kilkenny Report (McGuinness, 1993, p. 113), there has been little in the way of treatment for perpetrators of child abuse. Where the perpetrator is a child himself it falls within the scope of the children's services to provide treatment. This is not an uncommon problem and will need to be addressed. In itself, it falls within the section on prevention in that it should help prevent further abuse.

Finally, in realising these objectives and working effectively under the Act, training for professionals must be ongoing and reflect the current thinking about child abuse. Preconceived ideas are not good enough. As already mentioned, most consultant paediatricians see less than ten cases of child sexual abuse per year. No specific training is provided. Some gynaecologists see very few children in their practice and feel uneasy about definitive diagnosis of child sexual abuse.

References

Bunreacht na hÉireann: Constitution of Ireland (1937), Dublin: Stationery Office.

Butler-Sloss, Lord Justice E. (1988), *Report of the Inquiry into Child Abuse in Cleveland in 1987*, London: HMSO.

Colwell Report (1974), *Report of the Committee of Enquiry into the Care and Supervision Provided in Relation to Maria Colwell*, London: HMSO.

Department of Health (1987), *Child Abuse Guidelines*, Dublin.

Ferguson, H. (1994), 'Child Abuse Inquiries and the Report of the Kilkenny Incest Investigation: A Critical Analysis', *Administration*, Vol. 41, No. 4, pp. 385–410.

Kempe, R. S. and Kempe, C. H. (1978), *Child Abuse*, London: Fontana.

McGuinness, C. (1993), *Report of the Kilkenny Incest Investigation*, Dublin: Stationery Office.

Mrazek, P.B. and Kempe, D.A. (1981), *Sexually Abused Children and their Families*, New York: Pergamon Press.

Chapter 12

A PUBLIC HEALTH NURSING PERSPECTIVE

Anna Kelly

We in the health boards welcome the passing of the Child Care Act 1991 as the first major piece of child welfare legislation enacted by the state since the 1908 Act. The Act gives us the statutory responsibility for promoting the welfare of children who are not receiving adequate care and protection within our areas, and providing child care and family support services. As this responsibility reaches the public health nurses within the community at ground level, the Act must motivate us and structure our attempts to identify and respond to vulnerable children before situations deteriorate. Section 3(2)(a) requires a health board to 'take such steps as it considers requisite to identify children who are not receiving adequate care and protection and co-ordinate information from all relevant sources relating to children in its area'. The public health nurse, in assessing the early development of the children in her area, is at the centre and forefront of meeting this requirement.

It is in her duties of dispensing primary health care that the public health nurse can best embrace this new Act. Being family visitors, public health nurses have always had the responsibility of identifying any child at risk, and have done so pro-actively. The Department of Health's *Child Abuse Guidelines* (1987) are the main procedures guiding public health nursing practice in relation to child care in this area. The Donegal Community Care Area of the North Western Health Board has not produced an officially documented protocol on the appropriate action to take in cases of suspected abuse. The action that follows is heavily influenced by the quality of informal relationships between professionals, rather than an acknowledged formal understanding of roles and procedures

(186)

between the professionals involved. In the implementation of the section of the Act which requires us to 'co-ordinate' information on behalf of vulnerable children, inter-agency procedures will have to be written and guidelines set such that a nurse's suspicions of child abuse can be acted upon as efficiently and rapidly as possible. We need to devise new protocols for inter-agency communication at all levels within all organisations involved.

This conclusion has also been highlighted in the *Report of the Kilkenny Incest Investigation*, which recommends

> written agreed protocols for the investigation and management of child abuse within each health board. The roles and responsibilities of all staff should be outlined. There should be clear guidelines for inter-programme collaboration between hospital and community care staff on matters concerning the identification, notification and follow-up of child abuse. (McGuinness, 1993)

We must therefore examine the Act from the viewpoint of the public health nurse faced with operationalising it directly in her own community.

The Background to the Public Health Nursing Service

Gilligan (1991, p. 102) placed the current statutory responsibilities in the context of the evolution of the modern public health nursing service:

1851 Poor Relief (Ireland) Act enabled local authorities to appoint midwives to act as auxiliaries to district medical officers.

1907 Notification of Births Act heralds beginnings of child welfare service.

1915 Notification of Births (Extension) Act 1915 gives national effect to 1907 Act and makes grants available for the employment of nurses to visit mothers and children under five years of age

1919 Public Health Medical Treatment of Children (Ireland) Act lays the basis for the school health service.

1924 School Health Examinations, as provided for under the 1919 Act, are instituted.

1947   Section 102 of the Health Act provides that a health authority may, with the consent of the Minister, make arrangements for the provision of a nurse or nurses to give to any person requiring the same, advice and assistance on matters relating to health and to assist sick persons.

1956   Minister of Health urges health authorities to make nursing services (including home nursing and midwifery) available in each area.

1966   Ministerial circular (27/66) sets down policy for the development of the service. It envisages, among other things, a service available to families in each area of the country and a ratio of one nurse to 4,000 population. Among the services to be provided are the public health care of children from infancy to the end of the school-going period.

1970   Section 60 of the Health Act imposes a duty on health boards to provide without charge a nursing service to give to those persons (with full eligibility, or in other categories as specified by the Minister) advice and assistance on matters relating to their health and to assist them if they are sick.

1975   A major report on the workload of public health nurses is published (Department of Health, 1975).

1980   Institute of Community Health Nursing is founded.

1986   'Public Health Nursing Services in Ireland: Discussion Document' is issued by the General Medical Service Division of the Department of Health.

1987   National University of Ireland Diploma in public health nursing commences at University College, Dublin (replacing Bord Altranais course).

Of particular significance in shaping the present structure of the community nursing service was the policy initiated in 1966 through a Department of Health Ministerial circular (27/66) which, on foot of a wide-ranging policy review, set out the aims of the service and gave direction for future development. The aim of this new policy was the provision of services to individuals and families in each area throughout the country. More specifically, the objective was to provide domiciliary midwifery services as necessary, general domiciliary nursing, particularly for the aged, and, equally important, to attend to the public health care of children, from infancy to the end of the school-going period (Department of Health, 1966, pp. 2–3).

While public health nursing is mentioned in the 1970 Health Act, Section 60, there has been no fundamental change in the role and responsibility of the public health nursing service since the reforms were introduced in 1966.

Organisation of the Present Service

The public health nursing service is organised and managed within the community care programme in the eight health boards. The North Western Health Board provides a health service for a population of 208,174 (1991 Census) in counties Sligo, Leitrim and Donegal. The region is divided into two community care areas: Co. Sligo/Leitrim and Co. Donegal. In Co. Donegal the population (1991 Census) is 128,117. Public health nursing staff in Co. Donegal is comprised of 1 superintendent public health nurse, 2 senior public health nurses, 5 public health nurses on school and clinic duties and 52 public health nurses in the community.

Ratio of Public Health Nurses

The 1966 Ministerial circular (27/66) recommended a nurse/population ratio of 1:4,000. However, the public health nursing service has expanded and developed considerably over the past thirty years. This expansion, and a change in emphasis to health promotion and preventive measures, in addition to curative nursing, has brought about a change in the desired ratio. In 1986 the Institute of Community Health Nursing recommended a nurse/population ratio of 1:2,500. This contrasts with the actual ratio of 1:2,615 in the country as a whole in December 1990. In Co. Donegal, which is divided into 52 nursing areas based on the 1991 Census, the ratio is 1:2,464. While this looks very favourable and manageable when compared to the recommended ratio, it is important to remember that in Co. Donegal nursing areas are mainly rural and sparsely populated with few pockets of larger populations and nurses have long distances to travel.

Role of the Public Health Nursing Service

The public health nurse functions in a defined geographical area based on district electoral divisions. She is responsible for the organisation and provision of a comprehensive nursing service. As a practitioner, she identifies cases of need within her area using her initiative and making professional decisions. She seeks advice from, and is supervised by, the superintendent public health nurse, who is responsible to the director of community care and medical officer of health for the planning, management and development of the public health nursing and home help services. This includes the preparation of service estimates and the delivery of service within the allocated budget, the provision of nursing aids and equipment, stock maintenance, and staff supervision and training.

The superintendent public health nurse also monitors the liaison between hospital and community care nursing staff. She plays a supervisory/counselling role for public health nurses in connection with their work and continuing education. The Working Party Report on General Nursing found that the average ratio of public health nurses to superintendent was 33:1; the ratio is much higher in Co. Donegal (Department of Health, 1980). Two senior public health nurses assist the superintendent public health nurse. These four approved posts were established following the recommendations of the Working Party Report on General Nursing (Department of Health, 1980, pp. 52–6). The senior public health nurses report to the superintendent public health nurse and are responsible for:

- assisting and advising the superintendent public health nurse in the provision and monitoring of the public health nursing service and home help service in her area of assignment;

- assisting the training of student general nurses, trainee public health nurses and all newly appointed staff under her control;

- liaising with other health care professionals and general practitioners within her area in the development and provision of a comprehensive primary health care service.

Services Provided by the Public Health Nurse

The services provided by the public health nurse can be broadly classified under the headings 'curative nursing care' and 'preventive care'. In practice, within the wider dimensions of health, the public health nursing service has expanded and become more complex, taking into account the health implications, social conditions and lifestyles of its patients. This is borne out by the public health nursing home visit analysis survey (Kelly, 1987) carried out in the NWHB which showed that public health nurses are engaged in a variety of activities for patients, including some 'non-nursing' activities such as advising on diet, organising the connection or re-connection of electricity and water mains, liaising with county council and housing authorities about poor housing conditions and repairs needed, arranging financial support for needy people through statutory and voluntary organisations, arranging voluntary visitation for lonely and isolated patients, and initiating admission procedures for patients in order to relieve the stress of carers in the home.

However, public health nurses have to work without a workable, officially recognised structure to co-ordinate the appropriate mix of services to individuals and without a clear statement of the responsibilities of various health professionals involved in primary health care. In my experience public health nurses are in a unique position to identify problems and potential problems in the community. This has meant that considerable demands are placed on them by very vulnerable families and they take on an enormous variety of problems which affect the health of the individual.

Community nursing is a broad-based medico-social service. The concept of public health nursing interfaces with the medical and social models of health. Our survey showed that public health nurses were giving a service to many individuals who were not referred by a doctor but whom nurses recognised as not healthy or potentially 'at risk' as a result of various circumstances (Kelly, 1987, pp. 7–9).

In order to enter the Diploma Course in Public Health Nursing an applicant must be a registered general nurse and registered midwife with An Bord Altranais, with a minimum of two years' experience, working as a registered nurse/midwife, ideally with experience in paediatrics and geriatrics. She is required to hold the Leaving Certificate or equivalent and show evidence of recent study. The Diploma Course lasts for one year full-time at University College Dublin. Successful completion of the course leads to registration as a public health nurse with An Bord Altranais (An Bord Altranais, 1993, p. 11). The aim of this diploma course is to prepare the registered nurse/midwife to function as an effective, efficient and competent nurse in the community, carrying out primary, secondary and tertiary health care (Department of Nursing Studies, 1994).

Within the context of the maternity and child health service the public health nurse is charged with providing a service to the mother and child in the family setting following the notification of birth, which forms a major part of her workload. It includes a domiciliary service for post-natal mothers and infants up to six weeks old, followed by scheduled visits at specific stages of the child's development up to school entry. During these visits the nurse observes the physical, mental and social conditions of the family while giving advice on the physical and emotional needs of the child. She advises on the services available locally, with particular emphasis on the importance of immunisations and child development clinics. At the same time, she assesses social needs, remaining constantly alert to the possibility of puerperal depression, inadequate parenting or child abuse. She continues to provide a service to school-going children through the school health services and maintains a link between parents and school in connection with health matters.

The detection and prevention of child abuse are key areas in which the public health nurse must play a major role. Child abuse is not a new phenomenon. Unfortunately, children have been abused for centuries. In the sixteenth century a surgeon, Phelix Wurtz, wrote a clear account of some aspects of child abuse. Modern recognition of the problem began in Ireland at the end of the last century (Ferguson, 1993). Increased awareness of the medical aspects of child abuse owes much to the work of an American physician, Henry Kempe. In the 1960s he pointed out many of the manifestations of non-accidental injury to children. Kempe also stated that child abuse encompasses a much wider range of problems than was first diagnosed as battered baby syndrome (Kempe and Kempe, 1978). Numerous forms of abuse may damage a child both physically and emotionally (Evans, 1985). The fact that recognition of child abuse is often difficult and depends on awareness of the problem and careful observation is borne out by the Kilkenny incest case (Ferguson, 1994).

Needs of Children

Bearing in mind the legal implications of the Child Care Act 1991 we must encourage the development of initiative and apply our skills to child care problems in society today, maintaining a clear grasp of the needs of children. According to Pringle:

> It used to be thought that developmental needs come into play in a hierarchical sequence. Now it is held that all human needs are inter-related and inter-dependent in a subtle, complex and continuous way. (1980, p. 33).

This means that professionals need to develop skills that will enable them to deal with the numerous problems presented by individual families. According to Lestor (1993, pp. 162–3), the greatest stumbling block up to now in the protection of children is 'society's attitude towards children'. Historically they have been denied basic independent rights and their wishes and desires were superseded by their parents or guardians.

Under Section 3(2)(b) of the new Act we must now bear in mind that our actions should not only be in the best interest of the child but should also take account of the wishes of the child as far as it is feasible. In some cases we have seen the unmet physical and physiological needs of children speedily stabilised in a new and secure environment. However, it is usually desirable that the child be allowed to remain with his or her family, and that his or her family unit remain intact. Only as a last resort should any child have to be removed, or a member of the family segregated from the child, since such actions can have a detrimental effect on a child's development. Conversely, should a child have lost trust in those around him or her in the family unit, there is a definite case for removal to an environment where they can find new individuals to trust. Should this be the child's wish, then this should also be our primary concern. Of course, there will always be some untreatable families where the only course of action is the removal of the child from the life-threatening situation of its home environment.

It must be remembered that the 1991 Act extends the definition of a 'child' to include the sixteen–eighteen-year-old age group so that it becomes increasingly necessary to view certain individuals not as children but as young adults who are capable of making rational and sensible decisions about their own futures but who may also be less receptive to counter advice. In view of this, it is becoming increasingly necessary for professionals to be more skilled in dealing with these young adults.

Family Support

One of the primary functions of a public health nurse is to provide family support in her guise as a family visitor. Each public health nurse is required to make statutory visits to children from birth to five years for the purpose of child developmental assessment and to advise and educate parents. This affords her the opportunity to forge a relationship with families and children in her area and to observe the parenting and family relationships within the household. It also allows her to identify any deviations from the norm which would lead her to suspect child abuse, such as: a withdrawn, discontented or anxious child; physical evidence such as bruising, fractures or repeated physical illness; special cases such as young inexperienced mothers or a number of closely spaced pregnancies; a history of violence; developmental delay or other psychological factors such as a depressed mother. In addition, it may be obvious in certain circumstances that the nurse is unwelcome or indeed she may be refused admission to the family home as highlighted in the Kilkenny Report (McGuinness, 1993).

The public health nurse has the advantage that through her direct community involvement and relationship with families she is recognised as local, making her more readily trusted and respected as an easily acceptable confidant within the health board. This means that she is potentially better informed without the stress of involving social services. As professionals, public health nurses have built up over the years a vast knowledge of specialised information, skills and expertise, much of which relates to child care. They are experts in normal child development (Arton, 1985). One would therefore expect public health nurses to make major contributions to dealing with child care problems. Unfortunately, we find ourselves meeting frustrations both within and without our public health nursing discipline.

Present Situation within the Public Health Nursing Service

In order to understand the frustrations met in trying to implement this legislation, one must first be aware of the scope of the role of the public health nurse. She is by definition a generalist working with individuals, families and the community. Her duties bring her into contact with a wide range of people for the purpose of providing services to ante-natal and post-natal mothers, people needing rehabilitative care, children from birth to five years, school-going children, the disabled, the elderly, the sick and dying, the bereaved, and client groups such as travellers and high-risk groups. As an educator, adviser and professional health care worker she has an extensive caseload which, given demographic changes, advances in technology and techniques, de-institutionalisation of health care, and social problems such as unemployment, alcohol and other substance abuse and epidemiological changes, prompts the question whether public health nursing is sufficiently staffed to meet existing duties let alone the requirements introduced by the new legislation.

Public health nurses are assigned to geographical areas based on population rather than manageable caseloads or priority needs. They may have to enforce the legal implications of a situation of child abuse although their primary concern is to help the family rather than to police it. Many nurses find it hard to distance themselves from a family with whom they have established a relationship when it comes to deciding how to deal with their own suspicions about a child 'at risk', and the possibility that they may end up giving evidence in court. For this reason, the Kilkenny Report recommendation that there should be mandatory reporting of suspicion by health care professionals becomes all the more important. Further, once a report is made to the director of community care and medical officer of health, he or she should be obliged to arrange a case conference to identify the key person to follow through on the case. This policy would assist in the early identification and confirmation of suspected cases of abuse and would eliminate situations where in the past it may have taken years to confirm suspicions, such as in the Kilkenny case. The expertise and experience of the key worker are paramount in the investigation and management of suspected cases of physical abuse and neglect. Our approach should be multi-disciplinary, not only because of the management implications, but also because all professionals working with children have different but relevant skills which, taken together, present a far more accurate and complete picture and understanding of the child and his or her problems and needs (Hanks *et al.*, 1989, p. 142). Central to the successful practice of inter-disciplinary co-operation is the role of the key worker.

The primary defect in the present broad-based public health nursing service is the lack of a defined caseload. This limits the public health nurses' time commitment to focusing on the identification of community care needs and the implementation of this new piece of legislation. The second major defect is the absence of a clear policy statement in relation to inter-professional management of child care cases in the area of child neglect/abuse which often leads to a feeling of isolation and lack of multi-disciplinary team working and accountability. The present structure within which primary health care is delivered is not conducive to the realisation of the community nursing service or other primary health care services. Apart from the rare exception, the primary health care team is a myth and exists in name only. The word 'team' implies interdependence and shared responsibility and the integration of the individual contributions of a group of people for the accomplishment of an agreed purpose. But the rhetoric does not reflect the reality.

Initial investigations in our health board have indicated that health professionals are not working as a team towards the accomplishment of an agreed purpose with shared responsibility. For example, work boundaries are unclear, as are working relationships among professionals in dealing with different types of cases, and there is no clear understanding of the roles and responsibilities of various professionals in many cases. The reality is that in practice public health nurses can be left in limbo, feeling isolated and anxious with the delay in getting a referral accepted and followed through. How often have we heard when attempting to make a referral to social workers 'My caseload is full up,' 'I am not on intake' or 'It will be four weeks before I can get out.' These replies from our obviously overworked colleagues highlight the need for a trained case co-ordinator to regularly monitor and review ongoing cases and families who give cause for concern. None of us wishes to live with a question mark over our professional integrity.

The lack of understanding among professionals of their roles and responsibilities as members of a multi-disciplinary team appears to be at the root of the problem identified by public health nurses in the North Western Health Board survey. This manifested itself in the lack of feedback and backup from other professionals in many cases—particularly 'social type' cases. To realise the potential of public health nurses and other health care professionals there is a need to break down defensiveness among the various disciplines. Unfortunately, in the present health board structure the possibility of a primary health care team functioning effectively is extremely remote. In my opinion the main reason for this is that planning, management and budgeting for health care are done on a service-by-service basis. This encourages competition among the various service areas for the largest slice of resources.

Each manager plans for his or her own service without taking account of how the other services may influence the demand on other areas. For example, if public health nurses stop visiting social cases, would the work of the social workers increase? Similarly, how does the visiting pattern and work of the social worker influence the time the public health nurse needs to spend with children 'at risk'? The activity of one service obviously influences the other. These are factors which must be taken into account if we want to plan our resources in an informed way. I am convinced that any primary health care service must be clearly patient/client centred, based on the needs of the individual. Bearing in mind the concept of the wider dimensions of health we, as public health nurses, recognise the profound influence the environment can have on that individual. For this reason, public health nurses should continue to deliver services on the basis of a smaller geographically defined neighbourhood.

What Needs to be Changed?

To maximise the potential that exists for developing good practice under the Child Care Act, we must make improvements in the following areas.

- Protocols should be established clearly setting out the role and function of each member of the inter-disciplinary team, and allowing for inter-disciplinary liaison and communication. This would ensure that through continuous review of cases public health nurses, as well as other members of the inter-disciplinary team, can link in and contribute towards an optimum resolution of the case.

- Trust between professionals and support and mutual understanding of roles within the multi-disciplinary team should be developed.

- Knowledge and skills should be improved to enable staff to identify and cope with the challenges perceived in the legal framework of the new Act. Training at a multi-disciplinary level needs to be available locally for all who may come in contact with child abuse and families in need of support.

- In compliance with the new statutory duty on health boards to promote the welfare of children and provide family support services, all professionals and members of the team must regard themselves as having responsibility for highlighting the social and economic factors in society which affect the ability of parents to care adequately for their children.

- Staff records and reports will have to be kept correctly. The importance and need for this have been well documented in the Kilkenny Report (McGuinness, 1993).

- The statutory obligation to respond to all families where children are identified as being 'at risk' means committing ourselves to prevention and not just to an emergency service which can respond only to serious child care cases.

- More emphasis should be placed on the promotion of preventive rather than curative care. This could be done through the development of support services such as better ante-natal care and parentcraft teaching for parenting development, crèche facilities, day nurseries, mother and toddler groups, community mother schemes, support and counselling services, and a home maker scheme. None of this can be achieved, however, without adequate staffing.

- The provision of pre-school services by health boards should be welcomed.

- A balance needs to be struck between the surrendering of powers by professionals and ensuring that staff possess the relevant knowledge and skills to carry out duties appropriately.

- Adequate resources must be provided to avoid the present position where staff are physically and mentally stretched beyond their limits.

- People should be helped to prepare for parenting with more time and emphasis on pre-natal parenting courses. All of us have seen history repeating itself in cases where poor or less than adequate parenting was carried through to the next generation. Ongoing support and education should be available to parents of children in the pre-school, school and teenage years.

- Cases of suspected child neglect or abuse should not be left unresolved. The confirmation of such cases can be difficult where, due to personal involvement, the professional involved is uncertain. More emphasis on probing, and the support of skilled personnel, in the absence of obvious evidence of abuse or neglect is required (McGuinness, 1993).

- The targeting of children at risk of ill-treatment should go beyond the ideas of high and low risk. The development of child welfare services should not supersede the development of other family support services, and neither should it overshadow the need for supervision and organisational support.

- The commitment by health boards and joint planning between the Departments of Health, Education and Justice should be monitored.

Conclusion

Child abuse continues to demand a very high level of resources and professional commitment. The consequences of intervening too precipitously weigh heavily on the minds of professionals. For this reason, many child care professionals still hesitate to tackle this problem actively. If the truth be told, many are still very uncomfortable with having to deal with 'at risk' situations, especially when the individuals involved are known to them, as is often the case with public health nurses. It is for this reason that we must actively embrace this legislation and use it as a motivating force towards change and communication.

The commitment of the different departments to communication, co-operation and joint planning is paramount to the success of this legislation. The same can be said for the different services involved in child care within the health boards and all those working to support families. In this we welcome the creation of the child care advisory committees whose function is to advise the health board under the Act, and report on the actions taken. We, as public health nurses, see this legislation as a means of bridging the lack of awareness about the overall potential of our service. This legislation should indeed prompt the Minister to realise the true lack of resources within this field. Places for children who have been taken into care are sadly lacking at present as are walk-in clinics and the like. If the Department of Health and the health boards intend to use public health nurses as a resource to implement this Act, more consideration must be given to the provision of staff, and the setting up of adequate backup services. Child welfare should not come second to curative health care.

References

An Bord Altranais (1992), *An Bord Altranais News*, special feature: 'Public Health Nursing' (August).

An Bord Altranais (1993), *An Bord Altranais News*, 'Courses in Nursing', Vol. 5, No. 2 (August).

Arton, M. (1985), 'Spotlight on Children', *Nursing Times*, 27 November.

Central Statistics Office (1991), *Census 1991*, Local Population Report, 1st Series, No. 30, Co. Donegal.

Department of Health (1966), *Circular 27/66, District Nursing Service*, Dublin.

Department of Health (1970), *Health Act*, Dublin: Stationery Office.

Department of Health (1980), *Report of the Working Party on General Nursing*, Dublin: Stationery Office.

Department of Health (1987), *Report of a Working Group on Child Health Services*, Dublin.

Department of Nursing Studies (1994), *Diploma in Public Health Nursing Curriculum*, Faculty of Medicine, University College Dublin.

Evans, R. (1985), 'The Silent Victims', *Nursing Times*, 27 November.

Ferguson, H. (1993), 'Surviving Irish Childhood: Child Protection and the Deaths of Children in Child Abuse Cases since 1884', in H. Ferguson, R. Gilligan and R. Torode (eds.), *Surviving Childhood Adversity: Issues for*

Policy and Practice, Dublin: Social Studies Press.

Ferguson, H. (1994), 'Child Abuse Inquiries and the Report of the Kilkenny Incest Investigation: A Critical Analysis', *Administration*, Vol. 41, No. 4, pp. 385–410.

Gilligan, R. (1991), *Irish Child Care Services: Policy, Practice and Provision*, Dublin: Institute of Public Administration.

Hanks, H., Hobbes, C. and Wynne, J. (1989), 'Early Signs and Recognition of Sexual Abuse in the Pre-school Child', in K. Browne, C. Davies and P. Stratton (eds.), *Early Prediction and Prevention of Child Abuse*, Chichester: Wiley.

Kelly, A. I. (1987), 'Realizing the Potential of Community Nursing in Primary Health Care', paper presented to the Conference on Health Policy, Beaumont Hospital, Dublin (October).

Kempe, R. S. and Kempe, C. H. (1978), *Child Abuse*, London: Fontana.

Lestor, J. (1993), 'Changing Attitudes to Children', *Health Visitor, The Journal of the Health Visitors' Association*, Vol. 66, No. 5 (May), pp. 162–3.

McGuinness, C. (1993), *Report of the Kilkenny Incest Investigation*, Dublin: Stationery Office.

Pringle, M. K. (1980), 'The Needs of Children and How They Are Met', in *The Needs of Children*, 2nd edn, London: Hutchinson.

Chapter 13

A GENERAL PRACTICE PERSPECTIVE

Eamon Shea

The general practitioner's (GP) involvement in child health begins during the mother's pregnancy. A possible predictor of future child abuse is the mother's attitude to her pregnancy: is she ambivalent about the pregnancy? If yes, this should be noted by the GP (Boyd and Molden, 1982). After the baby is born, the GP's first contact with the baby is usually at six weeks when babies are brought for a routine check under the mother and infant scheme. Before the six weeks' check, the mother and child are visited by the public health nurse who brings any problems arising to the GP's attention. At this check, it is important to observe the bonding, or lack of it, between the baby and the mother. Later, the GP sees the baby and parent for routine immunisations at two, four, six and fifteen months. Although no official screening service for infants is carried out by GPs, he or she can observe the development of the child at these visits. Any sign of failure to thrive or a failure of the mother to cope should be noted.

In common with the majority of Irish GPs (59 per cent), I work single-handed. As a consequence, we work in professional isolation. This sometimes, though rarely, can be total isolation (Coomber, 1992). In my case, I work as a rural, dispensing GP with a General Medical Service (GMS) list of 1,500 plus. This includes 191 children (98 boys and 93 girls) in the age group from birth to fifteen years. Some fifteen consultations per doctor per week occur in this age group (Coomber, 1992, p. 26).

I have only one staff member in my practice—my receptionist/secretary. However, I share the health centre I work in with the local public health nurses and I am in daily contact with them. I am employed by the North Western Health Board. My contacts with the Board have, until recently, been directly with the local community care office. Recent changes in administrative structure have led to the formation of general practice units in the health boards and these have GP members.

What training did I receive to deal with child abuse? The answer is none. I cannot remember it being mentioned in medical school at all, but my memory of those days is hazy now. I worked as a paediatric senior house officer (SHO) for one year but I cannot remember dealing personally with any case of child abuse. My reading about child abuse probably started when I was studying for membership of the Royal College of General Practitioners. I read such journals as *Update, Journal of the Royal College of General Practitioners* (now the *British Journal of General Practice*). Since then, I have learned more through being involved with cases of child abuse in my practice.

Nowadays, doctors who intend to practise as GPs take vocational training courses, which include education on how to recognise and deal with child abuse. Professional isolation is of great importance when the GP, this one at least, is confronted by the possibility of child abuse and especially child sexual abuse in his or her practice. This may come to light in a routine consultation. In addition to seeing the child for immunisations, the GP often sees these infants for upper respiratory tract infections and other minor ailments. During these visits, the GP may come across some suspicious signs of non-accidental injury, such as unexplained bruises, grip marks on limbs, bites, cigarette burns or undisclosed fractures (Boyd and Molden, 1982). There are pitfalls to be avoided in that some accidental bruises may lead to unwarranted accusations of abuse. Would GPs consider the failure of parents to present their children for immunisations as evidence of neglect? The GP's attitude to this is important. Will he or she accept the explanations given for the presentation of bruises or delayed reporting of injuries because of a reluctance to open a can of worms which he/she feels he/she cannot cope with? Will the GP repress thoughts of ill-treatment because of reluctance to recognise that it may be occurring in families that the doctor knows well?

When the GP becomes aware of the problem by being told directly by the victim or the perpetrator that abuse has been occurring, he or she must inform the area medical officer as advised in the *Child Abuse Guidelines* (Department of Health, 1987). Otherwise the outcome may be similar to that noted in the *Report of the Kilkenny Incest Investigation* where it was revealed that the victim attended GPs on ten different occasions, on one occasion directly revealing abuse, without any response from the medical profession (McGuinness, 1993). There remains a great reluctance by GPs to involve outside agencies when confronted with child abuse for fear of breaking patient–doctor confidentiality. Suspected child abuse may also be brought to the attention of the GP by a relation or neighbour of the child in question, or the problem may be referred for his or her attention by other health care professionals.

Does the hapless GP rush to telephone the local director of community care or area medical officer as advised by the *Child Abuse Guidelines*? Yes, if the individual presentation of child abuse is clear cut. However, in the majority of abuse cases I have been involved with the presentation is not clear cut but there is a suspicion that something is amiss. I contact and talk directly to one or both parents involved and try to find out if there is, in their opinion, any possibility of abuse. In the great majority of cases, the parents are only too willing to co-operate in an attempt to get at the 'truth'. We usually agree to have the child in question referred to and examined by the local paediatrician. If he or she agrees that there is strong evidence of abuse, then we contact the local social worker who has responsibility for child abuse in the area.

In co-operation with all involved, the social worker begins a detailed examination of the problem. Hopefully, in cases of intra-familial child sexual abuse, for example, this ends with the perpetrator being willing to undergo treatment and thus he (as it usually is a he) is able to remain in the family, as is the victim of the abuse. This is the ideal outcome and it has occurred in at least one occasion in my practice. However, sometimes the investigation leads to the gardaí becoming involved and this almost inevitably leads to a court appearance for the family and the GP. This can be traumatic both for the family and the doctor. The problem becomes common knowledge, especially in the small communities of rural practices.

This can be most uncomfortable for the GP, especially when relatives of the family approach the GP and make their feelings felt, particularly in the case of relatives from the alleged perpetrator's side of the family.

The court experience itself can be traumatic for the GP and the patients as they end up as adversaries in the courtroom. Indeed, the GP can be questioned aggressively by the opposing (the family's) legal advisers and all his or her information questioned in depth. The written record becomes essential here and any contact with the family must be legibly recorded as all alleged information, even the most reasonable, will be challenged under oath; people's memories of events can differ considerably from your own when it comes to courtroom evidence. All this has its effect on the GP who has no counsellor to speak to. From personal experience, I see a need for such counselling to help individual GPs involved come to terms with their own feelings about the child abuse cases they deal with. These can affect their personal relationships, particularly those with other children, for example their own children. Perhaps the Irish College of GPs will give some consideration to this in the future. Child abuse cases also have a profound effect in the local community. It may lead to other cases of child abuse being hidden from the GP because most people in the community believe that the GP should not breach professional confidence by getting outside agencies involved. However, as we know, it is impossible for the GP alone to investigate or in any way deal with abuse cases in isolation. He or she would be most unwise even to contemplate doing so.

Thankfully, a court case occurs in only a small minority of cases, in my practice only once. On other occasions where child abuse was proven, again the minority of cases of suspected abuse, case conferences were held. It is essential that the GP attends such case conferences (even if he or she has nothing new to add) to hear the perspectives of other people involved and to gain a better understanding of the evaluation of the family involved. Indeed, that GP may learn a lot about his or her patients from the others at the conference. For GMS doctors, a fee is payable for attendance at case conferences called by the area medical officer.

The Child Care Act and General Practice

What effect will the Child Care Act 1991 have on GPs' approach to child protection and child welfare in general? Part II of the Act states that every health board has a function to promote the welfare of children in its area who are not receiving adequate care and protection. Section 3(2) goes on to specify that health boards must:

> (a) take such steps as it considers requisite to identify children who are not receiving adequate care and protection and co-ordinate information from all relevant sources relating to children in its area;

> (b) having regard to the rights and duties of parents, whether under the Constitution or otherwise—

>> (i) regard the welfare of the child as the first and paramount consideration, and

>> (ii) in so far as is practicable, give due consideration, having regard to his age and understanding, to the wishes of the child; and

> (c) have regard to the principle that it is generally in the best interests of a child to be brought up in his own family.

How is this to be done under the Act? A number of methods are mentioned in the Act: voluntary care; increased powers to the gardaí; emergency care order, interim care order, care order and a supervision order.

Voluntary care: with parental consent, the health board can take a child into care for as long as necessary for the child's welfare. This can only be done with the consent of the parents or someone acting *in loco parentis*. If the parents object, this voluntary care cannot apply. I note that the health board can take a child into voluntary care because the child is lost, or the parents are missing, or the child is abandoned ('Home Alone Syndrome'). This option would obviously be of help to GPs confronted with this rare event.

Increased garda powers: Part III, Section 12 can be used for the protection of children in emergencies:

> Where a member of the Garda Síochána has reasonable grounds to believe that
>
> (a) there is an immediate and serious risk to the health or welfare of a child, and
>
> (b) it would not be sufficient for the protection of the child from such immediate and serious risk to await the making of an application for an emergency care order by a health board under Section 13

the garda may take the child to a place of safety. The child must, as soon as possible, be delivered into the custody of the health board. The child can be held for three days under this section, at which time he or she must be brought by the health board to the District Court for a hearing. I can see that this may be of great help to GPs who are working at weekends, when they often get the impression that they are working alone in the community. I can foresee that the local GP will be calling on the local garda sergeant for help.

It is not feasible to contact the area medical officer at weekends or at night to take a child immediately to the District Court. However, this section will allow GPs to intervene quickly if they feel a child is at risk. Now they will be able to follow the advice given by Neil O'Doherty in his book *The Battered Child.* Discussing the issue of whether 'diagnosis demands immediate hospital admission', Dr O'Doherty states:

> The battered child is at serious risk of death or permanent damage and must be admitted immediately to hospital for his safety and protection. If his case presents in the doctor's surgery or health centre contact must be made by telephone with the duty consultant or the child abuse team where one exists. The child must be seen right away with his parents. There is no way of knowing that a battered child will not be killed or permanently damaged in the interval if he is allowed 'parole'; the relative mildness or age of the presenting lesions is no cause for delay. A pessimistic assumption is the only safe one. (1982, p. 38)

An *emergency care order*, which replaces the place of safety order under the old legislation, can be issued by the District Court if it deems it necessary on application by the health board. Social workers have no powers to remove a child without such an order. This order lasts for eight days only. Subsequently, the District Court can issue an *interim care order*. This can be sought when the retention of the child beyond eight days is sought on the following grounds: (a) the child has been or is being assaulted, ill-treated, neglected or sexually abused; or (b) the child's health, development or welfare is likely to be avoidably impaired or neglected (Section 18 (1)).

Where a case is found by the Court to be proved the judge has the option of making a *care order*, which replaces the fit person order, and lasts under the new legislation until the child/young person is eighteen years old. The other option available to the Court is a *supervision order* which is a new disposal in the Irish system. Lasting for a twelve-month period (after which the board may apply for it to be renewed), it empowers health board professionals to visit the child in his or her home or some other named place of supervision (such as a family centre). A supervision order may prove to be very useful in that it takes a lot of the burden off the GP's shoulders and this burden can be shared with the social worker and the Court. This order would not imply any guilt on the part of the family and the GP should be able to maintain the doctor–patient relationship intact in such cases. I do not see the GP being directly involved in the investigation after the social worker becomes involved.

Part v of the Act deals with jurisdiction and procedures and I feel Section 29(3) is encouraging:

> The District Court and the Circuit Court on appeal from the District Court shall sit to hear and determine proceedings under *Part III, IV* or *VI* at a different place or at different times or on different days from those at or on which the ordinary sittings of the Court are held.

A separate children's court might have been more appropriate at this stage. Also in Section 30, it is stated that the child in question does not have to appear in court. A court appearance for most of us is a traumatic affair; it is especially so for a child in distress and is most unhelpful. Section 31 states that none of the court proceedings can be published. I would have thought that the media voluntarily avoids this at present but, now it will be illegal to publish. This will give some reassurance to GPs who may be fearful of such publicity and the effect it may have on their other patients.

Having read and re-read the Act, despite having some problems with legal terminology, I feel that this legislation should be an improvement on the present state of affairs. The two most interesting aspects of it are the ability of the gardaí to get involved in an emergency situation and the supervision orders. The GP must make it plain to the parents of the child that involving the gardaí is a course of action he or she wants to avoid and if they allow their child to be admitted voluntarily to the care of the health board, perhaps to the local paediatric unit, this could be avoided. However, if the parents refuse and the timing is such that the GP cannot contact the area medical officer, he or she can contact the duty social worker who can approach the gardaí to act immediately if they agree that the child is at risk.

This clarifies the process between the identification of a child at risk and the ability of the GP to get him or her into care. Until now, the GP had to organise a visit to the District Court through community care and social workers. The only alternative was to ask the parents to voluntarily admit the child. A refusal to do this can now lead to further action by the GP. This, of course, will cause some GPs to worry about confidentiality. However, I disagree with this and believe that the safety of the child overrides any problems with breach of confidentiality. Others may not agree.

The other welcome change is the supervision order. This should prove very helpful to GPs who suspect a case of child abuse but have not enough evidence to proceed to the stage of a care order. Both of these changes will lead to increasing team work by the GP with social workers and the gardaí. Some GPs may feel uneasy about having a closer association with the gardaí, especially in small communities. However, the gardaí will be coming to enforce the law rather than being on the side of the doctor or the doctor being on the side of the police. Some public disquiet may arise from this. However, the public will be asked to think again whether they wish to leave children at risk in situations which may lead to them being further harmed. The new situation with the courts will also be helpful and hopefully most of the cases will be held away from the public view.

In conclusion, I hope that the Child Care Act 1991 will aid GPs in their task of diagnosing and treating child abuse. The general aim will be to protect the abused child, treat the abuser and maintain both in the family, wherever possible keeping the family intact.

References

Boyd, R. and Molden, R. (1982), *Paediatric Problems in General Practice*, Oxford: Medial Publications.

Coomber, H. (1992), *The First National Study of Workload in General Practice*, Dublin: Irish College of General Practitioners.

Department of Health (1987), *Child Abuse Guidelines*, Dublin.

McGuinness, C. (1993), *Report of the Kilkenny Incest Investigation*, Dublin: Stationery Office.

O'Doherty, N. (1982), *The Battered Child—Recognition and Primary Care*, London: Balliere Tindall.

Chapter 14

A SOCIAL WORK PERSPECTIVE

Val O'Kelly

I have been in social work for a considerable length of time, in fact from the early days of the formation of community care social work departments under the 1970 Health Act. For most of that time I have worked with the North Western Health Board in Co. Sligo and Co. Leitrim in the area of child care. I am currently a senior social worker in the Sligo/Leitrim area. Since we began the process of implementing the Child Care Act, I have found myself reflecting on the past eighteen years and the optimism and expectations I carried during that time about the possibility of new legislation and policies and practices affecting the families and children we were attempting to help.

The community care area I serve covers two counties, Sligo and Leitrim, with a total population of 85,000. A small area of West Cavan was added in April 1993, with an addition of 1,200 people. The area is largely rural, with one large urban centre in Sligo City and several smaller urban centres throughout the region. The team I head is comprised of fifteen social workers and four child care workers. In addition to my team, there are two social workers attached to Sligo Social Services Centre, which is a voluntary social service covering Sligo City area, partly funded by the Board.

The majority of my staff, eight in all, form a family and child care team. The work of this team covers all social work to do with families, children, children in care, foster care services and child protection. The remainder of the staff deliver a social work service to Sligo General Hospital, mental health services and geriatric services. There is one generic social worker who is involved in work with the mentally handicapped and one community worker whose work is largely concerned with liaison with voluntary organisations in the area.

The four social workers work in a small children's home, with a capacity for six children, which is funded by the Board. In addition to the social work service operated by the Board there is a large social service council in the one large urban centre, Sligo. This is substantially funded by the Board, employs two full-time social workers and provides an extensive range of services for the elderly. It also acts as an umbrella body to a variety of organisations, such as the Catholic Marriage Advisory Council, Home Liaison Scheme, CURA and St Attracta's Adoption Society. Both the Adoption Society and CURA have a social worker each and together with Sligo Social Services Council are grant-aided by the Board. The senior social worker's task is determined by this backdrop of services. I have an overall monitoring role on behalf of the Board with the voluntary organisations and in particular on the delivery of services on the ground. My role in relation to the other services can be described as manager. It includes supervision of the professional work offered by the services. A large part of the work involves having an input into health board and national policy on social work and related issues. I have budget responsibility for the entire pay and non-pay social work service in the area, with the exception of Section 65 grants payable to the voluntary organisations.

When I look at our services in Sligo today, having watched and been involved in some of their development down through the years, I consider that we are relatively well placed to implement the Child Care Act. We have one of the highest rates of social workers to population in the country. This I consider a good basis for the challenge of spreading widely the kinds of family support services listed in the Act, such as pre-school services, home liaison and community mother schemes, to cite a few.

The Challenges

I would now like to address some of the challenges, with particular reference to policy and practice issues that the implementation of the Act poses for my profession in the North West and, in particular, the implications at senior social worker level. It is important to begin by considering some of the Act's underlying principles. I see the enshrining of these principles as a major task of management in the formation and implementation of policies, procedures and provisions of services. Three major principles underlie the Act:

- The welfare of the child is paramount

- Due consideration should be given to the wishes of the child

- It is in the best interests of the child to be brought up in his or her own family

These principles, I feel, have influenced our practice in many areas even before the Child Care Act 1991. The difference, as I see it, is that these principles will now have a clear statutory base and must underpin policies and practices under the Act. In the guidance that accompanies the UK Children's Act 1989, the principles guiding that legislation are referred to as the colours of the social worker painter's palette, to be used in the combination and patterns required. Each picture painted represents a child care case handled (UK Department of Health, 1989).

It is vital, I feel, that the three principles outlined above are integrated through the thinking of the social workers and their managers. It is part of the management task to provide the means by which the principles can be put into practice and the effectiveness of such systems maintained. When I look at my own particular service in relation to the Act, I see a great need for getting things right within the service first, looking at developing services within the community. I am referring to the provision of basic facilities, such as adequate office and interviewing facilities, basic office equipment and adequate secretarial/administrative support, in respect of which we are currently under-resourced.

I have a total staff of nineteen. When it comes to consultation and supervision, such numbers do not lend themselves to adequate supervision. In social work, I define supervision as a process by which one practitioner enables another social work practitioner, who is accountable to him or her, to practise to the best of his or her ability. The key elements are enabling and teaching. The new responsibilities under the Child Care Act will require extra resources, including knowledge, skill and opportunities for consultation at senior social work level and with outside consultants and experts from other disciplines as appropriate, particularly in the legal field. In the social work field I see the role of the senior social worker under the new Child Care Act as supporting workers in decision-making, for example in the taking of emergency care orders or in the discharging of other orders such as supervision and care orders. The necessity to maintain a child-centred approach in child protection work will be an integral part of the consultation process under the new Child Care Act (Ferguson, 1994a).

The new responsibilities under the Child Care Act, such as supervision orders, will require an adequate level of available supervision to help decision-making in this area and in the maintenance of such orders. New regulations on foot of the Act in the area of pre-school registration and voluntary children's homes registration will also require an adequate supervision system to facilitate good practice in the social work field.

The Report of the Kilkenny Incest Investigation emphasised that supervision should facilitate liaison and provide an opportunity for professionals to plan, evaluate and gain support from each other in their child protection work (McGuinness, 1993). Adequate supervision will also promote good standards of practice for the benefit of all. The Kilkenny Report clearly saw child abuse as an issue for the health boards as a whole. The structures in place and the management at different levels and in different professions will determine the response to child abuse. Leadership and clarity of purpose and affirmation of the work are crucial ingredients in developing an adequate child protection service.

In addition to the professional work with the staff in my own agency, it is also important that managers such as myself are available for consultation with the voluntary social work agencies in the area. I have already referred to difficulties with the present system. These will be greatly compounded with the implementation of the new Act unless there is created without delay a supervisory grade to whom some of the management functions presently held by the senior social worker can be delegated. There is considerable urgency about this because parts of the Act have been implemented and discussions begun on the implementation of the remaining sections. The effect of this on the present structure is that the more discussion takes place on the Act, the less time is available for day-to-day consultation and monitoring of trends, particularly in the post-Kilkenny Incest Inquiry Report period. This is not a situation I would like to see continue much longer.

There will also be a need for more frontline social work staff to do the increased work created by the new responsibilities under the Act and the impact of the Kilkenny case. In the period between March and September 1993, after the Kilkenny incest case broke, our community care service experienced a 150 per cent increase in reported cases of child abuse. This is a direct result of increased public and professional awareness brought about by the publicity surrounding the case (see Ferguson, 1994b). The result of this increase has been to put the child protection service under considerable pressure. This is an example of the impact that changes in public awareness can have on a service. We need to have adequate resources in place to meet such contingencies. The Kilkenny Report recommended the creation of a child protection co-ordinator post in health boards. The exact duties of such a post are not spelled out in the report, but the management responsibility in child protection would still remain with the senior social worker.

The Implications of the Act for Social Work

I will now discuss specific sections of the Act and offer an overview of their implications for social work as I see them.

Part III, which places a duty on health boards to promote the welfare of children in their areas, is one of the most important and significant sections in the Act. It imposes a statutory duty on health boards in a number of important areas. Health boards must identify children who are not receiving proper care and attention and act to promote their welfare, having due regard to the child's wishes. It also requires health boards to provide family support services, taking cognisance of the principle that it is generally in the child's best interests to be brought up in his or her own family.

This strongly-worded section gives us the opportunity to move from a reactive approach to child care, as was largely the philosophy under the 1908 Children Act, to a pro-active approach. The Kilkenny case illustrates the need to be more pro-active on behalf of abused children. The victim at the centre of the Kilkenny case and her family were well known to services for many years, but there was real difficulty in actual disclosures. The task facing professionals in the post-Kilkenny era must be to advocate on behalf of abused children, no matter how difficult this may be. Waiting until the abuse is disclosed and validated is insufficient. Our services need, on an inter-disciplinary and inter-agency basis, to develop a much better understanding of the nature of the violence we are dealing with in the family and act on it.

Section 8 places a requirement on health boards to review services and the adequacy of the child and family support services available annually. The requirements of Section 3 and Section 8 are quite extensive, demanding the collection and evaluation of data from a number of services. The collection of this information involves very many disciplines and agencies. My own role as a senior social worker will be very central, as the categories of children identified in Section 8 are those with whom we are in contact. An adequate information database on these categories is essential.

Section 3 also states that it should be the function of every health board to 'co-ordinate information from all relevant sources relating to children in its area'. It does not state how this is to be effected. As highlighted in recent research in the field of services for the elderly (Browne, 1992), there are considerable difficulties in this area. It would appear that the Act requires consultation and communication between relevant services within the board and the establishment of formal channels of communication between health boards and schools, gardaí, probation and welfare services, youth services and housing authorities. Some structures do already exist for the exchange of information, of which the case conference is the focal point. But the Act appears to require more extensive arrangements as the case conference deals only with individual cases. The manager's job is to be involved in the setting up of more macro structures for co-ordination and policy development and monitoring trends in needs and in services. Such structures operate at another level such as agreed regional procedures. Other managers and senior managers have an important role in this.

Section 11 of the Act refers to the conducting of research in the area of child welfare and protection of children. It is a short section but an important one. We have very little research in Ireland in this area and as a result very little information on trends, which results in us having to work rather blindly in the area and to depend on UK or American sources. The manager's role is important in identifying areas in need of research and facilitating such research, possibly with professionals in the research field.

The protection of children in emergencies: The purpose of this section is to enable gardaí and health boards to intervene where there is an immediate and serious threat to the safety and welfare of the child. The emergency care order (ECO) replaces the place of safety order under the 1908 Act. Within three days of the gardaí removing a child, application has to be made to the District Court for an emergency care order. The health board is also given the power to apply for an ECO in situations of high risk to children. The ECO lasts for a maximum of eight days, following which the board must apply for an interim care order if it wishes to pursue the case. It is necessary for management to have in place an emergency procedure, including emergency placement and follow-up work. The application for an emergency order under this section is not very different from our present place of safety order. However, parents will now have the right to challenge the board's application for an interim care order. Thus, there are some extra requirements, and from a management point of view it will be necessary to have clear procedures in place so the necessary steps are taken in the required time for the emergency care order. What is important here, say in cases of alleged sexual abuse, is a joint garda/social work written protocol.

Part IV covers care proceedings. The main thrust of this part is to set out the grounds under which care orders can be applied for. What this section adds to the previous legislation is the introduction of an interim care order, the supervision order and a care order. The care order replaces the fit person order and the grounds for application for a care order have been extended to include sexually abused children and situations in which the child's health, development or welfare has been or is likely to be unavoidably impaired or seriously neglected. I see a great challenge ahead to establish in the courts exactly what is meant by the child's health, development or welfare being unavoidably impaired. From a child care point of view it is incumbent upon us to be very clear when presenting to the Court exactly what we are talking about when applying for an application under these headings. I see considerable work having to be done in this area.

Section 20 constitutes a major addition to the work already being done. This section allows for an application for a care order or a supervision order in respect of children who come before the Court under the Guardianship of Infants Act or Judicial Separation Act and allows the Court in certain circumstances to direct the health board to investigate the child's circumstances. With the number of cases coming before the courts under this Act, there will be considerable increase in work in this area; the presenting of this evidence requires skills that may not at present be available among our workers. The effect of the extended legal powers and the increase in the age range of children covered under the Act to eighteen years will mean an increase in the number of court hearings. Given the protracted nature of such cases, social workers will spend a considerable length of time doing court work. Such involvement in court work raises the question for managers of how workloads and administrative systems are designed to meet this, how decisions are made and case files are kept, and case conferences and reviews are recorded.

Court appearances tend to be stressful to the worker; the function of management is to set systems and training in place to facilitate the social worker in this work and help alleviate some of the stress. The supervision order, a new power introduced under Section 19 of the Act, is likely to be widely used as it will not require separating children from their parents and is partly in keeping with the concept of minimum intervention. Ferguson (1993), writing on the manifest and latent implications of the Kilkenny Report, stresses the importance of child-focused work and the use of professional power in confronting parents and violent men in particular. He stresses the importance of engaging children at risk directly and to this end the new supervision order seems to have potential in facilitating such work with involuntary families. We need to consider also the implications of putting the supervision order into practice and the legal requirements in this. This will result in a considerable increase in work, such as regular home visits and extensive reporting on such visits, and reporting back to the courts. The use of the supervision order to negotiate with family members and facilitate openness will be a crucial aspect of effective statutory work.

Jurisdiction and procedure: Part V emphasises that the welfare of the child is a first and paramount consideration and where practicable due consideration should be given, having regard to age and understanding, to the wishes of the child. This section poses a considerable challenge to our policies and procedures. We will have to ensure that systems are in place that will give us the information and facilitate our understanding of the wishes of the child. Participation of children and young people in regular case conferences and case reviews will be an important part of facilitating this understanding.

Part VI is an extensive section covering children who are in the care of the health boards, and incorporates some previous legislation. Provision for parents to contest access arrangements by the health board constitutes a major difference between this and previous legislation. The other major addition to previous legislation is the after care section. Very little after care facilities are in place in our present service and this is an area that needs to be developed. To give an effective after care service a variety of services need to be put in place. The transition from care to independent living is extremely important. The years of care could be undermined if the gap between leaving care and starting independent life is not bridged adequately. Managers need to ensure that social workers do the necessary direct work with children.

Part VII, which covers the supervision of pre-school services, is an extensive section and is a complete innovation in the work at present being done by health boards. Pre-school service has traditionally been provided by voluntary organisations and the people in the community and it is important that this voluntary expertise is incorporated when the new Act is put into operation. It will be the responsibility of health boards to set in place structures to encourage this voluntary effort while at the same time meeting the statutory requirements. It is important in implementing this section that the family support aspect rather than an inspectorial aspect of the school services is emphasised. In discussion with various people I feel there is a possibility of over-emphasis on the pre-school aspect. This section covers pre-school services, not just pre-schools, and does, as the Act says, concern playgroups, day nurseries, crèches and day care for those taking care of more than three children.

It is possible that some voluntary organisations, such as the Irish Pre-School Playgroups Association, who have been in the forefront of registering existing pre-schools on a voluntary basis, could do some of this work. A link-up with the boards in relation to this is essential, as the boards carry the statutory responsibility and will have identified specific areas of need arising from their caseloads, in addition to having the statutory responsibility to register the pre-schools.

Part VIII covers the registration of children's homes. It is intended to apply to those homes run by voluntary organisations rather than those run by health boards themselves. The only children's home in our area is run by the Board. The standards set down in the Act for registration of children's homes also apply to those run by the boards.

Resources

One of the functions of a senior manager is to act as gatekeeper in the provision of resources. The Child Care Act 1991 is about allocating (scarce) resources to construct an infrastructure for child care. Section 3.2(c) of the Act states that the health board should provide child care and family support services. It is a golden opportunity, and possibly the only one to resource services properly so that they reach the most vulnerable families. This can be done on two levels—at community level and the individual level of the family of the parents and children.

Commenting on the resource implications of the Act, Gilligan (1993) sees resources falling into different categories: those that will support families and reduce the need for admission into care; those required for provision for children in care; social worker backup services, including management; additional resources for training, research and specialist services. Management must identify and provide adequate resources in each area. The provision of adequate resources will have a major impact on the implementation of this legislation. The resources available will never be totally adequate to the needs; there will always be a deficit in the provision of any resources. It behoves us as managers to prioritise in accordance with the provisions of the Act and place resources where they will have the most effect. The demands of family support services and child protection services together with children in care services will have to be balanced. Keeping this balancing act going will not be an easy task. The child care advisory committees already set up under the Act will have important roles to play in the provision and evaluation of the adequacy of the services and in identifying resources. The role of top management, such as programme managers, is very important in allocating adequate resources based on the information received from the professionals in the field.

Conclusion

For managers, the Act constitutes a major challenge in managing change. The social work profession will be working with much more legislative backup than has been available in the past eighty-five years. This Act makes a serious attempt to balance the rights of parents and children. This represents considerable change for us in the way we are presently working. There is greater accountability envisaged in the Act for work undertaken.

Due to the massive increase in court work, much of our work will be under the microscope as never before. It will be like working in a goldfish bowl. That represents great change.

I have concentrated in this chapter largely on my own profession, but in so doing I am greatly aware of the need to work closely with other disciplines and other agencies in the area of child welfare and child protection. The aspiration to work together to help families and to protect children is not sufficient in itself, nor are structures to facilitate such working together. Hallett and Stevenson (1980), in their in-depth study of case conferences—a major forum of inter-disciplinary inter-agency work—differentiated between the content of the case conference and the process issues which arise in such meetings. They see the negotiation of the dynamics involved in such a forum of inter-agency work as a complex task. Similarly, we have to deepen our understanding of these dynamics in working with other disciplines and agencies in the identification and provision of services for families in the Irish context. This has to include partnership with parents; forms of inter-agency and inter-disciplinary work should develop which represent a considerable change in our ways of working.

From a management point of view strategic planning will be very necessary. At its best the Act and the accompanying regulations provide the framework, but there is a need to bring that down to specifics in policies and procedures at local level. Having these written and clearly understood at every level throughout the organisation is most important. To achieve this I would like to see a child care policy drawn up at local level, incorporating the principles of good child care practice and involving those who are directly involved in the delivery of the service.

Such a written policy would go a long way to enshrine key principles and ensure that good child care practice is implemented. I feel that not only would the content of such a policy statement be of tremendous use, but the process involved in drawing it up would of itself be a major step forward in the multi-disciplinary task of protecting children and helping families.

In the mammoth task facing my profession and other professions involved as we embark on identifying and providing services under the Act, we should build in an evaluation procedure. The need to evaluate on a regular basis will be extremely important, particularly when we go to look at the changes in practice prompted by the Child Care Act.

References

Browne, M. (1992), *Swimming against the Tide: Co-ordinating Services for the Elderly at Local Level*, Dublin: National Council for the Elderly.

Ferguson, H. (1993), 'The Latent and Manifest Implications of the Kilkenny Report', *Irish Social Worker*, Vol. 11, No. 4.

Ferguson, H. (1994a), 'Managing to Practise Child Protection: Key Elements of a Child Centred Approach', *Irish Social Worker*, Vol. 12, No. 1.

Ferguson, H. (1994b), 'Child Abuse Inquiries and the Report of the Kilkenny Incest Investigation: A Critical Analysis', *Administration*, Vol. 41, No. 4, pp. 385–410.

Gilligan, R. (1993), 'The Child Care Act 1991: An Examination of its Scope and Resource Implications', *Administration*, Vol. 40, No. 4, pp. 345–70.

Hallett, C. and Stevenson, O. (1980), *Child Abuse: Aspects of Inter-professional Co-operation*, London: Allen and Unwin.

McGuinness, C. (1993), *Report of the Kilkenny Incest Investigation*, Dublin: Stationery Office.

UK Department of Health (1989), *Children's Act 1989—England and Wales*, London: HMSO.

Chapter 15

A CHILD PSYCHOLOGY PERSPECTIVE

Kieran Woods

Perspective on Professional Group

The psychology service within the North Western Health Board area is divided into two departments, one servicing the Sligo/Leitrim region and one servicing the Donegal area. Both departments are headed by a senior clinical psychologist and there is a complement of eight basic grades attached to each department. The Donegal psychology service is based within the community care programme and thus the reporting relationship is to the director of community care. In the Donegal context about three-quarters of all the psychology services work is child-related in the broadest sense. This varies from the usual type of referrals to a child psychology service: from developmental delay, enuresis and school refusal through to our involvement in the investigation, monitoring and treatment of children at risk.

The Child Care Act 1991

The Child Care Act 1991 is to be welcomed in that it is an attempt to update the law in relation to child welfare and is the first major change in child welfare provisions since the 1908 Act. Before looking more specifically at what I regard as the major assumptions underlying the legislation, I would like to draw attention to the rather negative definition of child welfare implied by the tenor of the Act. While, understandably, the Child Care Act is concerned with the protection of children from abuse and neglect, the emphasis on this overshadows what I would regard as the need for a much more positive definition of what child welfare actually means.

The enormous pressure of large caseloads in the child care area often prevents professionals from acting where a child is not experiencing any overt abuse or neglect. However, as all of us know from our knowledge of the literature and our own common-sense experience, the absence of abuse or neglect is not sufficient to guarantee a child's welfare. As Jones (1977) stated in a review of the relevant research:

> regardless of whether they have been physically abused, many children who may never come to professional attention are living in sub-optimal environments and experiencing the kind of inadequate parenting which could permanently impair and disrupt their development.

In this country, huge inequity and disparity exist between different sections of society in terms of the facilities, resources and opportunities available to them. The Department of Health's own figures for 1987 suggest that 47 per cent of children in Ireland were living in households below the poverty line (Department of Health, 1988). I can only assume that, given the large increase in unemployment in the interim, the percentage of children living in poverty has increased substantially. That almost half of our children are living in poverty is a frightening statistic and one which we need urgently to address. It is not acceptable that such totally dependent and vulnerable people as children should have to exist in subsistence conditions. I do not wish to imply any criticism of their parents in making this statement, I wish rather to draw attention to the inequality with which our society is riven and which blights the prospects of so many of our children. Most people are aware that the possibility of the children of low-income families gaining access to third-level education is minimal.

However, equally disturbing but less touted are statistics showing that perinatal mortality rates are twenty times higher in low-income families than they are among the professional classes (Department of Health, 1994), rates of admission to psychiatric hospitals are six times higher in unemployed groups than they are in managerial classes (O'Connor and Walsh, 1986), and reading backwardness among disadvantaged children is three times higher than the national average (O'Connor *et al.*, 1989). An amount of healthy outrage on behalf of disadvantaged children is well justified but is obviously not sufficient to improve the quality of their lives. A charter of rights for all children, guaranteeing them decent housing and physical conditions under which to live, adequate access to material, resources and experiences which would permit appropriate development in all areas of functioning, lives free from inappropriate stresses such as the worry of seeing parents struggling to make financial ends meet and the rights to unconditional love and acceptance, is long overdue.

Such a charter of rights aimed at articulating and promoting the needs of children is also justified because of the lack of case law in this country articulating specifically children's rights. Children instead have to rely on a body of rights in the Constitution conferred on all citizens. In this regard, the Government's ratification of the United Nations Charter on the Rights of Children, with its emphasis on promoting the mental, physical, spiritual, moral and social development of children, is to be welcomed. However, a declaration of intent to provide for all what those of us lucky enough to have been born into the right circumstances can take for granted would be appropriate in a bill on child care.

I would now like to deal with the assumptions on which I believe the 1991 Child Care Act is predicated. These assumptions are:

1) The welfare of the child is to be given priority in arriving at any decision in child care cases.

2) The child's best interests are served by remaining with its family.

3) State intervention should be minimal.

1. The Welfare of the Child Should be the Paramount Consideration

Only with the Guardianship of Infants Act in 1964 was statutory force given to this principle. As a statement of principle, one would find it hard to disagree with the notion that the welfare of the child comes first. However, we know in both legal and clinical practice that things are not quite so clear cut. Courts and social service agencies do not make decisions about child care in a vacuum. Apart from trying to deal with and disentangle the complicated personal and familial context in which 'at risk' children live, the courts and agencies are also influenced by the norms prevalent in society, many of which are deeply antagonistic to the notion of interference with family privacy. Thus many different factors come into play once complicated decisions about families have to be made.

The lack of clear protocols and procedures for professionals, as well as the absence of explicit criteria against which to judge the quality of parenting which a child is receiving, further complicate the decision-making process. Different professionals have their own standards based on a combination of professional knowledge and experience and coloured by personal values. It is uncertain whether there is any consensus among professionals or within society as to what constitutes a minimal level of effective parenting. Professionals are not cocooned from the values of the society in which they operate; we are all influenced in our practice to a greater or lesser extent by values which are pervasive in society at any given time and by the body of law and constitutional rights which we as a society regard as reflecting those values which we hold most dear. In this regard, our Constitution bestows enormous powers on parents.

Article 41 of the Constitution talks of recognising the family as having inalienable and imprescriptible rights which supersede all positive law. The Constitution also tends to see children's rights located within their family and asserted through their parents. For instance, the 1985 judgment by the Chief Justice held that the duty of parents of a child to provide for its upbringing conferred a corresponding right on the child to be brought up by its parents. This ruling would seem to suggest that it is impermissible within the Constitution to regard the welfare of the child as having paramount consideration. Therefore, it is not always clear in conflicts of interest between parents and children as to what position the Court will adopt or even as to whether the notion of the child's welfare being paramount is not in fact unconstitutional. For these reasons, I warmly welcome the recommendation made in the *Report on the Kilkenny Incest Investigation* that the Constitution should include an overt declaration of the rights of children (McGuinness, 1993).

2. Children's Needs are Best Met by their Remaining within the Family

The second major assumption within the Act is that the child's needs are best met by remaining within its family. As already seen, this assumption is heavily buttressed by the Constitution and the law as things currently stand. The Constitution clearly states that the basic social unit in society is the family, which is defined very clearly as the family based on marriage, and that the protection of this unit is critical to the ongoing stability of society at large. This highlights the difficulties that courts may have in separating a child from its parents where such a separation may be seen as an attack on the basic social unit of society, and the fact that the Constitution is often out of step with actual changes taking place in society. For instance, the family based on marriage is no longer quite the absolute norm which it was at the time the Constitution was drafted in 1937. In 1989, there were 37,500 single-parent families in the state responsible for 81,000 children (Central Statistics Office, 1989).

Many more thousands of children live in two-parent families not based on marriage. Births outside marriage now account for nearly 20 per cent of total births. This represents a fourfold increase over the past ten years. Since 1987, the national marriage rate has declined by some 17 per cent and is now the lowest in Europe. Another factor affecting our thinking about families has been the large increase in the number of children identified as having been physically or sexually abused within their families. Some 3,000 children are in care at any one time in this country. The most common reason given for this is parents' inability to cope, which is usually a euphemistic phrase to cover the myriad horrors which are inflicted on these children. On the basis of the Department of Health's latest available statistics covering the year 1990, on average two children were taken into care each day of that year (Department of Health, 1992). Apart from children in care, all of us through our clinical work are aware of many thousands of other children who, while not being grossly abused or neglected, are none the less living in circumstances which we would not deem adequate. These children are being psychologically damaged by virtue of the atmosphere and conditions in which they live, both because of the adverse economic factors to which they are subjected and by ineffective parenting. Many children lead lives of what I would regard as quiet desperation and quiet destitution. The likelihood of children achieving their full potential in such circumstances is slim. While many professionals working in the area may not regard themselves as having a role to play in highlighting the economic and structural issues in society which have an impact on families and the ability of parents to care adequately for their children, most, if not all, professionals have comments to make on effective parenting.

One of the theoretical constructs which has gained currency in recent years has been that of the Good Enough Parent (Bettelheim, 1987). A good enough parent is one who is able to meet the physical, psychological, social and emotional needs of a child, thereby helping the child to become a functioning, contented adult. However, trying to decide what 'good enough' means has given rise to bitter arguments—partly because of the consequences of such a decision. This obviously has a critical relevance where the consequence may be the permanent separation of parent and child, enforced by the state. Although the courts have to make such decisions, legislation at present provides no clear definition of inadequate parenting. Physical and sexual abuse and gross neglect are clearly deemed not to be good enough parenting. But to jump from this to say that all other types of parenting are satisfactory is not borne out by clinical or common-sense experience. There is an urgent need to establish explicit guidelines for both professional and legal practitioners which would be widely accepted and respected.

This is all the more pressing because of the provision in the Act which allows the courts to obtain independent reports for the cases brought

(230)

before them. In the absence of explicit guidelines, it is not difficult to imagine a great deal of divergence in professional views which may only add to the Court's confusion rather than helping it clarify its decision. In this regard, the Kilkenny Report (McGuinness, 1993) makes welcome recommendations both in relation to giving statutory effect to the Child Abuse Guidelines and in recommending a much more precise set of procedures which would include workable definitions of physical, emotional and sexual abuse and neglect.

From a professional point of view, the process of identifying inadequate parenting and making relevant decisions involves a combination of knowledge of the relevant research in the field, the necessary professional skills and competence in the assessment and treatment of problematic families, recognition of the values which we all hold at personal, professional, organisational and societal levels, and the way these values may affect and impinge on our professional judgements. This places an onus on each of us individually, and also on the agencies for which we work, to ensure that we possess the relevant knowledge, skills and insights to perform our duties satisfactorily. These factors will be all the more compelling now with the duty which the new Act imposes on health boards to provide a range of family support services.

The single most important responsibility that any adult will undertake is that of rearing a child. Rutter *et al.* (1983) suggested that

> parenting resources need to be considered in terms of such variables as time available for parenting, parents' own emotional state, the presence of other life stresses and problems, the qualities of the spouse and the extent to which child rearing is shared, the existence of satisfactions and achievements apart from parenting and the availability of adequate social supports and housing conditions.

However, as a society we display a rather cavalier attitude to this process. No adult is ever expected to undergo any formal training for this task. Instead, we rely on people's vicarious experiences, especially that of having been parented themselves. Good practices of one's own parents may be internalised and reproduced when the child in turn becomes an adult and a parent. However, some adults are not satisfactory parents, so we must intervene to prevent bad models from being bequeathed to the next generation. Given the welcome and increasing tendency of secondary schools to offer lifeskills classes to their pupils, it is time for us to introduce a compulsory parenting module within this context for all final-year students.

Similarly, both pre-marital courses and ante-natal courses should all include a comprehensive and detailed input on parenting. Ante-natal courses, in particular, could give us an opportunity to target and support couples and single parents who might find the adjustment to a new arrival within the family particularly stressful. We need to move away from the notion of parenting as some intrinsic trait which will manifest itself appropriately and somewhat magically when the time comes. Parenting ability is not some all or nothing trait which we either possess or lack or which remains static throughout our parenting career. Each of us, as professionals, should set ourselves the objectives of highlighting and informing society's attitudes to the role of parents, and assisting through our agency work less effective parents to become more effective. We should support parents who, because of economic or personal stress factors, are experiencing problems in their parenting, helping them to re-establish adequate child care.

The laissez-faire attitude in society to parenting is intimately tied up with the emphasis on the privacy of the family. There is of course an element of self-protection for all of us in this in that none of us would readily wish to have the spotlight on our own parental behaviour. An unfortunate consequence of this, however, is the lack of reflection on parenting values and practices. A clear example of this is our whole attitude to corporal punishment. I strongly believe that all corporal punishment should be outlawed immediately; in this regard I quote a trenchant comment from Justice Kenny from as far back as 1972, who stated (in J. O'C v M. O'C):

the parent who uses corporal punishment on children may think that it is for their good, but civilised human beings have long since abandoned this barbaric practice. (Kenny, 1972)

There is far too much condoning of corporal punishment as a way of disciplining children. Discipline should be imparted through information and not chastisement. A parent with self-respect doesn't need to buttress his or her security by demanding respect through threatening the child. A secure parent does not see the child as an extension of him- or herself but rather as an individual in his or her own right with whom one has to negotiate and reason. Secure parents know that when the child shows lack of respect for them this is not a personal assault but rather an immaturity of judgement which time and experience will rectify. The demand for respect, on the other hand, reveals an insecure parent who lacks the conviction that this will be given naturally. Punishment will make a child obey orders, but it will not inculcate the values of self-restraint, which only come from recognising and affirming individuality and which will nurture the process of becoming a responsible adult.

As Bettelheim (1987) eloquently states:

> The younger the child, the more he admires his parents. In fact, he cannot do otherwise; he needs to believe in their perfection in order to feel safe. In what image can he form himself but that of the persons who act as parents to him? Who else is so close and important to him? And if things are as they should be, nobody loves him so well, takes such good care of him as his parents do. Every child wishes to believe that he is his parents' favourite.

The Child Care Act is disappointing in its failure to address these issues of parenting standards, corporal punishment and the need for an educative and preventive focus in our work. While I realise that many of these issues would be difficult to enforce and achieve, none the less their appearance on the statute book would be a statement of intent and a symbol of our changed attitude towards children. While, in many instances, the law has changed in response to changing social norms, the reverse process can also take place, whereby changes in the law can lead to an

(233)

altering of social attitudes and behaviours. Once these new norms have been established and accepted, there is usually far less need for the heavy hand of the law to ensure their enforcement.

3. Minimal State Intervention

By and large child protection agencies in this country operate on the basis of taking into care only those children who have been abused or neglected. The histories of such children are an indictment of our tardiness in responding to their tragic dilemmas. Too many have had their bodies penetrated and their trust despoiled by our failures to act in time. Many children in care have reported dozens of incidences of physical and sexual abuse before they were removed. How many children are today living in families where they are being physically and sexually abused? It's no longer enough to assert that, in the absence of strict legal evidence of children being abused or neglected, they can continue to live in circumstances which clinically we know to be damaging. We need a much more positive statement of what is required of families and a more positive intent to take action and help families who on their own are unable to meet these standards.

If we accept, as most of us do, that the early formative years are critical in determining a child's subsequent ability as an adult to enter into and maintain satisfying relationships and in turn to become an effective parent, we should not be shy about intervening and assisting families in providing a positive growth-enhancing atmosphere in which their children can flourish. If we do not try, the cost of human misery, unfulfilled potential and loss of happiness condemns us all. If state intervention and support, in whatever form, are necessary to reverse these blightings of human development, then let us ensure that we provide it. Children's lives are too precious to be allowed to be spoiled by experiences which we know to be damaging, but for which we as society have too elastic a tolerance in not insisting on intervention. As a society, we have too permissive an attitude to what happens within the four walls of a home. Misery is misery irrespective of under what guise it befalls us. Because their options are so few, children are left in a particularly invidious position in this regard. Too many children continue to suffer because their parents refuse help or because the situation in which they find themselves is not deemed serious enough to warrant care. The process of minimalist state intervention and its dreadful consequences were graphically illustrated in the Kilkenny case.

Although the raising in the Child Care Act of the legal age at which children can be taken into care from sixteen to eighteen is a positive step, it fails to protect those young adults who have passed that chronological landmark and who continue to live in abusive situations. One of the great difficulties in the Kilkenny case lay in the inability of the child protection agencies to invoke the law to protect the person in question beyond the age of sixteen (under the 1908 Children Act). Obviously, from a legal perspective it is necessary to have some chronological cut-off point, but this fails to recognise the dynamics and complexities that exist within families where abuse occurs and which ensure that the victims of such abuse continue to put up with the most harrowing of circumstances because they themselves are unable actively to take the steps to protect themselves legally. The power and control which abusers display over their victims and the consequent undermining and fear which is inherent in all victims of abuse usually prevents them taking effective action for many years, if at all.

Due to my concern that we are often too late in intervening with families, I am also rather concerned that what appears to be an extra string to our bow, namely supervision orders, may, in fact, become a soft option and an alternative to care in cases where the bullet needs to be bitten. The language of the Act in relation to supervision orders gives me some ground for concern. The Act states:

> that where on the application of a health board, the court is satisfied that there are reasonable grounds for believing that a child has been or is being assaulted, ill-treated, neglected, abused or his welfare has been avoidably impaired or neglected, a supervision order may be made.

I would argue that it is not at all reasonable to leave a child in a situation where there are reasonable grounds for believing that it is being abused. The Act also fails to specify minimum visiting periods in relation to supervision orders and we all know from hard cases the difficulties of interviewing children in their own homes where we have concerns for their safety.

I do not mean to imply from all the above that care is always the best and only option for children. Obviously all of us know that the removal of a child from its natural family is usually just the end of one process and the beginning of another. We all also know or have read about too many cases of children who have jumped from the frying pan into the fire and have been subjected to as much abuse in the foster family or in residential centres as they were in their natural homes. Even in situations where the provision of alternative care has worked well, there are many difficulties attached to it. Usually children become more and more separated from their natural family, the transition into their new foster family can be difficult, the frequent changing of field workers can constrain their capacities for meaningful attachments, not to mention the effect that an abrupt termination of foster care and return to the natural family can have. A child's long-term future is not always considered, so that children often come into long-term care on an unplanned basis. We as professionals, therefore, need to be more accountable for our decisions. We should be capable of outlining and providing a series of logical and comprehensive steps in an evaluation process. This process should start with clear indicators as to whether we should or should not intervene and the likely consequences of either decision.

The intermediate steps in such an assessment would include an evaluation of environmental factors impinging on the family, parental and family functioning, development of the particular child, the potential for change and the changes necessary to resolve the difficulties. It is imperative that the process of such an assessment, and the criteria used, are shared with parents, as this not only makes it more possible for parents to understand what is happening but is also more likely to increase their co-operation with the intervention process. This would also provide professionals with secure parameters against which they could measure what has been done and what needs to be done and facilitate the clear enunciation at national level of standard protocols and procedures which would allow for uniformity of best practice across community care areas.

References

Bettelheim, B. (1987), *A Good Enough Parent*, London: Thames and Hudson.

Central Statistics Office (1989), *Summary Population Report*, 2nd Series, Dublin: Stationery Office.

Department of Health (1994), *Perinatal Statistics 1991*, Dublin: Stationery Office.

Department of Health (1988), *Health Statistics 1987*, Dublin: Stationery Office.

Department of Health (1992), *Survey of Children in the Care of the Health Boards 1990*, Dublin: Child Care Division, Department of Health.

Jones, C. (1977), 'The Fate of Abused Children', in A. W. Franklin (ed.), *The Challenge of Child Abuse*, London: Academic Press.

McGuinness, C. (1993), *Report of the Kilkenny Incest Investigation*, Dublin: Stationery Office.

O'Connor, A., Ruddle, H. and Gallagher, M. (1989), *Cherished Equally? Educational and Behavioural Adjustment of Children: A Study of Primary Schools in the Mid-West Region*, Limerick: Mid-Western Health Board.

O'Connor, A. and Walsh, D. (1986), *Activities of Irish Psychiatric Hospitals and Units*, Dublin: Health Research Board.

Rutter, M., Quinton, D. and Liddle, C. (1983), 'Parenting in Two Generations: Looking Backwards and Looking Forwards', in N. Madge (ed.), *Families at Risk*, London: Heinemann.

CONCLUSION

TOWARDS AN INTEGRATED SYSTEM OF CHILD CARE SERVICES

Harry Ferguson and Pat Kenny

The aim of this book has been to provide a comprehensive analysis of the content and implications of the Child Care Act 1991 for child welfare and protection from a range of perspectives. A clear message that has emerged is that there are a great number of people working in a caring way on behalf of children experiencing a variety of adversities. A common thread running through the book is the difficulty that arises nowadays from the tendency to equate child care with child protection. Over recent years an increasing proportion of professional time and scarce resources has been directed at child abuse work. There are a number of reasons for this development. The huge increase in child abuse referrals has been dealt with by a static number of social workers. Comparatively, a large proportion of cases involve suspected child sexual abuse, with all the complexities involved in confirming that such abuse has happened. One result has been that the activities of child care professionals have received much more public and media attention.

We have tried to show that child protection, for all its importance, is only part of a range of services which needs to be developed. What is required is an integrated system of child care services. It is clear from this book that many professionals are dissatisfied with their limited ability to respond early to the needs of vulnerable children and their families in a preventive way. The need for a more preventive service has been highlighted, and in the case of the North Western Health Board is a frequent theme in debates and discussions. Authoritative interventions by the state are often seen as failures by professionals who torment themselves

(238)

with the conflicting emotions brought about by trying to help children who are being abused or neglected by their carers, and their wish to be more helpful to parents who are under enormous strain in caring for their highly valued children. Constantly responding to child abuse is like trying to mop up water from a leaking pipe without the time or resources to fix the pipe.

Clearly, the possibility that they might have to intervene in a way which separates children from their parents causes great anxiety to health professionals at all levels. The Child Care Act has the potential to clarify the criteria by which such agonising decisions are made and to modernise the socio-legal decision-making process itself. However, the separation of children from parents does not imply that the essential bond which exists between children and their parents is not recognised. This is demonstrated by the efforts made by health boards to provide suitable access for parents and other significant people in children's lives. As this book has shown, the level of access is already respectably high in the NWHB's current practices. The example of access (child abuse work is another) illustrates very well how essential it is to evaluate and give due recognition to the constructive practices currently followed in health boards; such work provides the bedrock upon which the future development of child care services will be based.

This book has also highlighted a number of gaps in services and identified challenges raised by current trends in child welfare and protection. Implementing the Act in full is the main priority. But implementation will not of itself necessarily mean that child care will improve. This is illustrated by the fact that implementation of Section 5 has led to only minimal improvements in services for homeless children across the country.

Three things are at issue here. Firstly, there is the way in which child care problems are thought about and conceptualised. Homelessness and after care provision for teenagers in care are examples of the difficulties apparent in viewing adolescents as children in danger, as opposed to dangerous children. With the extension of the legal definition of a child to eighteen years, conceptualisation of the needs of children across the age range will be crucial to the effective development of services. What is required is the development of a comprehensive means of understanding the adversities which affect all children today.

Secondly, our response to child care problems—or indeed, in some respects, the lack of response—is shaped by the social and political context in which we view the family and in which policy and practice are formulated. Thirdly, there is the sheer weight of effort and strategic planning that are required to make implementation actually mean something constructive in the lives of children and their caretakers. This book has tried to illustrate the kinds of issues that such implementation raises, to provide insights into the variety of professional perspectives relevant to working under the Act, and to give some pointers to the appropriate direction of policy and practice.

Simply harnessing and channelling the goodwill and energy of child care professionals, already sorely challenged, will not be enough. Sufficient resources must be allocated. This, in turn, will be determined by the level of political will. The then Minister for Health, Brendan Howlin, committed the Government to an expenditure of £35 million to implement the Child Care Act in full by 1996. While this will provide much valuable help in the development of services, there can be little doubt that more will be needed. It is sobering to think that in 1994 the Irish state incurred an estimated bill for the same amount (£35 million) for the Beef Tribunal (Hamilton, 1994). Some legal professionals reputedly even became millionaires as a result of their roles in that tribunal.

Yet health care professionals continue to struggle to make ends meet and are too often forced, for example, to place homeless children in unsuitable bed and breakfast accommodation because no alternative resources have been made available. Equally, our ability to provide the range of supports to the many vulnerable children and parents whose lives are characterised by poverty, disadvantage and marginalisation is severely limited. While there is no denying that the beef industry is crucial to the continued wealth and well-being of this nation, surely our collective responsibility to provide children with adequate care and healthy childhoods is at least as deserving as any obligation to industry. Just as huge resources and effort have been put into inquiring into the activities of relatively few people in the beef industry and into the causes of the problem they encountered, the same level of resources and effort must be devoted to understanding and responding to the nature and causes of childhood adversity.

The Kilkenny Report (McGuinness, 1993) usefully highlighted how a greater understanding of child abuse is crucial in preventing similar cases. Most health boards responded by setting up training programmes for their staff. In addition, however, we also need to establish a national database of child care cases which focuses on the types of service provided and which, as Michael McGinley among others has stressed in this book, evaluates the outcomes as well as the inputs of service provision and the ways in which scarce resources are being deployed. It is crucial that Section 11 of the Child Care Act is used to facilitate research into how services are responding to the whole spectrum of childhood adversity and that a commitment is found to disseminate research findings.

The practical implication of what we are arguing here is not that we can in any sense afford to walk away from abused children. It is rather that a concerted effort also has to be made to reach other children who are, to paraphrase the Act, at risk of not receiving adequate care and protection. Achieving this is not simply a matter of changing attitudes. It will only come about if more actual systems are put in place to respond to the categories of vulnerable children covered under the Act. Thus, as well as Child Abuse Guidelines, the Department of Health and health boards need to develop 'Family Support Guidelines'. These should include provision for services directed at preventing many of the problems referred to in this book. The guidelines, and the professionals who operate them, should work alongside those relating to the protection of children from abuse and not in any sense separate from them.

Operational definitions of child care problems are very difficult to arrive at in practice. Thus, as the book has shown, child abuse, for example, is not simply a taken-for-granted phenomenon, but a problem that is defined through a process of social construction by professional gatekeepers. Nevertheless, all the evidence presented in this book suggests that some attempt at least should be made to define thresholds of entry to different child care systems and services. Thus, definitions should be sought of what constitutes a legitimate referral to family support systems, child protection, the homeless child unit, and alternative care services.

To some degree, this kind of guidance will be provided in revised Department of Health Child Abuse Guidelines in response to the recommendations of the *Report of the Kilkenny Incest Investigation* (McGuinness, 1993) and also in regulations which are drawn up by the Department to outline operational criteria for the various sections of the Act. In addition, it is desirable that, at a local level, health boards formulate clear and explicit procedures for putting into practice the nationally agreed policies on services for the range of child care problems this book has addressed. This should not only involve guidance on defining cases that are most relevant to particular services, but must also involve the clarification of quality control guidelines as well as criteria for defining successful outcomes for service users as well as the agency. In sum, the Act affords an opportunity for the state to define in qualitative terms the nature and content of the child welfare and protection services it provides. The extent to which the philosophical, policy and practice challenges outlined in this book are met will determine how far the promise of the Child Care Act 1991 is realised and the degree to which our efforts to work fairly and effectively on behalf of the child will be enhanced.

References

Hamilton, L. (1994), *Report of the Beef Tribunal*, Dublin: Stationery Office.
McGuinness, C. (1993), *Report of the Kilkenny Incest Investigation*, Dublin: Stationery Office.

Index

Abuse, *see* child abuse

access, 14, 23, 34, 110, 122, 155, 156 167,
239
  activities during, 134–5
  average length of visit, 127–8
  contact time, 137–8
  Donegal study of, 121–40
  emotions involved, 116–17
  frequency of visits, 126–7
  legal perspective, 160–1
  organisation and supervision, 131–2
  and parents, 12, 32–3
  quality of experience, 138–9
  role of social workers, 110, 116, 124–5, 155–6
  siblings, 129–30
  study findings, 126–39
  survey methodology, 122–3
  transport, 132–4
  venues, 135–7

Accused Parents Aid Group (APAG), 37

adolescents, 74–5, 77, 162, 239–40
  in care, 108–9

adoption services, 10, 14, 23, 108–9

after-care services, 14, 23, 30, 86, 220–1

attachment, 106–9

audit, clinical, 166

battered baby syndrome, 193

Bayley, Nessie, 107

Beckford Report, 51–2

Beef Tribunal, 240

befriending schemes, 173

Belfast, 76–7

birth rate, 229

bonding, 106–9

Bord Altranais, An, 188, 192

Boys' Hope—Ireland, 91

Brinich, Paul, 108–9, 113

care orders, 12, 32, 53–6, 159, 167–8, 209, 219
  legal perspective, 159–60
  time limits, 53–4
  variations in use, 45–6

case conferences, 196, 206, 218, 220
  study of, 223

Cavan, County, 45, 212

Cavan/Monaghan Community Care Area, 44

chief executive officer, 145, 146, 154
  functions of, 16

child abuse, 20, 57, 183, 200
  children at risk, 24–31
  child's perspective of, 109–10
  confidentiality, 155
  definitions of, 30, 48–53, 241–2
  diagnosis of, 151, 177–8
  false accusations, 37
  GP's perspective, 204–6
  increased referrals, 43–4
  mandatory reporting, 25–6, 179–80, 196
  and neglect, 27–8
  number of cases, 24
  prediction of, 51–2
  pro-active approach, 217, 238–9
  reporting patterns, 25
  role of GP, 207–11
  role of paediatricians, 177–9
  role of PHN, 192–3
  sexual abuse units, 43–4
  treatment of perpetrators, 184
  variations in response, 45–53, 56, 57

Child Abuse Guidelines, 18, 25, 73, 186,
205, 231, 241
  mandatory reporting, 179–80
  revision of, 242
  variations in usage, 57

Child Abuse Prevention Programme, 118–19

child care
  adversities other than abuse, 25–31
  co-ordinating provision, 152–3, 238–9
  entry to, 29–31
  evaluation of services, 149–50
  history of, 17–20
  identification of need, 24–31, 150–1
  key issues in, 17–38
  legal proceedings, 12–13, 219
  and legalism, 35–6
  numbers in care, 32, 44–5
  philosophical issues, 20–2
  political issue, 36–7
  social context of, 44–57
  state intervention, 234–7
  threshold of entry, 27, 242
  variations in approach, 150

written policy needed, 223
Child Care Act 1991
    categories of children, 23
    description of, 10–15
    historical background, 17–20
    implications of, 22–3
    jurisdiction and procedure, 167–8
    overview, 9–16
    resources promised, 240–1
    role in child protection, 53–6
    Section 02, 113
    Section 03, 23, 53, 98, 114, 186, 193, 207,
        217–18, 222
    Section 04, 98
    Section 05, 84–102, 239
        origins of, 93–6
        provisions of, 96–102
    Section 7, 149
    Section 8, 90, 96, 102, 217
    Section 11, 218, 241
    Section 12, 32–3, 53, 159, 181–2, 208
    Section 13, 33, 53–4, 115, 208
    Section 16, 55
    Section 17, 33, 182
    Section 18, 33, 55, 160
    Section 19, 33–5, 99, 160, 182–3, 220
    Section 20, 219
    Section 24, 21–2, 115–16
    Section 25, 36, 115–16, 160
    Section 26, 160
    Section 27, 159
    Section 29, 159–60, 209
    Section 30, 209–10
    Section 36, 99
    Section 37, 32, 116, 121, 140, 155, 160–1
    Section 41, 117
    Section 44, 32
    Section 68, 57
    Section 69, 57
    sections in operation, 16
    variations in practice, 45–8
child care advisory committees, 11, 150,
    159, 165–7, 170, 181
Child Care Policy Unit, 9
child development programme, 68–9
child guidance clinics, 162
child neglect, 25–31, 231
child party to proceedings, 13, 16, 115–16,
    160, 169–70
child protection, *passim* especially

Chapter 3
    27–31, 36, 37, 38, 61, 73, 90, 216, 238
    dominance of, 29
    emergency, 11, 218
    policy, 4
    powers, 33
    registers, 29–30
    system, entry to, 27
child psychiatry
    perspective on Act, 162–74
child psychology
    perspective on Act, 225–37
children
    definition under Act, 10, 22, 92, 113, 174,
        176, 181, 194, 239–40
    disadvantaged, 226–7
    emotional development, 106–9
    family needs conflicting with, 50–1
    numbers in care, 229–30
    protection of identity, 14
    sense of identity, 111–12
    welfare paramount, 150–1, 183, 193–4,
        214, 227–9
Children Act 1908, 10, 17, 18, 21, 33, 45,
    164, 174, 217, 218, 225
Children Act 1989 (England & Wales), 29–30
Children Act 1989 (UK), 165
children in care. *see also* access
    perspective of, 109–13
    theoretical perspectives, 106–9
    without access, 128
    working with, 105–19
Circuit Court, 209
Cleveland Inquiry, 51–2, 177
clinical audit, 166
Colwell Report, 178–9
Combat Poverty, 76, 78
community
    and child abuse, 178–9
community care
    no written policies, 56
    role of director, 42–3
'community mothers', 69
community paediatrics, 181
Community Welfare Service, 91
confidentiality, 155, 205
Cork, 85
corporal punishment, 232–3
counselling, 54, 56, 65
    for GPs, 206

courts. *see also* District Court
  appearance of child, 209–10
  dilapidation of, 161
  GPs in, 206
  increased role of, 35–6
  perspective of, 158–61
  reports for, 168–9, 230–1
  social workers in, 219–20
cultural relativism, 49–50
Cyrene House, Galway, 91

depression, 69, 77
developmental family support, 66
Dingwall, Robert, 48–50, 51, 56, 57
District Court, 22
  access orders, 14, 23
  care orders, 12, 32
  emergency care orders, 11, 33, 53–4, 115,
    159–60, 209, 218
  interim care order, 182
  residential care registration, 15
  supervision orders, 12–13
divorce referendum, 158
domiciliary nursing, 188–9, 192
Donegal Community Care Area, 42–4, 45,
  146, 186, 189
  access, 121–40
  child protection team, 105–6
  child psychology, 225
Drysdale, Barbara Dockar, 108
Dublin, 85

Eastern Health Board, 77
  child abuse, 27–8
  child development programme, 68–9
  child psychiatry, 163
  homeless children, 87, 92, 100, 102
Edmund Rice Home, Galway, 91
Education, Department of, 14–15, 85, 86, 200
  Special Schools, 99
elderly, services for, 217
emergency care orders, 11, 33, 35, 53–4,
  115, 181–2, 209, 218
  legal perspective, 159–60
emergency protection, 11, 32–3
Environment, Department of, 14

family
  and child development, 67–8
  in Constitution, 20–1, 50–1, 228–9
  definitions of, 62

difficulty of replacing, 69–70
extended family, 112, 116, 117, 130
  role of, 227, 229–34
family resource centres, 31, 135
family support, 22, 29, 30, 31, 53, 114–15,
  150, 231–2
  child psychiatry perspective, 171–3
  and children in care, 112–13
  community services, 76–7
  compensatory, 66
  definition of, 61
  formal and informal, 64–7
  identification of need, 152–3
  importance of, 67–71
  key conceptual issues, 62–7
  key principles of, 71–2
  lay helpers, 73
  mechanics of, 72–6
  and other child care functions, 70–1
  paediatric perspective, 183–4
  prospects for, 77–8
  protective, 66–7
  role of Child Care Act, 60–79
  role of health board, 154–5
  role of PHN, 194–5
Finance, Department of, 158
Finlay, Mr Justice, 51
fit person orders, 10, 54, 209, 219
Fitzgerald, Kelly, 28
Flood, Chris, 99–100
fostering, 14, 61, 112–13, 119, 159
  abuse by fosterers, 236
  and access, 116–17, 122, 136
  breakdowns in, 105
  day fostering, 66
  role of health boards, 155

Galway, 91
Garda Síochána, 179
  emergency care order, 218
  and the GP, 205, 210–11
  powers under Act, 11, 16, 22, 32–3, 53,
    181–2, 208, 210
  protection from legal challenges, 158, 159
  role in child abuse, 205
  general practitioners, 151
  identification of abuse, 24
  perspective of, 203–11
  role under Act, 207–11
Gibbons, Jane, 29–30

Good Enough Parent, 230
grandparents, access to, 130
Greenland, Cyril, 51
guardian *ad litem*, 13, 36, 160
    child psychiatry perspective, 169–70
Guardianship of Infants Act 1964, 13, 219, 227

Health, Department of, 9, 57, 61, 226. *see
    also* Child Abuse Guidelines
    and family support, 73, 78, 241
    and health board organisation, 146, 148–9
    and homelessness, 86
    inter-departmental co-operation, 200
    pre-school services, 14
    report on nursing, 190
    statistics, 229–30
    survey of children in care, 44
Health Act 1947, 188
Health Act 1970, 18, 145, 154, 188, 189
Health and Social Services, Department
    of (DHSS), 179
health boards, 18, 51
    care orders, 54–6
    case reviews, 14, 23, 32
    children in care of, 14, 31–2, 44–5, 119
    competition for resources, 197–8
    duties of, 10
    duties under Act, 21–3, 31, 53, 61, 114,
        155–6, 216–17
    evaluation of child care services, 149–50
    and family support, 70–1, 72–3, 78, 154–5
    functions of CEOs, 16
    and homelessness, 84, 86, 87, 90–2,
        97–8, 115
    lack of co-ordination, 217–18
    management structure, 146–8
    organisation of, 42, 145
    policies and procedures, 153–4, 242
    policy formulation, 148–9
    programme manager's perspective, 145–56
    reports required, 11, 90, 149–50
    and residential centres, 15
    variations in practice, 56, 57
    and voluntary agencies, 173
    and welfare of children, 150–1
home
    family support in, 75
    inviolability of, 159
    venue for access, 136–7
'Home Alone' cases, 28, 207

home help staff, 151, 152, 171–2
home-making services, 152, 171
homeless children, 10, 23, 30, 31, 38, 61,
    115, 239
    B & B accommodation, 99–102
    criminalisation of, 99
    definition of youth homelessness, 92–3
    determinants of homelessness, 85–6
    extent of homelessness, 87–92
    lack of facilities, 97
    Section 5 of Act, 84–102
hospitals, 24, 151, 162, 184
Housing Act 1988, 92
Howitt, Denis, 37
Howlin, Brendan, 19, 94, 240

Institute of Community Health Nursing, 188
institutional care, 86
inter-agency co-operation, 156, 184, 187,
    196–7, 215–18, 223
interim care order, 12, 33, 54–5, 182, 209,
    218, 219
Irish Constitution, 182, 227
    amendments needed, 57
    role of family, 20–1, 50–1, 228–9
Irish Medical Organisation, 146
Irish Pre-School Playgroups Association, 221
Irish Society for the Prevention of Cruelty to
    Children (ISPCC), 17–18, 20–1, 25, 36
    cases of neglect, 27

Judicial Separation Act, 219
Judicial Separation and Family Law
    Reform Act 1989, 13
jurisdiction, 13–14, 33–5, 183
Justice, Department of, 78, 86, 200
juvenile crime, 77

Kempe, Henry, 193
Kennedy Report, 18
Kenny, Justice, 232–3
Kilkenny Incest Investigation, Report of the, 9,
    194, 205, 241
    difficulties of disclosure, 26, 179, 193,
        217, 235
    effects of, 19–20, 36–7, 216, 220
    on family support, 77
    mandatory reporting, 25–6, 196
    recommendations, 57, 117–19, 183,
        187, 215, 231, 242
    on record-keeping, 199

on rights of children, 51, 229
kinship, 117
Knight, Philip, 163

Law Reform Commission, 25–6
legal proceedings, 12–13. *see also* courts
    protection of identity, 14
legal representation, 13, 16, 115–16, 160,
    169–70
Letterkenny Hospital, 176
Limerick, 90
Local Government Superannuation
    Scheme, 15
Longford/Westmeath care area, 44
Louth, County, 45
Louth Community Care Area, 44

McGuinness, Catherine, 19
Madonna House, 37
mandatory reporting, 25–6, 179–80, 196
marriage rate, 229
maternity leave, 62
media, role of, 36–7, 52
Mid-Western Health Board, 90, 128, 140
mortality rates, 226
Mulberry Bush Therapeutic School
    Needs Assessment, 107–8

National University of Ireland, 188
natural love, 50
neglect, 25–31
neighbourhood
    family support in, 76
neighbourhood youth projects, 75, 77
New Zealand, 117
Newpin Project, 70
Ney, Professor Philip, 108
North Eastern Health Board, 91–2
North Western Health Board, 42, 43–4,
    186, 203, 225, 238, 239
    access, 132–3
    child psychiatry, 163
    paediatric care, 176–84
    programme manager's perspective, 145–56
    public health nursing, 189, 191
    social workers, 212–13
Notification of Births Act 1907, 187
Notification of Births (Extension) Act
    1915, 187
Nursing Board. *see* Bord Altranais, An

O'Connell, Dr John, 97

O'Doherty, Dr Neil, 208

paediatricians
    identification of abuse, 25
    implications of Act, 180–4
    perspective of, 176–84
parents, 28, 63. *see also* access
    and care orders, 54, 56
    and children in care, 110–13
    natural love, 50
    number of single parents, 229
    rights of, 20
    and supervision orders, 34–5
    support for, 68–9
    training for, 171, 199–200, 232
place of safety order, 33, 181, 182, 209, 218
play therapy, 114
playgroups, 74
Poor Relief (Ireland) Act 1851, 187
poverty, 29, 31, 226
pre-school services, 14–15, 23, 31, 66, 199, 221
    and family support, 74
    registration, 215
    study of, 69
prevention programmes, 53
primary health care team, 196–7
procedure, 13–14, 16, 33–5, 183, 220, 242
professionals
    caseloads of, 226
    and child psychiatry, 164
    in child sexual abuse, 44
    co-ordination of provision, 152–3, 196–7
    court reports, 168–9
    criticisms of, 37–8, 51–3
    and family support, 72–3, 155
    and health board policy, 148, 149
    on parenting, 228, 230
    variations in approach, 46–7, 150
    and welfare of children, 151
programme manager
    perspective of, 145–56
    role under Act, 148
prostitution, 99
protective family support, 66
psychiatry. *see* child psychiatry
Public Health Medical Treatment of
    Children (Ireland) Act 1919, 187
public health nursing, 31
    background to, 187–9
    identification of need, 24–5, 151

improvements needed, 198–200
in NWHB, 152
organisation of, 189
perspective of, 186–201
present situation, 195–8
qualifications, 191–2
role of, 190–3
services provided, 191

relatives, care by, 14, 15, 32, 112, 117, 127
Report on Child Sexual Abuse, 25–6
reports, 11, 90, 149–50
    child psychiatry perspective, 168–9
research, 218, 241
Resident Managers Association, 99
residential centres, 14, 15, 61, 114, 119, 182
    abuse in, 236
    registration, 215, 221
    religious orders, 18
resource centres, 76
resources, 38, 113–14, 149, 160–1, 174, 201
    and family support, 171
    lack of, 214–15, 240–1
    possibility of waste, 165
    social worker perspective, 221–2
Roscommon, County, 45
Rowe, Jane, 112
Rule of Optimism, 49–50
Ryan, Brendan, 95, 96

scapegoating, 28
schools, 77, 99
    family support in, 76
    health examinations, 187
    lifeskills, 232
    truancy, 85–6
sibling attachment, 112, 116, 129–30
Sligo, 92
Sligo General Hospital, 212
Sligo/Leitrim Community Care Area, 43,
    44, 45, 146, 189
    child psychology, 225
    social workers, 212–13
Sligo Social Services Centre, 212
Smyth, Fr Brendan, 20, 37
social deprivation, 29, 31, 63–4, 226–7
social workers, 35, 43, 56, 125, 177
    see also access
    caseloads, 31, 32, 197
    and child abuse, 205
    and child neglect, 25–31

criticisms of, 51–2
cultural relativism, 49–50
as guardians, 169–70
perspective on Act, 212–24
role under Act, 32, 216–21
shortage of, 32, 184, 216
solicitor
    appointed to child, 13, 36, 115–16, 160,
        169–70
solvents, 16
South Eastern Health Board, 90
Southern Health Board, 91
Stay Safe Programme, 118–19, 184
Streetwise National Coalition, 99
supervision orders, 12–13, 55, 160, 167,
    209, 210, 219–20
    child psychology perspective, 235–6
    description of, 33–5
    and homelessness, 99
    increased workload, 180–1
    paediatric perspective, 182–3
    and social workers, 215
    types of supervision, 34–5
Supreme Court, 159

Task Force for Child Care Services, 18–
    19
Thoburn, June, 111, 117
Tipperary, County, 45
total quality management, 122
transport
    access visits, 132–4
travelling community, 31, 77
Treacey, Noel, 93–6, 100
truancy, 64, 85–6
unemployment, 86, 226
United States, 25, 69, 74, 173
University College, Dublin, 188, 192

vocational education committees, 76, 78
voluntary care, 10, 23, 32, 207
voluntary organisations, 11, 76, 173
    and health board policy, 149

Western Health Board, 90, 100
Wexford, County, 45
Working Party Report on General
    Nursing, 190
Wurtz, Phelix, 192

youth programmes, 66, 75